FREEDOM OF EXPRESSION®

Overzealous Copyright Bozos
and Other Enemies of Creativity

KEMBREW McLEOD

DOUBLEDAY

NEW YORK LONDON TORONTO SYDNEY AUCKLAND

PUBLISHED BY DOUBLEDAY

a division of Random House, Inc.

DOUBLEDAY and the portrayal of an anchor with a dolphin are registered
trademarks of Random House, Inc.

The author gratefully acknowledges permission to reprint from the following
works:

"Adolph and Nevilline" by Woody Guthrie, copyright © by Woody Guthrie
Publications, Inc. All Rights Reserved. Used by permission.

"Clowns," written and performed by Too Much Joy, published by
People Suck Music.

Book design by Chris Welch

Library of Congress Cataloging-in-Publication Data

McLeod, Kembrew, 1970–

Freedom of expression® : overzealous copyright bozos and other enemies of
creativity / Kembrew McLeod.—1st ed.

p. cm.

1. Intellectual property—United States. 2. Copyright—United States.
3. Freedom of expression—United States. 4. Creation (Literary, artistic, etc.)—
Economic aspects—United States. I. Title.

KF2979.M348 2005

346.7304'82—dc22

2004055289

ISBN 0-385-51325-9

Visit Kembrew McLeod's Web site at www.kembrew.com

PRINTED IN THE UNITED STATES OF AMERICA

February 2005

First Edition

1   3   5   7   9   10   8   6   4   2

FOR LYNNE

CONTENTS

CHAPTER SIX **THE DIGITAL FUTURE**   270

and the analog past

AFTERWORD **FREEDOM OF EXPRESSION®**   328

INTRODUCTION

I n 2003 Fox News sued Al Franken and his publisher, Penguin, for naming his book *Lies and the Lying Liars Who Tell Them: A Fair and Balanced Look at the Right.* The veteran satirist, who had publicly quarreled with Fox News host Bill O'Reilly in the months leading up to the book's release, used the news channel's slogan "Fair and Balanced" in the title. The company claimed this use trespassed on its intellectual property. By associating Al Franken's name with Fair and Balanced®, the Fox lawyers argued, it would "blur and tarnish" the good reputation of the trademark. The suit went on to state that Franken "appears to be shrill and unstable." He was also described in the lawsuit as "increasingly unfunny," a charge Franken responded to by saying that he had trademarked "funny" and was considering a countersuit.

Later that week on his daily radio talk show, O'Reilly grew testier, lashing out at Franken and his alleged theft. Despite O'Reilly's bluster and the earnest legal arguments of Fox's lawyers—who drew laughter from the courtroom when they advocated their indefensi-

ble position—U.S. District Judge Denny Chin dismissed the injunction against the book. "There are hard cases and there are easy
cases," Chin stated. "This is an easy case in my view and wholly
without merit, both factually and legally." The O'Reilly-Franken
dustup was the prelude to an increasingly aggressive trademark
rampage. That year, the news channel threatened to sue a Web-site
outfit that was selling a satirical T-shirt that mimicked its logo with
the words "Faux News" and tweaked its motto: "We distort, you
comply." It also targeted *The Simpsons* (which airs on its sister network) for parodying the news channel's right-wing slant. During
one episode, the cartoon imitated the Fox News ticker, running
crawling headlines such as "Oil slicks found to keep seals young,
supple" and "Study: 92 percent of Democrats are gay."

Fox News eventually backed down, opting not to file a lawsuit
against the show. "We called their bluff," said Matt Groening, *The
Simpsons'* creator, "because we didn't think Rupert Murdoch would
pay for Fox to sue itself. So we got away with it." It's probably the
first time that media consolidation has actually *enabled* freedom of
expression®. Still, *The Simpsons* writers got a slap on the wrist by
the parent company when it imposed a rule that the cartoon could
no longer imitate news crawls. "It might confuse the viewers into
thinking it's real news," Groening drily noted. As for the Web site
that sold the "Faux News" T-shirt, Fox News dropped its threat after
the American Civil Liberties Union intervened on its behalf. The
ACLU sent Fox a " 'get stuffed' letter," as the site's operator Richard
Luckett put it.[1]

"Blur and tarnish," the choice of words used by Fox's lawyers in
the Franken case, might sound absurd to the average person, but it's
the language of trademark law. Unlike copyright law, which protects creative works such as books and movies, and patent law,
which covers inventions and the like, trademark law is designed to

prevent consumer confusion and unfair competition. In other words, you can't place the Coca-Cola logo on your own newly minted soft drink or use the company's trademarked advertising slogans to trick people into buying your product. It also protects companies from having their trademarks associated with something unsavory, which is where the blurring and tarnishing comes in. The problem—at least as far as freedom of expression® is concerned—is when trademark holders go too far in trying to protect their property. The *Fox News v. Franken* case is but one of many examples of this kind of overkill.

By wielding intellectual-property laws like a weapon, overzealous owners erode our freedoms in the following ways: (1) we, or our employers, engage in self-censorship because we think we *might* get sued, even if there's no imminent threat; (2) we censor ourselves after backing down from a lawsuit that is clearly frivolous; (3) worst of all, our freedoms are curtailed because the law has expanded to privatize an ever-growing number of things—from human genes and business methods to scents and gestures. (Donald Trump not only trademarked "You're Fired," but also his hand gesture that accompanied the phrase on *The Apprentice*.)

In the first case, the makers of the anti–Fox News T-shirts didn't back down and instead brought in the ACLU, which forced Fox News to call off its attack dogs. Victory for freedom of expression®. In the second case, Penguin Books fought Fox's lawsuit and easily won because the law allows us to parody or criticize intellectual properties. Franken's publisher didn't make him change the title or cower from what was obviously a lawsuit that was "wholly without merit." Another victory for freedom of expression®. These two instances remind us that we can fight back and win, especially because many recent court decisions have upheld free-speech rights in the age of intellectual property. The problem is that lots of individuals and companies either don't know this or don't want to take a risk.

The third case is far more troubling, because in some important respects the law *does* curtail our rights. The rise of the Internet has served as a wonderfully effective boogeyman used by intellectual-property owners to legitimate the same one-dimensional arguments they've been asserting for years. Those claims go something like this: *Anyone* who does *anything* to *any* of their properties is a "pirate" (such as VCR owners and music fans who made cassette-tape copies of works in the 1980s). Courts and Congress fortunately rejected this line of reasoning twenty years ago, giving consumers far more options—including the option not to be sued. However, Internet-fueled fears have changed the legal and cultural landscape in dramatic ways.

In 1998 Congress passed the Digital Millennium Copyright Act (DMCA) in response to the megabyte-sized specter that haunted American business interests. Although well-intentioned, the DMCA is a terrible law. It was written to protect digital property by making it illegal to bypass "digital locks" such as copy-protection technologies on CDs or simple passwords on software. It's a bad law because it has failed to prevent unauthorized duplication of copyrighted goods—surfed the Internet lately?—and has only succeeded in curtailing freedoms, criminalizing legitimate research, and arresting the development of worthwhile software. (Sometimes it has led to the arrest of software developers themselves.)

One of the DMCA's unintended consequences is that companies have tried to use it to squash competition on things such as garage-door openers and aftermarket ink cartridges. A few years ago, for instance, Lexmark placed in its printers an "authentication regime"—a fancy way of referring to a kind of password that lets the ink cartridge and the printer "talk." Then it invoked the DMCA to eliminate competition from less-expensive aftermarket ink cartridges that "hacked" the digital lock on Lexmark's printer. It took many months and many more thousands of dollars to convince courts that these competing products weren't illicit materials. Only in America, you might think, but draconian DMCA-like laws are spreading around the globe like digital wildfire. In 2004 thirty-three-year-old Isamu Kaneko, an assistant professor at the University of Tokyo, was arrested because he developed file-sharing software similar to the popular KaZaA application. The same year, the Italian parliament passed a law imposing jail time of up to three years for anyone caught sharing copyrighted material via the Internet.

These sanctions are another unfortunate outcome in the drive to privatize every imaginable thing in the world, including genetic material. The peculiar case of John Moore couldn't have happened without the expansion of patent law in the past quarter century. When Moore's spleen was removed to treat a rare form of leukemia, his University of California doctor patented a cell line taken from his organ, without Moore's knowledge or permission. The long-term market value of the patent has been estimated at roughly $3 billion, and Moore's doctor received $3 million in stocks from Genetics Institute, the firm that marketed and developed a drug based on the patent.[2]

When Moore found out about these shenanigans, he sued—and lost. The California Supreme Court claimed that giving Moore any rights would lead to the commodification of the human body—an argument that ruffled the feathers of Judge J. Broussard, who dissented from the *Moore v. Regents of the University of California* decision. "Far from elevating these biological materials above the marketplace," Broussard wrote, "the majority's holding simply bars *plaintiff,* the source of the cells, from obtaining the benefit of the cells' value, but permits the *defendants,* who allegedly obtained the cells from plaintiff by improper means, to retain and exploit the full economic value of their ill-gotten gains."

Patents not only allow companies to have a monopoly control over human and plant genes, but also business methods, such as Amazon's "one-click" procedure. U.S. Patent No. 5,960,411 gives Amazon the right to extract money from any business that wants to let customers purchase items on the Internet with only one click of the mouse. The online retailer exercises the monopoly right that this patent gives it, bullying small and large companies into purchasing a license for this "technology." For instance, Amazon won a court order that prevented barnesandnoble.com from using this feature for two holiday-shopping seasons before the two parties reached a settlement. Today, every company from Apple's iTunes to the smallest of businesses that Amazon's lawyers can shake down are compelled to license the "one-click" feature. Otherwise, they'll be sued.

Clear Channel Communications, which controls more than one hundred live venues and over thirteen hundred radio stations in the United States, bought what is considered in the music industry to be an important patent. It covers selling recordings of concerts immediately after a performance, something that has recently become popular with fans who want to take home live CDs. Other companies had been providing this service, but Clear Channel intends to enforce its patent to squeeze licensing fees from other small businesses and bands and to eliminate competition in this area of commerce. "It's one more step toward massive control and consolidation of Clear Channel's corporate agenda," says Mike Luba, the manager of the jam band String Cheese Incident, which was prevented by the corporate Goliath from using CD-burning equipment. Pixies manager Ken Goes grumbled, "I'm not fond of doing business with my arm twisted behind my back."[3]

Another terrible law is the Sonny Bono Copyright Term Extension Act of 1998, which extended the length of copyright protection by twenty more years. To put this into perspective, nothing new will enter the public domain until 2019—that is, until Congress likely extends copyright protection again for its corporate campaign donors. Previously, copyright law was written in such a way that, between 1790 and 1978, the average work passed into the public domain after thirty-two years. Stanford University law professor Lawrence Lessig notes that this honored a constitutional mandate that copyright protections should last for "limited times," something today's Congress interprets quite liberally. U.S. copyright protection now stretches ninety-five years for corporate authors, and for individual authors it lasts their entire lifetime, plus an additional seventy years.

Copyright protectionists argue that extending a work's copyright ensures that there will be an owner to take care of it. But the opposite is often true. "Long copyright terms actually work to *prevent* a lot of stuff from being preserved," argues film archivist Rick Prelinger. "There's a lot of material that's orphaned," he tells me. "It's still under copyright, but the copyright holders are gone, or we don't know who they are. The copyright could be obscure." Many archives won't preserve a film if they don't know who the owner is, which means there are thousands of films, records, and other fragile works that aren't being protected because nobody knows their status. "The interesting thing about film, what's actually scary about film," Prelinger tells me, "is that the term of copyright is now longer than the average lifespan of film as a medium. So you've got this film in a cage and you can't get to it until the copyright expires, and the cage melts down. But in the meantime the film may disintegrate. That's a real issue."

John Sorensen, a high school friend and an independent documentary producer who has worked for A&E and PBS, shares

Prelinger's concerns. "From the perspective of a historian," he says, "after spending a lot of time looking at film and photo collections from the early part of the century, one realizes that the things that still exist, the images that are chosen to be preserved, are those images that are perceived by corporate or government bodies to have potential value. So the visual record that is kept is totally subject to the laws of the marketplace." Of the works produced between 1923 and 1942—which were affected by the Bono Act—only 2 percent have any commercial value. This means we are allowing much of our cultural history to be locked up and decay only to benefit the very few, which is why some have sarcastically referred to this law as the Mickey Mouse Protection Act. If not for the Bono Act, *Steamboat Willie,* the first appearance of the rodent, would be in the public domain.[4]

INTELLECTUAL PROPERTY V. FREEDOM OF EXPRESSION®

When companies try to use intellectual-property laws to censor speech they don't like, they are abusing the reason why these laws exist in the first place. Copyright was designed to, as the U.S. Constitution puts it, "promote the progress of science and useful arts, by securing for limited times to authors and inventors the exclusive right to their respective writings and discoveries." Copyright exists—and the U.S. Supreme Court has consistently repeated this—as a means to promote the dissemination of creative expression, not suppress it. The overzealous copyright bozos who try to use the law as a censorious weapon mock the idea of democracy, and they step on creativity. As culture increasingly becomes fenced off and privatized, it becomes all the more important for us to be able to comment on the images, ideas, and words that saturate us on a daily basis—without worrying about an expensive, though meritless, lawsuit. The right to express one's views is what makes these "copy fights" first and foremost a free-speech issue. Unfortunately, many intellectual-property owners and lawyers see copyright only as an economic issue.

By using intellectual-property law as a thread that ties everything together, I gather what may seem to be a wild array of subjects: hip-hop music and digital sampling; the patenting of seeds and human genes; folk and blues music; education and book publishing; the collage art of Rauschenberg and Warhol; filmmaking, electronic voting, and the Internet. However, all of these topics are connected to the larger trend of privatization—something that pits economic values against the values of free speech, creativity, and shared resources. The latter aren't airy dreams. They're the very reasons why the framers of the Constitution established copyright and patent law: so that society would benefit from a rich culture accessible to all. Thomas Jefferson and the other Founding Fathers were thoughtful, and got it right.

They articulated a theory of intellectual-property law that rewarded authors and inventors for their creativity, but they did not intend the law to be so rigid that it would give creators (and their heirs) *complete* control over their work. In the influential 1984 Betamax case that legalized the VCR, Supreme Court Justice John Paul Stevens reminded us of copyright's Constitutional mandate. He made clear that the monopoly power of copyright was designed *first and foremost* to benefit society by stimulating new creative works. Copyright's purpose, he argued in the majority opinion, is *not* to provide a special private benefit to an individual or corporation.

"Rather, the limited grant is a means by which an important public purpose may be achieved," wrote Stevens. "It is intended to motivate the creative activity of authors and inventors by the provision of a special reward, and to allow the public access to the products of their genius after the limited period of exclusive control has expired. The copyright law, like the patent statutes, makes reward to the owner a secondary consideration."[5] Despite Hollywood's fears, it turned out that the VCR generated *more* money for movie studios. Box-office revenues have continued to rise since the 1980s—even in the age of digital downloading—and video rentals and sales now generate twice as much money as box-office receipts.

Since this 1984 decision, the hypnotic drumming of privatization has grown louder and more persuasive. Some pundits believe it makes sense to place as many things as possible under the control of property owners, because it would be best for business. This is a false assumption, and it is filled with many dangerous trapdoors. The risk we face today is that the free exchange of ideas could be halted by recent trends in intellectual property—with dire consequences for creativity and the human spirit. This book documents a *Lord of the Rings*–size battle between a more than two-hundred-year-old tradition that encourages openness and the total monopoly control that many copyright protectionists advocate. It's also a story about how activists aren't letting the erosion of our freedoms happen without one smackdown of a fight. The situation isn't hopeless, though there are plenty of areas where the conflict is getting worse for freedom of expression®. We still have a way to go.

ONE LAST THING

To address an issue I'm sure will be raised: No, I wouldn't mind earning some extra income from this book's sales, as I've accrued massive student-loan debt over my decade of higher education. However, I thoroughly approve if you copy this book for noncommercial uses. The point of copyright law is to provide *limited* incentives to promote creativity and the spread of knowledge, not total control in perpetuity. My copyright comrade at NYU, Siva Vaidhyanathan, told me that some professors in India have photocopied his book *Copyrights and Copywrongs* in its entirety. The cost of a book is almost an entire month's salary for some university workers in that country, so Siva's feathers aren't ruffled over this kind of "piracy"—though it makes him sad that in the era of globalization such things as books aren't affordable for certain people.

In this book, I don't argue for the abolition of intellectual-property laws. Nor do I believe that those who think their intellectual property is worth protecting are automatically "overzealous copyright bozos." But I do contend that we need to roll back the recent restrictions that have been imposed on us in the digital age. Today, copyright and trademark owners repeatedly invoke the Internet as something that will surely devastate them. Jack Valenti, the recently retired Motion Picture Association of America (MPAA) CEO, has claimed that Hollywood would be brought to its knees by the digital anarchy perpetrated by "twelve-year-olds." Valenti has argued, "If the value of what [movie studios] labored over and brought forth to entertain the American public cannot be protected by copyright, then the victim is going to be the American public." He went on to assert that if people were able to freely copy and watch movies whenever they wanted, this would lead to a "lessened supply of high quality, expensive high budget material where its investment recoupment is now in serious doubt."[6]

VALENTI SAID THIS over twenty years ago, and he was talking about the VCR.

CHAPTER ONE

THIS GENE IS YOUR GENE

fencing off the folk and genetic commons

This gene is your gene," sang Francis Collins, playfully reworking an old Woody Guthrie song, with electric guitar in hand. "This gene is my gene," he continued, backed up by the lumbering roar of a middle-aged rock band. This was no ordinary club gig; he was singing at a post–press conference party for scientists. Collins was the man who headed up the Human Genome Project (HGP), funded by the National Institutes of Health, and he was trying to make an ethical and political point. Since the mid-1990s, Collins's HGP had raced against a private effort to map the human genome in order to make our genetic information freely accessible, not privately owned and patented by a handful of corporations. Any scientist could examine HGP's genome map for free—unlike the Celera Genomics' privately owned draft, which was published with strings attached.[1] Over the din, Collins chided his competitors in song by genetically modifying Guthrie's lyrics:

This draft is your draft, this draft is my draft,
And it's a free draft, no charge to see draft.

It's our instruction book, so come on, have a look,
This draft was made for you and me.

Dr. Francis Collins reworked "This Land Is Your Land" to argue that genetic information should be freely available to the scientific community. However, his use of that Woody Guthrie song was sadly ironic, on multiple levels. "This Land Is Your Land" is a song written by an unabashed socialist as a paean to communal property: "This land was made for you *and* me." Another key lyric goes, "A sign was painted 'Private Property' but on the backside it didn't say nothin.'" The folk-song tradition from which Guthrie emerged valued the open borrowing of lyrics and melodies; culture was meant to be freely created and re-created in a democratic, participatory way.

If this was so, then why was Collins's use of "This Land Is Your Land" painfully ironic? Even though it was written over sixty years ago, the song is, to quote Woody Guthrie himself, still "private property." Guthrie based the melody of "This Land Is Your Land" on the Carter Family's 1928 recording "Little Darlin' Pal of Mine," which in turn was derived from a nineteenth-century gospel song, "Oh, My Loving Brother."[2] This means that, in the twenty-first century, the publishing company that owns the late Guthrie's music can earn money from a song about communal property, which was itself based on a tune that is over a century old. Far more disturbing, Guthrie's publishing company prevents musicians from releasing altered, updated lyrical versions of that song. We won't be hearing Collins's mutated "This Gene Is Your Gene" anytime soon.

What's the connection, you might be wondering, between folk music and genetic research? Although obviously very different endeavors, the practitioners of both used to value the open sharing of information (i.e., melodies or scientific data). In these communities, "texts" were often considered common property, but today this concept has been fundamentally altered by the process of privatization, that is, the belief that shared public resources—sometimes referred to by economists and social scientists as the *commons*—can be better managed by private industries. And in recent years, there's been a significant erosion of both the *cultural* commons and the *genetic* commons, resulting in a shrinking of the public domain. The fact that folk melodies and lyrics are now privately owned rather than shared resources is a depressing example of how our cultural commons is being fenced off. As for the genetic commons, the patenting of human and plant genes is but the furthest logical extension of privatization—taken at times to illogical lengths.

HAPPY BIRTHDAY, SCREW YOU

Like with many things relating to copyright, the story of how Time-Warner's music-publishing division came to own "Happy Birthday to You" is long, convoluted, and absurd. It's also a telling narrative about folk music—how it evolved from a living, breathing part of culture to little more than one musical genre among many, a mere section of a record store. When I first began cobbling together a legal and social history of "Happy Birthday to You," I was surprised to discover that there was virtually nothing published on the subject. Unearthing the song's genealogy was difficult because Warner-Chappell Music, then a subsidiary of TimeWarner, ignored my repeated requests for internal documents that might shed light on the song's origins. Finally, Don Biederman—an executive vice president at the company—informed me in a faxed letter that the company does in fact maintain "files concerning HBTY in various departments of our company." However, he could not provide me with any information on "Happy Birthday to You" because "we regard this information as proprietary and confidential."

Despite the "owner's" lack of cooperation, I can now tell the story—after nearly ten years of digging through journals, books, music-trade papers, old master's theses, and other dusty sources. It goes like this: Schoolteacher Mildred J. Hill and her sister Patty published the song's melody in 1893 in their book *Song Stories for the Kindergarten,* calling it "Good Morning to All." However, the Hill sisters didn't compose the melody all on their own. There were numerous popular nineteenth-century songs that were substantially similar, including Horace Waters's "Happy Greetings to All," published in 1858. The Hill sisters' tune is nearly identical to other songs, such as "Good Night to You All," also from 1858; "A Happy New Year to All," from 1875; and "A Happy Greeting to All," published 1885. This commonality clearly suggests a freely borrowed melody (and title, and lyrics) that had been used and reworked throughout the century. Children liked the Hill sisters' song so much that they began singing it at birthday parties, changing the words to "Happy Birthday to You" in a spontaneous form of lyrical parody that's common in folk music.[3]

It wasn't until 1935 that the Hill sisters finally got around to registering a copyright on the melody *and* the new birthday lyrics, claiming both as their own. The years rolled on, and so did the lawsuits, of which there were many. Then, in 1988, Birch Tree Group, Ltd., sold "Happy Birthday to You" and its other assets to Warner Communications (which begat TimeWarner, which will one day give birth to OmniCorp, or a similarly named entity). The owners of Birch Tree told the *Chicago Tribune* that it was too time-consuming for a smaller company to monitor the usage of "Happy Birthday to You" and that "a major music firm could better protect the copyright during its final 22 years."[4] It turns out TimeWarner hit the jackpot when the U.S. Congress added twenty more years of protection to existing copyrights. As a result, "Happy Birthday to You" won't go into the public domain until 2030.

How better to protect an investment than to aggressively police the song's use? The current owner does this job quite well, much like the song's previous stewards. One person who was very well acquainted with royalty payments and copyright law was Irving Berlin, the famous American popular-music composer. His 1934 Broadway play *As Thousands Cheer* included a scene where actors sang the litigation-prone birthday song. Although the *lyrics* of "Happy Birthday to You" had not yet been copyrighted—that wouldn't happen for another year—the Hill sisters' publishing firm nevertheless claimed that his use of the song was an infringement on the *melody* of "Good Morning to You." The illicit singing was in all probability very innocent, but as was the case with later lawsuits against other infringers, they didn't take pity on Berlin.

Postal Telegraph, a company that began using "Happy Birthday to You" for singing telegrams in 1938, found itself treading in copyright-infringement waters, as did Western Union. Western Union career man M. J. Rivise remembers, "From 1938 to 1942, most of our singing telegrams were birthday greetings, and 'Happy Birthday to You' was the cake-taker." Postal Telegraph apparently received permission from the American Society of Composers, Authors, and Publishers (ASCAP)—the organization that collects royalties for song-publishing companies—to use "Happy Birthday to You" without paying royalties. By 1941, ASCAP changed its mind and hiked the royalty rates. Western Union and Postal Telegraph refused to pay, commissioning birthday songs based on the public-domain melodies of "Yankee Doodle" and "Mary Had a Little Lamb." The public thought they were pretty lame, as you might imagine, so by 1950, the singing of "Happy Birthday to You" resumed, with the licensing problem sorted out. It's likely that singing telegrams were instrumental in popularizing and ritualizing the birthday song throughout the United States.[5]

Roy Harris, a twentieth-century composer of classical music, got into trouble when he used part of the song in his "Symphonic Dedication," which honored the birthday of another American composer, Howard Hanson. *Variety* reported, "Keeping the occasion in mind, Harris brought his composition to a climax with a modern treatment of 'Happy Birthday.' After Harris' piece had been introduced by the Boston Symphony he was compelled by the copyright owners to delete the 'Happy Birthday' passage from his score." P.D.Q. Bach, the "Weird Al" Yankovic of the classical-music world, avoided using any strains of "Happy Birthday to You" in a birthday ode to his father because he was afraid of being sued. Instead, he based it on a traditional German birthday song. Even Igor Stravinsky was slapped on the wrist when he cited a few bars of "Happy Birthday to You" in one of his symphonic fanfares (the composer reportedly assumed it was an old folk tune).[6]

Although I found little evidence to suggest that "Happy Birthday to You" was an old folk song dating back to the eighteenth century, as I had first suspected, it obviously came out of the folk-song tradition that valued borrowing and transformation. As with most folk songs, there was no single "author"; instead, the tune slowly evolved over the years with anonymous contributions by many people. The Hill sisters based "Good Morning to All" on an existing melody, and the lyrics were spontaneously generated by a bunch of five- and six-year-olds. Because the melody, first published in 1893, is now in the public domain and the lyrics weren't even written by the Hill sisters, there is little reason why the copyright to "Happy Birthday to You" should still be enforced. But that hasn't stopped the song's stewards from taking every measure to prevent others from singing it without paying royalties.

In the mid-1990s ASCAP sent letters to Girl Scouts and other summer camps, informing them that they had to purchase a performance license in order to sing certain songs. The fact that such a notice hadn't been issued before illustrates the rising level of entitlement among copyright owners by the end of the twentieth century. Under the guidelines set forth by this ASCAP letter, songs such as "This Land Is Your Land," "God Bless America," and, of course, "Happy Birthday to You" could not be sung at the summer camps without buying a license us. Copyright law defines a "public performance" as something that occurs "at a place open to the public, or at any place where a substantial number of persons outside of a normal circle of a family and its social acquaintances is gathered." For instance, around a campfire.

The rules governing public performances are quite convoluted, like tax code, and enough to scare off anyone who wants to turn on a TV or radio outside his or her living room. For instance, "bars and restaurants that measure no more than 3,750 square feet (not including the parking lot, as long as the parking lot is used exclusively for parking purposes) can contain no more than four TVs (of no more than 55 inches diagonally) for their patrons to watch, as long as there is only one TV per room." Radio broadcasts can be played through no more than six loudspeakers, with a limit of four per room. Any more, and you're in trouble. The only exception is if the restaurant is run by "a government body or a nonprofit agricultural or horticultural organization, in the course of an annual agricultural or horticultural fair or exhibition conducted by such a body or organization." In that case, you can use more speakers.[7]

Girl Scout camp officials were told that the penalty for failing to comply with copyright laws would range from five thousand dollars and six days in jail to one hundred thousand dollars and a year in jail for every unauthorized performance. After the American Camping Association (ACA) was approached by ASCAP, the ACA sent out a newsletter warning its members of the possible risks of litigation. Some took the warning very seriously, including a Girl Scout Council director who advised future counselors at a training session to limit their repertoire exclusively to Girl Scout songs. The *Houston Chronicle* reported that "several cash-strapped camps stopped singing the songs" altogether.

ASCAP CEO John LoFrumento defended his organization's hardball tactics: "They buy paper, twine and glue for their crafts—they can pay for the music, too. We will sue them if necessary."[8] This climate of fear resulted in the following surreal scenario reported by the *Minneapolis Star Tribune*, which sounds like an episode of *Sesame Street* directed by David Lynch.

Something is wrong in Diablo Day Camp this year. At the 3 p.m. sing-along in a wooded canyon near Oakland, Calif., 214 Girl Scouts are learning the summer dance craze, the Macarena. Keeping time by slapping their hands across their arms and hips, they jiggle, hop and stomp. They spin, wiggle and shake. They bounce for two minutes. In silence. "Yesterday, I told them we could be sued if we played the music," explains Teesie King, camp codirector and a volunteer mom. "So they decided they'd learn it without the music." Watching the campers' mute contortions, King shakes her head. "It seems so different," she allows, "when you do the Macarena in silence."[9]

Finally, however, ASCAP backed down after the kind of public-relations smackdown that comes when you threaten to beat up Girl Scouts and take their lunch money. Soon after national wire services picked up the story, ASCAP entered into negotiations with Girl Scout leaders and hammered out guidelines that waived full royalty payments for nonprofit camps. After an agreement was reached, ASCAP released a statement claiming that it "has never sought, nor was it ever its intention, to license Girl Scouts singing around a campfire," a direct contradiction of the statements made before the public-relations debacle came to a head. Today, ASCAP charges the Scouts $1 a year, which allows the company to save face while at the same time reminding everyone that the kids are allowed to sing only because of ASCAP's good graces.[10]

MAKING FOLK MUSIC

One year, I was taking a shuttle van back from the airport, glad to be back in Iowa City but exhausted from the Christmas holidays and feeling mute. However, I was alone with a driver who obviously wanted to chat, so I answered his questions about what I do. I mentioned my interest in music, which got the full attention of Jim Bazzell—the grizzled, fiftysomething man behind the wheel. It turned out that Bazzell's father had been in a band called Jimmy and the Westerners, one of the many country-music combos that roamed the land in the 1940s and 1950s. They once performed at Nashville's Grand Ole Opry and had their own radio show, though the group mainly made a living playing in honky-tonk bars around the Southwest. "My dad couldn't read music and would play by ear," says Bazzell. "I remember my mom would scramble to write down song lyrics as they came on the radio." He chuckles, "Of course, she'd get a lot of 'em wrong because she couldn't write as fast as they sang, so my dad would just make up the lyrics he didn't know."

This kind of improvisation used to be a common practice, especially in folk and country circles where lyrics and melodies were treated as raw materials that could be reshaped and molded in the moment. When writing my last book, for instance, I happened to be listening to a lot of old country music, and I noticed that *six* country songs shared the same vocal melody, including Hank Thompson's "Wild Side of Life."[11] In his exhaustively researched book *Country: The Twisted Roots of Rock 'n' Roll,* Nick Toches documented that the melody these songs used was both "ancient and British." It's unlikely that the writers of these songs simply ran out of melodic ideas and decided to pillage someone else's music. It wasn't artistic laziness. Rather, it's probable that these six country songwriters, the majority of whom grew up during the first half of the twentieth century, felt comfortable borrowing folk melodies. They probably didn't think twice about it.

This was also a time when more people knew how to play musical instruments, like Bazzell's family, which performed small gigs at local hospitals and the like. His dad was proficient on fiddle and guitar—"any stringed instrument, really," Jim says—and the kids learned to play at an early age, as did his mom. The stories he told reminded me of the song "Daddy Sang Bass," which Carl Perkins wrote and Johnny Cash popularized. "Mama sang tenor," the song's chorus continued. "Me and little brother would join right in there." It describes how the singer's parents are now in heaven and how one day he'll rejoin the family circle in song, concluding, "No, the circle won't be broken . . ."

The chorus makes an overt reference to an important folk song that dates back to the nineteenth century: "Will the Circle Be Unbroken," which the Carter Family made famous. Starting in the 1930s, Woody Guthrie drew direct inspiration from a lot of songs associated with the Carter Family, recycling their melodies to write his own pro-union songs. For example, Guthrie wrote in his journal of song ideas: "Tune of 'Will the Circle Be Unbroken'—will the union stay unbroken. Needed: a sassy tune for a scab song." Guthrie also discovered that a Baptist hymn performed by the Carter Family, "This World Is Not My Home," was popular in migrant farmworker camps, but he felt the lyrics were counterproductive politically. The song didn't deal with the day-to-day miseries forced upon the workers by the rich and instead told them they'd be rewarded for their patience in the next life:

This world is not my home
I'm just a-passing through
My treasures are laid up somewhere beyond the blue
The angels beckon me
From heaven's open door
And I can't feel at home in this world anymore.

The hymn could be understood to be telling workers to accept hunger and pain and not fight back. This angered Guthrie, so he mocked and parodied the original—keeping the melody and reworking the words to comment on the harsh material conditions many suffered through. "I ain't got no home, I'm just a-ramblin' round," he sang, talking about being a homeless, wandering worker who gets hassled by the police, rather than a subservient, spiritual traveler waiting for an afterlife door prize. Instead of looking to heaven—because "I can't feel at home in this world anymore"—Guthrie wryly arrived at his song's punch line: "I ain't got no home in this world anymore."[12]

In 1940 Guthrie was bombarded by Irving Berlin's jingoistic "God Bless America," which goes, in part, "From the mountains to the prairies / to the oceans white with foam / God bless America, my home sweet home." The irritated folk singer wrote a response that originally went, "From California to the New York Island / From the Redwood forest to the Gulf Stream waters / God blessed America for me." (Guthrie later changed the last line to "This land was made for you and me.") Continuing with his antiprivatization theme, in another version of this famous song Guthrie wrote:

As I was walkin'—I saw a sign there
And that sign said—no trespassin'
But on the other side . . . it didn't say nothin'!
Now that side was made for you and me!

He set the lyrics to a beautiful melody he learned from the Carter Family, giving birth to one of the most enduring (and endearing) folk songs of all time. Guthrie's approach is a great example of how appropriation—stealing, borrowing, whatever you want to call it—is a creative act that can have a powerful impact. Before Guthrie, the Industrial Workers of the World, the Wobblies, borrowed from popular melodies for their radical tunes, which were published and popularized in the *Little Red Songbook*. These songs also parodied religious hymns, such as "In the Sweet By-and-By," which was changed to, "You will eat, by and by."[13]

For Guthrie and many other folk musicians, music *was* politics. Guthrie was affiliated closely with the labor movement, which inspired many of his greatest songs; these songs, in turn, motivated members of the movement during trying times. That's why Guthrie famously scrawled on his guitar, "This Machine Kills Fascists." Appropriation is an important method that creative people have used to comment on the world for years, from the radical Dada art of the early twentieth century to the beats and rhymes of hip-hop artists today. Guthrie drew from the culture that surrounded him and transformed, reworked, and remixed it in order to write moving songs that inspired the working class to fight for a dignified life. Instead of passively consuming and regurgitating the Tin Pan Alley songs that were popular during the day, Guthrie and other folk singers *created* culture in an attempt to change the world around them. They were truly part of a counterculture, not an over-the-counter culture.

Curious about the copyright status of Guthrie's decades-old music, I called up Woody Guthrie Publishing and spoke to a very nice gentleman named Michael Smith, the general manager of the organization. He was clearly familiar with the folk-song tradition and obviously knowledgeable about Guthrie, but he nevertheless had a lot of trouble accepting the idea that copyright extension was a bad thing for art and culture. I was surprised when Smith told me that the song-publishing company that owns Guthrie's music denies recording artists permission to adapt his lyrics. And I was shocked when Smith defended the actions of the company, called The Richmond Organization (TRO), even after I pointed out that Guthrie often altered other songwriters' lyrics. "Well," Smith explained, "he admitted to stealing, but at the time that Woody was writing . . ." He paused. "I mean, things have changed from Woody's time."

They certainly have. During the 2004 election season, a year after I spoke to Michael Smith, a small-time team of cartoonists posted a Guthrie-invoking political parody on their Web site. Not surprisingly, TRO threatened to sue. The animated short portrayed G. W. Bush and John Kerry singing a goofy ditty to the tune of "This Land Is Your Land," where Bush said, "You're a liberal sissy," Kerry replied, "You're a right wing nut job," and they sang together, "This land will surely vote for me." Guthrie's copyright managers didn't think it was funny at all. "This puts a completely different spin on the song," TRO's Kathryn Ostien told CNN. "The damage to the song is huge." Perhaps more damage is done to Guthrie's legacy by practicing such an aggressive form of copyright zealotry.

"If someone changed a lyric in Woody's time," said Michael Smith, "chances are it wasn't going to be recorded and it was just spread through campfire singing, you know, family-time singing and stuff like that. You know, now you can create your own CD at home and distribute it any way you want to, and so the dissemination is a lot broader, a lot faster, and can be a lot more detrimental to the integrity of the song." *Detrimental to the integrity of the song?* I pressed him further on Guthrie's own alterations of others' songs and asked what Woody would think of TRO locking up his folk-song catalog. "The answer to that is, you know, 'Hey, you're going to have to ask him, because we have a duty,'" Smith said. "We don't know what Woody would have wanted—we can't tell."

Soon Michael Smith began to make a little more sense to me—at least economic sense. "If you allow multiple rewrites to occur, then people will think it's in the public domain, and then you have a hard time pressing people to prove to them that it's not in the public domain." Then the publishers can no longer generate revenue from it. That a company can still make money off "This Land Is Your Land" is exactly the type of thing I believe Woody Guthrie *would not* have wanted. Even worse, that TRO prevents musicians from releasing altered, updated versions of his music probably makes Guthrie roll in his grave. But don't trust me; listen to the man himself. When Guthrie was still alive, for instance, Bess Lomax Hawes told him that his song "Union Maid" had gone into the oral tradition, as folklorists call it.

"It was part of the cultural landscape, no longer even associated with him," said Hawes, the daughter of the famous song collector and archivist Alan Lomax. "He answered, 'If that were true, it would be the greatest honor of my life.'"[14] In a written statement attached to a published copy of his lyrics for "This Land Is Your Land," Guthrie made clear his belief that it should be understood as communal property. "This song is Copyrighted in US," he wrote, "under Seal of Copyright # 154085, for a period of 28 years, and anybody caught singin' it without our permission will be mighty good friends of ours, cause we don't give a dern. Publish it. Write it. Sing it. Swing to it. Yodel it. We wrote it, that's all we wanted to do." Notice that he mentioned the song's copyright lasted twenty-eight years, though the term was later lengthened.

Also note that Guthrie said, "We wrote it" not "*I* wrote it," something that indicates Guthrie didn't see himself as the song's sole author. Since much of the song's power comes from that lovely melody passed down to him, how could he? In light of Guthrie's view, how sad it is that others continue to taint this socialist musician's ideals by keeping his songs private property, turning them into a lucrative revenue stream rather than a shareable part of our common cultural heritage. If Woody Guthrie had to make his art under the overly restrictive policies his song-publishing company imposes on today's musicians, it would have been very hard for him to make his music at all. In some cases it would have been impossible, for "things have changed."

In a dramatic turn of events, Ludlow Music, the subsidiary of TRO that controls Guthrie's most famous copyrights, backed off from its legal threats against JibJab.com's parody. This was after the Electronic Frontier Foundation (EFF)—a nonprofit organization that defends civil liberties online—came to the Web site's rescue, providing legal council. What made the aftermath of the JibJab.com flap remarkable wasn't merely that the copyright bullying ended. More interesting was the discovery by EFF senior intellectual property attorney Fred von Lohmann that, according to his research, "This Land Is Your Land" has been in the public domain since 1973! He writes:

> Fact#1: Guthrie wrote the song in 1940. At that time, the term of copyright was twenty-eight years, renewable once for an additional twenty-eight years. Under the relevant law, the copyright term for a song begins when the song is published as sheet mu-

sic. (Just performing it is not enough to trigger the clock.) Fact #2: A search of Copyright Office records shows that the copyright wasn't registered until 1956, and Ludlow filed for a renewal in 1984. Fact #3: Thanks to tips provided by musicologists who heard about this story, we discovered that Guthrie published and sold the sheet music for "This Land Is Your Land" in a pamphlet in 1945. An original copy of this mimeograph was located for us by generous volunteers who visited the Library of Congress in Washington, D.C. This means that the copyright in the song expired in 1973, twenty-eight years after Guthrie published the sheet music. Ludlow's attempted renewal in 1984 was eleven years tardy, which means the classic Guthrie song is in the public domain. (I'll note that Ludlow disputes this, although I've not heard any credible explanation from them.) So Guthrie's original joins "The Star-Spangled Banner," "Amazing Grace," and Beethoven's Symphonies in the public domain. Come to think of it, now that "This Land Is Your Land" is in the public domain, can we make it our national anthem? That would be the most fitting ending of all.

Because art isn't made from thin air, the existence of a large and thriving public domain enriches the quality and diversity of creative expression. It's an important resource used by creative people to make new works, such as the musicals *Les Misérables* (based on the nineteenth-century novel by Victor Hugo) and *West Side Story* (based on Shakespeare's *Romeo and Juliet).*[15] The public domain also promotes artistic freedom of expression®, because it eliminates the rigid control some copyright owners exercise over the context in which their works appear. For instance, Gilbert and Sullivan's comic operas were tightly controlled by the D'Oyly Carte Opera, which required that all performances be staged exactly as the originals were. Not a note could change. But when the copyrights were released into the public domain the musicals were freed from the shackles of artistic mummification.[16]

Disney—which strongly lobbied for the Bono Act—made billions of dollars recycling "Snow White," "Pinocchio," "Beauty and the Beast," and many other old stories and fables. Like Guthrie, it would have been much harder for Walt Disney to legally make his fortune if he had to work under the intellectual-property laws his corporate heirs advocate. In his dissenting opinion in the challenge to the Bono Act, which the Supreme Court upheld, Justice Stephen Breyer argued that this law threatens the endangered ecosystem that is our cultural commons. "I cannot find," wrote Breyer, "any constitutionally legitimate, copyrighted-related way in which the statute will benefit the public. Indeed, in respect to existing works, the serious public harm and the virtually nonexistent public benefit could not be more clear."

Copyright protectionists defend the Bono Act by pointing out that Congress was only adhering to international copyright standards. However, this assertion ignores the fact that U.S.–based corporations such as Disney had a hugely influential role in setting these standards. In 2003 Illegal Art—a label hosted by Steev Hise's collage-centric Web site detritus.net and run by the pseudonymously named Philo Farnsworth (after the inventor of the television)—fought back. The label began work on its latest project, a compilation CD named *Sonny Bono Is Dead*. In its press release soliciting the input of artists, Illegal Art stated, "We encourage artists to liberally sample from works that would have fallen into the Public Domain by the year 2004 had the Sonny Bono Act failed," adding slyly that "artists are also encouraged to create new works by sampling Sonny Bono's output."

BORROWING FROM THE PAST

Musical borrowing has a long history within African American culture, from blues and jazz music to the black folk-preaching tradition of Martin Luther King Jr.; music was treated as communal wealth, not private property. Legendary blues musician Willie Dixon explained, "You get their things mixed up with your ideas and the next thing you know, you're doing something that sounds like somebody else." This kind of borrowing also happened in black gospel music. Artists such as Sister Rosetta Tharpe, who began recording in the 1930s, authored songs that imitated earlier gospel songs without being called a plagiarist. African American religious music, from its very beginnings, was based on appropriation. Slaves commonly used African folk melodies with the Christian lyrics forced upon them by their white owners.

Blues, folk, and gospel music are formulaic, though by "formula" I should point out that I don't mean "cliché." The rise of print culture cultivated an "anxiety of influence," where every newly created work has to stand on its own as *wholly original,* untainted by earlier works. This was not the case with oral cultures. One reason the oral tradition was central to African American culture is because laws forbade slaves from learning to read or write. During and after slavery, the way African American folk preachers gained stature in their community was by merging words and ideas in their sermons with those of older, more established preachers. "In this context," argues scholar Keith Miller, "striking originality might have seemed self-centered or otherwise suspect. While growing up, Martin Luther King Jr. absorbed this tradition, hearing religious themes and metaphors that originated during slavery."[17]

Two sermons King surely heard as a child, "The Eagle Stirs Her

Nest" and "Dry Bones in the Valley," date back to the end of slavery and continue to be heard in black churches today. Earlier black folk preachers worked from the assumption that language is created by everyone and that it should not be considered private property. Like many who straddle two cultures, King found a way to create a hybrid system that integrated the Western print tradition of academia with African oral culture in a way that seemed natural to him. King synthesized many cultural traditions in ways that allowed him to make sense of the world—and to make it a better place. One of the greatest things about King was his ability to integrate different belief systems (Christianity, Gandhi's teachings, Thoreau's ideas about civil disobedience), remixing and rearticulating ideas that white America held dear. In doing so, he made whites aware of why the black freedom struggle was important not just for blacks, but for society as a whole.[18]

King was posthumously criticized for plagiarism in his doctoral dissertation, which spun off into criticisms that some of his sermons and speeches also contained phrases that were not his. The *Wall Street Journal* broke the story on its front page in 1990, and it was also front-page news for the *New York Times* and other major U.S. newspapers. Many journalists emphasized that King was well aware of the principles of academic citation, and they wondered why King swiped the words and ideas of others without giving proper credit. This confusion was intensified by the fact that King didn't attempt to hide what he did. One story quoted a researcher as asking, "Why didn't he know better?" and "Why did he do it? Was he so insecure that he thought this was the only way to get by?"[19]

So in 1993, when King's estate filed suit against *USA Today* you might expect it would have been for slanderously questioning King's integrity. Instead, it was for copyright infringement. The newspaper had the audacity to reprint King's "I Have a Dream" speech on the thirtieth anniversary of the day he delivered it on the steps of the Lincoln Memorial. "It is unfortunate that we were forced to bring this action against *USA Today*," the estate declared in a press release. "Because of the blatant nature of the infringement, however, we felt we had no choice." The King estate has a history of tightly controlling the late civil-rights leader's copyrights, and has pursued matters legally numerous times, all while selling his image to advertisers.

In 1995 King's son Dexter consulted with the estate managers of another King—the "King of Rock 'n' Roll"—and returned from Graceland with a new kind of dream: to aggressively control his father's image for profit's sake. I'll never forget the bolt of anger I felt when I first saw the Cingular cell-phone commercial that digitally doctored footage of King delivering his "I Have a Dream" speech. As the camera pans across the Washington Mall, the entire crowd has been erased, and King is speaking to no one. "Before you can inspire," went the voice-over, "you must first connect." I'd like to connect my foot to whoever's ass approved this commercial. It would be inspiring.

The King estate clearly doesn't care how much significance those words hold within our culture, or that the mass circulation of that speech in *USA Today* might be of more benefit to society than a hardship. The estate doesn't even allow fragmentary quoting without payment; for it, there is no such thing as fair use. For instance, in the 1970s Bruce Gronbeck—a world-renowned scholar of political rhetoric and a colleague in my department—discovered that the cost of reprinting sections of "I Have a Dream" exceeded the publication budget for a speech-communication textbook he coauthored. This meant that it had to be deleted from the 1974 version of *Principles and Types of Speech Communication* and all later editions.

As a little experiment, I sent the King estate an e-mail inquiry about reprinting four sentences from "I Have a Dream" in a scholarly book. A few weeks later I received a contract in the mail from Writers House LLC, which licenses King's copyrights. The only way I could reprint those four sentences was to hand over two hundred dollars and adhere to nine other restrictive contractual stipulations. "I have a dream that one day . . . my heirs will shill my image in cell-phone ads and charge scholars fifty dollars a sentence to reprint this speech." Inspiring.

WHO STOLE THE SOUL?

The blues was a popular musical genre that whites have heavily borrowed from through imitation or swiping songs wholesale. For instance, on the first two Led Zeppelin albums, the British megagroup used significant elements of Willie Dixon's compositions without credit. They slightly altered the songs and assigned themselves the copyright. "My daughter first brought 'Whole Lotta Love' to my attention," said Dixon. "She was all raging about it and that's what really turned me on to it. . . . We made a deal where I was satisfied and that was a very great thing as far as I was concerned because I really wasn't expecting very much."[20] His attitude reflects the bleak resignation of many blues artists who watched whites make millions from their music.

Of course, there's an obvious contradiction happening here: Dixon and virtually all other early blues artists borrowed from each other, just as Zeppelin did from them. Many of Dixon's copyrights incorporated material from the cultural commons, such as the song "My Babe," which was part of the Southern country-blues tradition long before he claimed it. Others did the same. It's doubtful that blues artists such as Leadbelly "authored" every single song for which they held a copyright. Leadbelly's song "In the Pines," which Nirvana reworked as "Where Did You Sleep Last Night?" has antecedents in the nineteenth century. Nirvana, incidentally, shares a copyright license with Leadbelly for their cover version on their *MTV Unplugged New York* album.

In his autobiography, Willie Dixon described how Chuck Berry's "Maybellene," was based on a country song named "Ida Red." Dixon convinced Berry to simply change "the country & western pace" of the original and give it more of a rhythm-and-blues feel, something that contributed to it becoming the rock 'n' roller's first hit.[21] Professor Siva Vaidhyanathan detailed how Muddy Waters explained the origins of "Feel Like Goin' Home," a revised version of an earlier song, "Country Blues." After a recording session on the front porch of Waters's Mississippi home, the musician told folk archivist Alan Lomax, "I made up that blue in '38. . . . I was fixin' a puncture on a car. I had been mistreated by a girl, it was just running in my mind to sing that song. . . . Well, I just felt blue, and the song fell into my mind and it come to me just like that and I started singing." Lomax was aware of a similar song by Robert Johnson, and he asked Waters if he knew of any other songs that borrowed the same tune.

"There's been some blues played like that," Waters replied. "This song comes from the cotton field and a boy once put a record out— Robert Johnson. He put it out as named 'Walking Blues.' . . . I heard the tune before I heard it on the record. I learned it from Son House. That's a boy who could pick a guitar." In this short passage, Waters offers no fewer than five accounts of where "Country Blues" came from. Vaidhyanathan writes,

At first, Waters asserts his own active authorship, saying he "made it" on a specific date under specific conditions. Then Waters expresses the "passive" explanation of authorship as received knowledge—not unlike Harriet Beecher Stowe's authorship of

Uncle Tom's Cabin—that "it come to me just like that." After Lomax raises the question of Johnson's influence, Waters, without shame, misgivings, or trepidation, says that he heard a version of that song by Johnson, but that his mentor Son House taught it to him. Most significantly, Waters declares in the middle of that complex genealogy that "this song comes from the cotton field."[22]

Muddy Waters had no problem slipping into and believing all five versions of the song's origins, because blues artists saw little distinction between improvisation and composition. Each time they sang a song, it was both old and new. They felt free to draw upon common musical and lyrical themes shared by others in their community. But even though Led Zeppelin and other rock groups engaged in the same type of borrowing that these early blues artists did, the power dynamics in the two cases are quite different. Something else is going on when African Americans borrowed from one another as opposed to a white English group, backed by a powerful record label and its lawyers, doing the same.

For blues musicians to protect themselves from being ripped off by whitey, they had to buy into the European ideas of authorship embedded in copyright law, and by midcentury there was a notable shift away from the borrowing practices of their musical ancestors. The folk and blues music-making tradition is, quite simply, a thing of the past. Some might say that I'm arguing for a return to a kind of pre-industrial utopia where everything is shared, and that the idea of a commons is irrelevant in modern life. They might contend that only strong and inflexible intellectual property–law protections will give incentives to create. This is simply not true. To give but one major counterexample, the Internet owes its very existence to the fact that most of its foundational protocols, codes, applications, and architecture were *not* heavily protected.

Less copyright policing gave the programming community

enough freedom to improve upon what already existed in the commons of ideas and to develop the Internet from the ground up. Building the Web was done with the participation of thousands of creators and innovators who had no guarantee that their innovations would be rewarded. Many of those people were indirectly compensated for their creativity because of the economic opportunities that the Internet opened. Not only did they benefit, society benefited. The Internet of today would not exist if five, ten, fifteen years ago overzealous software companies such as Microsoft tried to restrict access to their proprietary information the way they do now.[23]

PATENTLY ABSURD

The public domain, a commons that anyone can freely draw from, runs counter to the guiding ideology of our hyper-commercialized, free-market age. The dynamic of privatization is an overpowering one. Much of what we hear from the mainstream news media is a coded neoliberalist message that says *everything* should be up for sale, including our genetic heritage: our bodies, our selves. The pressure to pin down every gene and place it in a locked safe has fundamentally altered the long-standing scientific norms of sharing and openness in the field of genetics, replacing them with secrecy and closure. This has eroded the scientific commons of genetic information, and many insiders have argued it has made it more difficult for researchers to do their scientific work.

The existence of a commons encourages creativity and innovation in both art and science, because this kind of openness allows people to build on others' discoveries or creations. As Sir Isaac Newton put it three centuries ago, "If I see further, it is because I stand on the shoulders of giants." But the shrinkage of the genetic commons increases the need to obtain permission from patent owners if a researcher wants to use certain privately "owned" genes. Similarly, rather than being able to freely draw from melodies and lyrics, as Woody Guthrie did, today's musicians have to get the consent of song publishers before they can alter a folk song such as "This Land Is Your Land." In both cases, the creative process is bureaucratized and monetized, lowering the chances of the kinds of accidental epiphanies that occur when we have more freedom to experiment—musically or scientifically.

Today, in the field of genetics, the idea of an open scientific commons where knowledge is freely shared almost seems quaint rather than something that was central to Western science for centuries. Noted microbiologist Emmanuel Epstein says, "In the past it was the most natural thing in the world for colleagues to swap ideas on the spur of the moment, to share the latest findings hot off the scintillation counter or the electrophoresis cell, to show each other early drafts of papers, and in other such ways to act as companions in zealous research." Now, he says, simply, "no more." The logic of privatization has fundamentally transformed legal and philosophical assumptions about human life, converting it into a product—an immensely profitable one. This has created a significant shift in the way we think about our world, where life has been transformed (or reduced, depending on your point of view) to commodified information. As Monsanto CEO Robert Shapiro obliquely put it, "information" was replacing "stuff."[24]

I'm often asked, "How can you patent a gene?" For some, it doesn't seem to make sense, but it's not completely illogical. To put it another way, gene patenting is based on its own kind of logic. But before you can understand how genetic material can be owned, it's important to know what it is, so here's a crash course. *DNA* is a device that stores information, like the hard drive of a computer, and within the DNA molecule are individual units called *genes.* DNA's double-helix structure is like a long, twisted ladder that can be composed of thousands of base pairs of nucleotides. These nucleotides are known as *letters:* specifically, A, T, C, and G. A *chromosome* is a long piece of DNA that can contain as little as one gene, or thousands of genes, depending on the complexity of the organism. And a *genome* is the sum total of all that is needed to build a living being.

To recap: chains of nucleotide molecules create DNA, which contain multiple genes, which make up chromosomes, which make up a genome. Think of a genome as an encyclopedia that has multiple volumes (chromosomes), each volume has several thousand terms (genes), and the definitions of those terms are written in an alphabet that only contains the letters A, T, C and G. This is why the genome is often referred to as "the book of life," but rather than being copyrighted as a Stephen King novel would be, genes fall under patent law. To return to the computer analogy, you can fit all the information contained in a human genome (all the data necessary to create you) on a compact disc. The human genome contains 1.5×10^9 bytes of information, which is roughly the same amount contained in a seventy-five-minute hip-hop CD by Snoop Dogg.

Much like computer software, genetic information is "programmed" to stimulate the production of proteins, which is facilitated by *RNA*—a close relative of DNA that only has one strand of nucleotides. RNA is transcribed from the DNA, creating a messenger RNA, or mRNA. This is known as a *transcript* because it carries a copy of a section of DNA that can assemble amino acids into proteins (much like how information is sent via e-mail). Following this metaphor of communication, it's in this transcription that a gene is "expressed" (the gene "tells" the mRNA to build a protein that tells the cell to do stuff).

Genetic expression occurs when molecules obey physical forces, similar to the way electrical impulses sent to speakers re-create music. Think of the gene in charge of producing the growth hormone protein as being like an MP3 file that contains Snoop Dogg's "Gin & Juice." The data contained in the MP3 file triggers the software program that translates the 1's and 0's into something recognizable. The computer sends an electronic signal to your speakers, which hurtles sound waves through the air, which vibrates in your ear so that you can hear Snoop rap, "It's kinda hard bein' Snoop D-O-double-G / but I, somehow, someway, keep comin' up with funky-ass shit every single day." In much the same way, the gene directs the growth hormone protein to initiate a cascade of signals that produces cell growth and division, which results in a gain in height and weight. Information, whether it's stored in an MP3 file or a gene, directly creates a physical response.

Incorrect recording can result in problems. The mere substitution of a T for an A in one particular gene causes sickle-cell anemia, for instance. In addition, genetic information is conveyed not just in the order of letters, but also how the letters are spaced out. For the sake of argument, let's say that the gene that controls the growth hormone protein might contain the following letters—CTAGG repeated—organized like this: CTAGG, CTA, GGCT, AGG, CTAGG, CTAG, GCTAGG. Information is embedded *not just in the ordering of letters, but also in the spacing* (just as the timing of a joke's punch line, the pause, makes all the difference in the world). There's a huge difference between "notjustintheorderingoflettersbutalsoin-thespacing" and "not just in the ordering of letters but also in the spacing" and "no tj us tint he or de ring of let ters bu tals ointh es pacing."[25] If this gene were a rapper, then MC DNA might bust something like, "It's kinda hard bein' the C(noop) T A double G / but somehow, someway, I keep comin' up with funky-ass growth hormone proteins every single day."

Defenders of gene patents argue that they aren't patenting the genes themselves (as they exist in nature, in our bodies). They are instead patenting "isolated and purified" DNA sequences or synthetic analogs. This means the DNA sequence is removed from its original biological context to trigger the creation of therapeutic proteins, or other such things, much like chemical compounds are invented in the laboratory. The problem with this logic is that DNA sequences look more like pure *information* than invented physical compounds, and control of that patented information can limit others' ability to create medicines and therapies. "At the moment," argues Nobel Prize–winning geneticist John Sulston in his memoir *The Common Thread,* "the practice of granting biological patents is not heeding the distinction between discovery and invention." Despite the fact that companies say they don't technically own a gene, they have *de facto* control over the way that gene's sequence can be used—which is only a slight rhetorical distance from actual ownership.

PRIVATIZING LIFE

Because of a landmark Supreme Court case and congressional legislation, 1980 was a pivotal year for genetic research. In the *Diamond v. Chakrabarty* decision, a five-to-four majority ruled that a living, genetically altered microorganism could be patented under U.S. law. Previous to this ruling, it was the policy of the U.S. Patent and Trademark Office (PTO) that living organisms—in the case of *Diamond v. Chakrabarty,* a bacterium that helped clean oil spills— could not be patented. But the Supreme Court ruled otherwise, stating that "anything under the sun that is made by the hand of man" is patentable subject matter. That same year, Congress passed the Bayh-Dole Act to encourage the commercialization of inventions produced by universities and other recipients of federal funding. An influx of private money poured into university science departments, and since the act's passing, the private funding of university biomedical research has increased by a factor of 20.

This growth in subsidies provided the legal justification for researchers to exploit human genes. And when I use the word "exploit," I'm not using it in an ideological way—I'm simply using the terminology of a patent lawyer. During an interview with a *New York Times* reporter, Todd Dickinson, the former U.S. Patent and Trademark Office's commissioner, took exception to the idea that patents allow a "government sponsored monopoly," a phrase he found imprecise. Instead, Commissioner Dickinson corrected the reporter, saying candidly and without irony, "We like to say 'right to exploit.' " Today, private pharmaceutical companies (many of which are partnered with universities) are engaged in a manic—maniacal, even—race to patent every imaginable human gene, protein, and cell line that might be profitable.

The BRCA-1 and BRCA-2 genes are linked to breast cancer and are owned by Myriad Genetics, whose literature reports, "Women with a BRCA mutation have a 33 to 50 percent risk of developing cancer by age 50 and a 56 to 87 percent risk by age 70." Myriad has a monopoly right over the use of the gene in diagnostic tests or therapies, which means that every time a woman is tested to find out if she carries those mutated genes, a hefty royalty has to be paid to Myriad. Also, if a researcher discovers a therapy that prevents cancerous mutations in these genes, he or she is obligated under the law to secure a license from Myriad, and the company has used its patent to block research on the gene. This is one of the ways that these kinds of gene patents contribute to the skyrocketing costs of drugs and medical care in the United States and throughout the world.

Helena Chaye, like many I've spoken with in the business of

drugs and science, feels uncomfortable about these kinds of situations. As the director of Business Development at the biotech corporation MediGene, she secures and sells gene patent licenses for the company. Chaye finds herself in an uneasy position. She has both a Ph.D. in molecular genetics and a degree in law, and is intimately familiar with both areas. "From a private company's perspective," she tells me, "you want everything to be protected. You want the ability to block other people, and you want the ability to monopolize a certain sector or a certain product and block others from entering, even though you may not be the one [who's] actually developing it." For many commercial entities, it simply makes no business sense to put anything in the public domain.

"I personally don't believe in that," Chaye says. "From what I do for a living, it's a struggle, philosophically, that I'm having to patent everything." She continues: "If genetic sequencing was publicly available for diagnostics, for example, you wouldn't have to go through Myriad and pay four thousand dollars for a breast cancer test. If that was available to other parties, then you could have somebody else develop it at a much cheaper rate and be available for everyone." She pauses. "I mean, the flip side of that is they say, 'Well, we're not going to be able to develop something so expensive unless there's some sort of monopoly that protects us in the future.' But I think there's a reasonable level at which certain things should be protected, and certain things should be left to the public domain."

My favorite patent request was submitted by a British waitress and poet who protested the gobbling up of the genetic commons by filing patent application GB0000180.0. She wanted to patent herself. "It has taken 30 years of hard labor for me to discover and invent myself," Donna MacLean drily wrote in the application, "and now I wish to protect my invention from unauthorized exploitation, genetic or otherwise. I am new. I have led a private existence and I have not made the invention of myself public." MacLean added, "I am not obvious." The provocateur poet didn't receive her patent, but she made her point.

PATENTS AS STUMBLING BLOCKS

While many are still happily riding the moneymaking bandwagon, there are a growing number of scientists, medical researchers, and even companies that believe certain gene patents can inhibit research. The chief scientific officer at Bristol-Myers Squibb, Peter Ringrose—hardly a radical anticapitalist Luddite—said that there were "more than fifty proteins possibly involved in cancer that the company was not working on because the patent holders either would not allow it or were demanding unreasonable royalties." Dr. Gareth Evans, a consultant in medical genetics, also believes that the economic value of genetic patents make research more secretive and restrictive, and therefore lessens the chances of scientists finding cures.

The hoarding of these kinds of patents threatens to create a "tragedy of the anticommons," as Rebecca Eisenberg, a National Institutes of Health–affiliated law professor at the University of Michigan, calls it. The phrase "tragedy of the commons" was coined by Garrett Hardin in his classic essay of the same name, and its primary argument goes like this: If anyone can use common property—a pasture where farm animals can freely graze, for instance—then it can be overused and trashed. While this can happen to physical resources, a patented gene won't suffer the same fate, but as Eisenberg points out by inverting the phrase, tragedies *do* occur from fencing off the genetic commons. Yes, it's true that patent protection provides the financial incentive for companies to invest in research and development, which, in turn, generates many useful drugs and inventions. Patents aren't inherently bad, but Eisenberg argues that certain patents can be problematic when the protected materials resemble a discovery, rather than an invention.

This kind of patent ownership creates bureaucratic stumbling blocks and economic disincentives that can dissuade laboratories from dealing with certain genes. This was the case with hemochromatosis, a hereditary condition that can cause liver or heart failure (the gene that carries the disorder is found in one in ten people). In 1999 two companies were fighting over the ownership rights of the patented gene connected to hemochromatosis. This created confusion over who owned the patent and to whom medical laboratories should pay licensing fees, helping to shut down research on DNA tests that screened for the condition. Five labs halted testing for hemochromatosis, and twenty-one others decided not to offer the test at all.[26]

Professor Eisenberg argues that the existence of a genetic commons speeds efficiency in medical research because it eliminates the need to track down and negotiate with numerous patent owners. This point was highlighted in 1999 when ten of the world's largest drug companies created an alliance with five of the leading gene laboratories. The alliance invested in a two-year plan to uncover and publish three hundred thousand common genetic variations to prevent upstart biotechnology companies from patenting and locking up important genetic information. The companies (including Bayer AG and Bristol-Myers Squibb) wanted the data released into the public domain to ensure that genetic information could be freely accessed and used for research. Its mission undermined the assertion that a genetic commons inevitably leads to commercial suicide and the end of research incentives.[27]

What's most troubling about thousands of DNA sequences being owned by a handful of companies is the fact that genes are deeply interrelated. For instance, there is no single gene that causes Alzheimer's disease, which instead results from a variety of environmental factors and interactions with other genes. Scientists have mapped much of the human genome, figuring out that there are roughly one hundred thousand pieces of a genetic jigsaw puzzle. But in order to effectively fight diseases with genetic technologies, researchers have to learn how each privately owned gene connects and reacts with the ones around it. Imagine trying to put together a puzzle if you had to buy a random assortment of jigsaw pieces from dozens of companies. You might get frustrated, even give up. When you have to secure multiple licenses from several companies just to begin research, it is all the more difficult for scientists to efficiently and affordably do their job.

"It's a really big problem if you have to sign lots of agreements," Eisenberg told *New Scientist.* "Licenses and material transfer agreements with companies are taking longer to negotiate, so it may take weeks or months." Similarly, Jeffrey Kahn, director of the University of Minnesota's Center for Bioethics, cautioned that high licensing fees can hold medical progress hostage. "If you're a start-up company, you need to have those licenses bagged," MediGene's Helena Chaye tells me. "You need them in your back pocket to go and raise money or to entice investors to put more money into it because you've got new licensed technologies." Not having those licenses, she says, "could definitely hinder your operations." And if you think that many of these companies aren't aggressively guarding their genes, just listen to Human Genome Sciences CEO William A. Haseltine, who openly stated: "Any company that wants to be in the business of using genes, proteins or antibodies as drugs has a very high probability of running afoul of our patents. From a commercial point of view, they are severely constrained—and far more than they realize."

Geneticist John Sulston argues in his book *The Common Thread* that it seems unlikely "that patent laws combined with untrammeled market forces are going to lead to a resolution that is in the best interests of further research, or of human health and well-being." Advocates of privatization argue that having a commons that anyone can freely draw from will mean the end of creativity and innovation, but the opposite is often true. The way patent law is applied in genetics can limit researchers' choices, which means the scientific imagination becomes routinized and stifled. There's little room for the kinds of visionary ideas and accidental discoveries that evolve into real breakthroughs. An argument for the commons—whether it's the genetic commons or a folk-song commons—is an argument for more creative elbow room.[28] But because of our blind faith in privatization, freedom of expression® has been limited artistically, socially, and scientifically.

SEEDS = INFORMATION

I live in Iowa, and I am surrounded by corn, pork, pickup trucks, and, from what I hear, meth labs. Over the past few years, I've been inundated by plenty of weird and wonderful stories about farming and rural living. However, one of the most unsettling, science fiction–sounding scenarios I've come across is the "Technology Protection System," or "terminator technology," as it is known in the press. This technology enables seed companies to genetically alter their patented seeds so that crops become sterile after one planting, turning off life like a light switch. It's a way of preventing farmers from retaining seeds from the previous year's crop and replanting them.

Saving and replanting seeds is something we humans have been doing since we stopped being nomadic creatures, but the practice is now illegal with seeds that are patented. The terminator seeds were developed by the U.S.–based Delta and Pine Land, whose president trumpeted, "We expect the new technology to have global implications." Delta and Pine Land claimed that the terminator seed would be marketed primarily in developing countries to prevent farmers from saving, trading, and/or replanting seeds that are sold by U.S. corporations. Interestingly, the seed industry experienced many aspects of the Napster file-sharing controversy a few years before it hit the music industry.

While there are obvious differences, there are also striking similarities. MP3 music files circulate on the Internet because someone had to purchase a CD, which was then inserted into a computer and "ripped" into digital files. These files can then be exactly duplicated, and copies are made of these copies, then shared. This is also true of privately owned seeds, though the earth (rather than a computer) "reaps" this information without permission. These copied seeds can then be given to other farmers through informal trading systems, delivering them from person to person, a sort of rural peer-to-peer file-sharing network. Even though the seeds are patented, much like music is copyrighted, this can't stop someone from creating a facsimile of someone else's intellectual property. This is why the terminator technology was invented.

Sterile seeds may be an inconvenience for American farmers who, for various reasons—including being riddled with debt—want to continue saving seeds. But they may prove devastating for their poorer counterparts in Third World countries who rely on subsistence farming. U.S. Department of Agriculture (USDA) spokesperson Willard Phelps stated that the goal of the terminator technology is "to increase the value of proprietary seed owned by U.S. seed companies and to open new markets in second and Third World countries." The primary creator of the terminator seed, Melvin J. Oliver, made clear his invention's purpose to *New Scientist:* "Our system is a way of self-policing the unauthorized use of American technology," he asserted, comparing it to copy-protection technologies that prevent the duplication of music. And we wonder why so much of the world hates us.

In mid-1998 Monsanto made an attempt to purchase terminator seed–patent owner Delta and Pine Land. However, this technology met with heated worldwide protests that targeted Monsanto as the next Great Satan, and in early 1999 the company stepped back in "recognition that we need some level of public acceptance to do our business." Although Monsanto backed out of the merger, Delta and Pine Land, which still holds the terminator-seed patent with the USDA, has continued to develop the technology. Just as in the movies, the Terminator lived on. Delta and Pine Land official Harry Collins stated in January 2000, "We've continued right on with work on the Technology Protection System. We never really slowed down. We're on target, moving ahead to commercialize it. We never really backed off." Since then, more terminator-technology patents have been awarded.

Four-fifths of the sixteen hundred patents issued for genetically modified crops are owned by just thirteen companies, and some of the most significant patents belong to Monsanto. The St. Louis–based operation was founded in 1901 as a chemical company, and it gained notoriety in the 1970s because it was responsible for creating Agent Orange. This chemical compound was used by the military to clear jungles in Vietnam, which led to illness and death in thousands, and the company has also been implicated in several cases of employee and residential contamination. A Monsanto production plant contaminated the Missouri town of Times Beach so much that it had to be evacuated in 1982, and in 2002 Monsanto lost a case against lawyers representing a small Alabama town that had been poisoned as well.[29]

By the mid-1990s Monsanto moved much of its chemical operations to biotechnology, and it is now a global leader in transgenic crops. The contract for Monsanto's Roundup Ready soybeans allows the company to search a customer's farmland for signs of saved seeds, and, to nab offenders, the company can track purchase records and check with seed dealers. Among other things, the company has hired Pinkerton detectives—the same private police force hired by the Rockefellers to murderously bust unions in the 1920s—to investigate tips on seed saving. In addition, the company created and advertised the existence of hotlines for neighbors to report farmers who save seeds. "Dial 1–800–ROUNDUP," said a Monsanto ad. "Tell the rep that you want to report some potential seed law violations or other information. It is important to use 'land lines' rather than cellular phones due to the number of people who scan cellular calls."[30]

Monsanto also developed a kit that determines whether or not a plant was derived from patented seeds by using a principle similar to a pregnancy test, but applied to leaves. Scott Good was one of the many farmers who dealt with the wrath of Monsanto when he saved his seeds and replanted the company's intellectual property. "They showed up at my door at six o'clock in the morning. They flipped a badge," said Scott of Monsanto's agents. "They acted like the FBI. I was scared." Farmers who infringe on Monsanto's patents have been fined hundreds of thousands of dollars, and some face bankruptcy. Much like other large seed companies, Monsanto offers incentives for seed distributors to carry their patented seeds rather than public-domain seeds.

A farmer's choice to plant public-domain seeds becomes increasingly difficult or impossible when near-monopolies exist within the agribusiness industries. Factory farming has flooded the market with low-priced crops, which forces farmers to purchase the patented, high-yield seeds or go out of business. University of Indiana seed geneticist Martha Crouch commented to *Science* magazine, "Free choice is a nice idea, but it doesn't seem to operate in the real world." Although critics have blasted the existence of these so-called Frankenfoods, we should keep in mind that farmers throughout history have manipulated the genetic makeup of crops by selecting for certain favorable traits. Also, these genetically modified crops often grow in more abundant quantities, need less labor, and sometimes require fewer chemical pesticides or herbicides. In other words, there are reasons why North American farmers plant these seeds.

One of the trade-offs, however, is that these patented crops are also uniform in their genetic makeup. This is a problem because when we rely on fewer varieties of food, we increase our chances of exposing ourselves to major food shortages. For instance, the biological cause of the Irish Potato Famine in the mid-1800s was rooted in a reliance on two major varieties of potatoes. The *Phytophthorainfestans* fungus precipitated the destruction of Ireland's primary food staple for five years, spreading to the Highlands of Scotland and elsewhere. Although the same blight affected the Andes, because South American farmers preserved hundreds of varieties of potatoes, the effects of the fungus were minimal. In fact, the only reason the Europeans could restock their food supply was that they could draw on varieties of potatoes from the Andean region.[31]

The spread of uniform, patented seeds has accelerated the loss of thousands of varieties of crops. Today, 97 percent of the vegetable varieties sold by commercial seed houses in the United States at the beginning of the century are now extinct, and 86 percent of the fruit varieties have been lost. These numbers are actually quite conservative because there were surely more varieties that weren't collected in the nineteenth century. Over the twentieth century the varieties of cabbage dropped from 544 to 20; carrots from 287 to 21; cauliflower from 158 to 9; apples from 7,089 to 878. The list goes on. In sum, roughly 75 percent of the genetic diversity of the world's twenty most important food crops has been lost *forever*. Because biodiversity is a key factor in the ability of plants to adapt to changing conditions, and humans' ability to do the same, reduced biodiversity seriously threatens ecological support systems.[32]

Despite skepticism from Europe, the planting of altered (and patented) soybeans, corn, potatoes, and canola in the United States and Canada has exploded, and the market for such crops is expected to grow to as much as $500 billion in the next few decades. The dramatic rise in the growing of patented crops in North America will likely be followed by the same expansion in other countries throughout the world—one way or the other. It's a biological fact that, once the pollen from genetically modified crops travels through the air, it can pollinate nongenetically modified crops. This invasive pollination has happened to many organic farmers, such as Laura Krouse, based in Iowa. Because of the presence of the Bt gene in her corn, Krouse's crop can no longer be certified as organic, and she lost half her business in the process.

Why can't these farmers prevent this contamination? The answer, my friend, is blowing in the wind. "I don't know if there's room for a business like mine anymore," said Krouse. "Biologically, it doesn't seem like it's going to be possible because of this sea of genetically engineered pollen that I live in, over which I have no control."[33] In 1998 Monsanto sued Canadian farmer Percy Schmeiser after the company discovered its patented canola plants growing on his property. The seventy-three-year-old Schmeiser argued that he shouldn't have to pay Monsanto a licensing fee because the pollen had blown onto his property from neighboring farms. Although Monsanto said this might be the case—in fact, the company acknowledged that Schmeiser never placed an order for its Roundup Ready canola—he was still infringing on their patent.

In a narrow 5–4 decision, Canada's Supreme Court ruled in favor of Monsanto in 2004, stating that it wasn't concerned with
"blow by" dissemination of patented plants. It simply determined
that the farmer "actively cultivated" Monsanto's property. These
patented seeds have also traveled south because the North American Free Trade Agreement (NAFTA) allows five million tons of corn
to be sold in Mexico. Many residents of the country, and the Mexican government itself, are up in arms over what they see as an un-
welcome invasion of their farmlands. But Dr. Michael Phillips, an
executive director at the Biotechnology Industry Organization
(BIO), isn't very sympathetic. "If you're the government of Mexico,
hopefully you've learned a lesson here," he bluntly told *NOW with
Bill Moyers.* The lesson? "It's very difficult to keep a new technology
from, you know, entering your borders—particularly in a biological
system."

GLOBALIZATION AND ITS DISCONTENTS

Much of the developing world—primarily rain-forest countries—is
loaded with what some gene hunters refer to as "green gold." This
refers to medically useful plant materials that can yield massive
profits. However, identifying a valuable DNA sequence is a very difficult task, like finding a needle in a mountainous biological
haystack. Scientists working for Western companies get around this
problem by relying on tribal shamans and medicine men to point
them to plants that are medically useful. Using the knowledge developed by indigenous people in developing countries increases by
400-fold a scientist's ability to locate the plants that have specific
medicinal uses. In another estimate, by consulting with the local
communities, bioprospectors can increase the success ratio from
one in ten thousand samples to one in two in their quest to find active ingredients that can be used in medicines.

For instance, using an active ingredient extracted from an indigenous plant in northeastern Brazil, the U.S.–based MGI Pharma developed a drug to treat symptoms of xerostomia, or "dry-mouth syndrome." The drug's development capitalized on the local knowledge about the properties of the jaborandi plant, which literally means—I love this—"slobber-mouth plant." Knowledge about the plant's properties had been passed down for generations, but the company did not compensate the native Brazilians in any way. Nor did MGI Pharma have to, even though it was the local knowledge that led the U.S. researchers to the drug discovery in the first place.[34]

Over the centuries, indigenous communities have significantly contributed to the diversity and cultivation of our most basic and important crops. The reason why we can purchase blue corn tortilla chips in stores is because of the centuries of care Mexican farmers gave to cultivating varieties of blue corn (as well as yellow, white, red, speckled, and hundreds of other varieties). This cultivation is a form of labor; that this corn still exists is no mere accident. However, only the knowledge developed in scientific laboratories is protected as patented "property," while the traditional systems are open to plundering because they are communally maintained. This illustrates the double-edged nature of "the commons," a reason why this concept shouldn't be blindly celebrated in all situations.

Under the global patent system, intellectual property can only be produced by people in white lab coats employed by companies with huge amounts of capital at their disposal. The time and labor and collective achievements of indigenous farmers are rendered worthless, devalued as being merely "nature." These kinds of bioprospecting patents—or, as globalization critic Vandana Shiva calls them, *biopiracy* patents—are built on the fiction of individualistic scientific innovation. This false premise ignores the collective nature of knowledge and denies communities patent protection.[35]

It would be as if someone came along and copyrighted the stories in the Bible. The Old Testament's narratives were passed down from generation to generation through the oral tradition, preserved by hundreds and thousands of years of active storytelling. Those who set the stories into print certainly had a strong editorial hand, crafting the sentences and ordering the stories in unique ways. But there are still strong echoes of that oral tradition: the use of repetition, mnemonics, formula, and other devices common to oral folk narratives. The written version of the Old Testament simply could not exist without the effort of the communities who passed the stories on. The same is true of useful plants in Third World countries. Western scientists would have never "discovered" these plants if not for the cultivative labor of indigenous communities over hundreds and thousands of years. Unfortunately, this is not an argument that makes sense in most established theories of economics—so, to paraphrase Woody Guthrie, the poor people lose again.

The U.N.'s 1999 *Human Development Report* pointed out that more than half of the most frequently prescribed drugs throughout the world have been derived from plants, plant genes, or plant extracts from developing countries. These drugs are a standard part of the treatment of lymphatic cancer, glaucoma, leukemia, and various heart conditions, and they account for billions in annual sales. According to the United Nations Development Project study, developing countries annually lose $5 billion in unpaid royalties from drugs developed from medicinal plants. The United States sees it differently. It calculates that developing countries owe its pharmaceutical companies $2.5 billion for violating their medical patents.[36]

The case of the yellow Mexican bean patent is symbolic of how patents can enable economic colonialism, where resources are drained from developing countries. In the early 1990s, bioprospector Larry Proctor bought a bag of dry beans in Mexico and proceeded to remove the yellow varieties, allowing them to pollinate.

After he had a "uniform and stable population" of yellow beans, his company, POD-NERS, exercised its legal right of monopoly by suing two companies that imported the yellow Mexican beans. The president of Tutuli Produce, Rebecca Gilliland, stated: "In the beginning, I thought it was a joke. How could [Proctor] invent something that Mexicans have been growing for centuries?" POD-NERS demanded a royalty of six cents per pound on the import of these yellow beans, which prompted U.S. customs officials to inspect shipments and take samples of Mexican beans at the border, at an additional cost to Gilliland's company.

Her company lost customers, as did other companies, which meant that twenty-two thousand Mexican farmers lost 90 percent of their income. The Mexican government challenged the U.S. patent on this bean variety, but the process would be long and costly, running at least two hundred thousand dollars in legal fees. In the meantime, Proctor remained defiant, filing lawsuits against sixteen small bean-seed companies and farmers in Colorado, and he amended the original patent with forty-three new claims. Poorer countries typically don't have the resources to battle these types of patents, especially when there are more pressing domestic concerns such as clean-water availability and health emergencies.[37] This lack of means to challenge bioprospectors is a real concern for countries targeted by patent-happy multinationals. It's a problem because the economies of some African countries rely on only one export, and others, on only four or five.

These exports are essentially raw biological materials, and they make up roughly 40 percent of all the world's processing and production. But once corporate biotechnology reduces active ingredients found in developing countries to their molecular components, the commodity can be manufactured rather than grown. Western multinationals hold a vast amount of patents on naturally occurring biological materials found in the Southern Hemisphere. These companies own 79 percent of all utility patents on plants; Northern universities and research institutions control 14 percent; and parties in Third World countries have almost no holdings. In Mexico, for example, in 1996 only 389 patent applications came from Mexican residents, while over 30,000 came from foreign residents. In this way, intellectual-property laws help to exacerbate the unequal distribution of wealth among rich and poor nations.[38]

Although patent law carries with it a Western bias, that doesn't mean the future is a bleak, foregone conclusion for developing countries. In recent years, these nations and their allies within nongovernmental organizations have lobbied strongly to better protect the resources of countries rich in traditional knowledge and biodiversity. For instance, the World Intellectual Property Organization (WIPO) convened the "Intergovernmental Committee on Intellectual Property and Genetic Resources, Traditional Knowledge, and Folklore"—which met seven times between 2000 and 2004. The committee's goal is manifold, but with regard to genetic resources it aims to encourage "benefit sharing" agreements between companies and countries rich in valuable biological material.[39]

An example of this is a 1991 deal linked between the pharmaceutical company Merck and the Costa Rican nonprofit Instituto Nacional de Biodiversidad (INBio). The agreement held the potential for Costa Rica to earn more than $100 million annually, money generated from INBio's 10,000 collected samples of biological material. Although INBio signed more than ten similar contracts with other companies, it should be noted that these kinds of agreements are entirely voluntary and continue to be rare. In fact, Merck ended its association with INBio in 1999, and no royalties had been earned as of 2004. Lorena Guevara, the manager of bioprospecting at INBio, told me that negotiations with companies over the terms of benefit sharing are quite difficult. Still, Guevara remains optimistic, even in the face of forces that are much more powerful than the nonprofit for which she works—or, for that matter, Costa Rica itself.

North American and European countries, and particularly the United States, have led an unrelenting battle to force developing countries to adopt acceptable (to them) intellectual-property systems. The Trade-Related Aspects of Intellectual Property Rights (TRIPS) has been an instrumental tool that forces member countries of the World Trade Organization (WTO) to adopt standardized intellectual-property laws. The general public in the First and Third World had no say in writing TRIPS. A senior U.S. trade negotiator remarked that, "probably less than fifty people were responsible for TRIPS."[40] TRIPS forces developing countries to adopt intellectual-property laws that often run counter to their national interests, and if they don't comply, they're threatened with economic blackmail in the form of trade retaliations.

Strengthened intellectual-property laws in developing countries decreases the ability of local communities to gain access to technological information (through reverse engineering and other imitative methods). This makes technological catching-up all the more difficult. In this brave new privatized world, the only way to have market power is to innovate. But the only way to innovate is to have lots of capital to invest in the first place, and developing countries only account for 6 percent of global research and development expenditures. As poor nations strengthen their intellectual-property regimes, their markets increasingly are dominated by imported goods, because their local industries can't compete.

The WTO acts as a policing mechanism that allows countries to bring "unfair competition" charges and other actions against offending countries. For instance, the Bush 2.0 administration has been under pressure from the biotech industry to bring charges against the European Union for its ban against genetically modified food. In a letter to Bush signed by virtually every agribusiness and biotech firm, it claimed that the ban stigmatized biotechnology and "may be negatively affecting the attitudes and actions of other countries." As if other countries should not dare form their own opinions and policies.

For years, the United States opposed in WTO courts the waiving of patents in countries that have been overwhelmed by AIDS and other deadly diseases, making it illegal for those countries to import generic versions of drugs at a fraction of the cost. Economic studies of Taiwan, China, and India have shown that when patent laws are strengthened, drug prices go up because these countries can no longer manufacture generic drugs. This pattern has been repeated numerous times in poorer countries, where price increases can be devastating. During the 1990s, the Brazilian government was proactive in dealing with AIDS, allowing local pharmaceutical manufacturers to produce low-cost generic HIV therapies. It wrote its patent laws to allow for what's called compulsory licensing, which legally compels owners to license their patents at a rate regulated by the government.

This approach allowed Brazilian manufacturers to produce Nevirapine—which helps prevent mother-to-child HIV transmission—for an affordable amount. It cost $0.59 U.S. dollars a day to treat each victim, which resulted in a 50 percent drop in AIDS-related mortality between 1996 and 1999. As a reward for this achievement, the United States took Brazil to the WTO dispute panel to force the country to undo its liberal patent laws.[41] "The power of the rich countries and of the transnational corporations," argued John Sulston, "was being used in a bullying and inequitable fashion to achieve ends that benefit them rather than mankind as a whole." After years of worldwide pressure, the United States granted concessions in the WTO that were largely meaningless, like a provision that allowed countries to manufacture lifesaving drugs without penalty. However, most of these African countries had no such pharmaceutical production base, making it impossible for them to legally acquire the drugs.

Years dragged on, millions upon millions died until, in 2001, the United States agreed on a proposal that allows countries to import manufactured generic drugs. But under pressure from the pharmaceutical industry, the Bush 2.0 administration quietly changed its position and sent its trade representative to the WTO to kill the proposal. Much of the world reacted with rage to this shift, and finally in 2003 the United States signed on to an agreement that technically allowed countries with no manufacturing base to import cheap lifesaving drugs. I use the word "technically" because the agreement contains so much red tape that it severely limits the amount of supplies it can import. "Today's deal was designed to offer comfort to the U.S. and the Western pharmaceutical industry," said Ellen Hoen of the medical-aid group Doctors Without Borders. She told the Associated Press, "Unfortunately it offers little comfort for poor patients. Global patent rules will continue to drive up the price of medicines."

I only hope that she is wrong, though given the WTO's and the pharmaceutical industry's track record on this issue, I have little faith. The kinds of constraints intellectual-property laws impose on culture may be bad for music and creativity, but in the case of drug patents it's literally a life-and-death matter. Patent policy is as much a moral issue as it is an economic one, solid proof that property rights trump human rights nine times out of ten. Yes, I realize that these pharmaceutical companies invest millions of dollars in research and development, but there are times when profits alone shouldn't guide us and empathy and compassion should take over. However, we're living in a time when, increasingly, money is the only thing that matters.

I'm not claiming that all patents are bad things, because it's demonstrable that they can encourage investment in the development of products. However, I am arguing for two things. First, there should be some flexibility in the way patent protections are enforced, especially in situations such as the worldwide AIDS crisis. It simply should not have taken ten years for the WTO to adopt half-hearted rules about importing generic drugs, and I believe that those who tried to block it have blood on their hands. Second, there are too many instances when overly broad patents are awarded, which can cause information flow to be slowed and research and innovation to be stunted.

ONE FINAL IRONY

The most shameful detail in all of this is that all developing countries—whether they were the United States and Switzerland in the nineteenth century or Brazil and Thailand in the twentieth century—had very weak patent and copyright laws. Historically, countries left out of the technological-development loop have emphasized the right of their citizens to have free access to foreign inventions and knowledge. The United States in particular had extremely lax intellectual-property laws at the turn of the twentieth century, which allowed it to freely build up its cultural and scientific resources. Also, the United States' agricultural economy depended on the importation of crops native to other countries because the only major crop native to North America was the sunflower.[42]

Even the music for the U.S. national anthem, "The Star-Spangled Banner," was swiped from a popular eighteenth-century English song, "To Anacreon in Heaven." This old drinking song was written by a group of English dandies in the Anacreonic Club, which was devoted to an orgy-loving Greek bard who lived during the 500

B.C.E. era. (Little do people know when they patriotically sing the anthem at sports games that the tune originally celebrated Dionysian explosions of sex and drinking.) In 1812 lyricist Francis Scott Key borrowed the tune, and in 1931 it became the national anthem.[43] Then in 1969, at Woodstock, Jimi Hendrix famously reappropriated the anthem and drenched it in a purple haze of feedback that fit the violent and dissonant Vietnam era. We are a nation of pirates.

Now the United States and other rich countries want strict enforcements of intellectual-property laws that ensure developing countries will remain uncompetitive within the globalized economy. Again, we wonder why much of the world hates us. Defenders of overbroad gene patents, terminator seeds, and global intellectual-property treaties argue that without technologies and legal protections that safeguard their investments, there would be no incentive to develop new, innovative products. Companies such as Monsanto (whose comforting motto is "Food—Health—Hope") insist that their motivations for doing business are grounded in a desire to prevent world hunger. By creating more efficient products, biotech, agribusiness, and pharmaceutical companies can contribute to the betterment of humanity, they say.

HOWEVER, IF YOU buy that selfless line of reasoning, then I have a genetically altered monkey-boy I want to sell you (all sales final).

CHAPTER TWO

COPYRIGHT CRIMINALS

this is a sampling sport

Tim Quirk's first unpleasant encounter with copyright law came in the form of a cease-and-desist letter sent by a clown. The word "clown," by the way, isn't a mean-spirited jab at greedy lawyers. No, I'm talking about Bozo himself.

Quirk was the lead singer, songwriter, and guitarist for Too Much Joy, a poppy, punky band whose career spanned the 1980s and 1990s. Much to his chagrin, Quirk's old band is probably better known for getting into trouble than for their sometimes goofy, sometimes sophisticated, and often catchy music. Over the course of a decade, Too Much Joy was arrested for performing obscene 2 Live Crew songs in Broward County, Florida; Quirk was detained by the Secret Service after drunkenly joking onstage about strangling Bill Clinton when Chelsea was in the audience; and they pissed off Bozo the Clown.

In the larger scheme of things, Too Much Joy is just a footnote in pop-music history, and Quirk's new band, Wonderlick, probably won't even qualify for that status. I don't mean this as an insult; on the contrary, not-even-a-footnote is the level at which almost all working musicians live. Comparatively speaking, Quirk has done pretty well for himself. When I first met him during the course of writing this book, he was happily married, the proud father of a nine-year-old daughter, and had somehow spun his love of music into a respectable career in the music industry—in the form of a nine-to-five job at Real Networks, one of the companies to get in early on the legal music-download business. In the time since Quirk first recorded "Clowns," he has gained some weight and lost a little hair. But even though he's not quite the same person who rocked the stage ten years ago, he's still a spry guy.

How exactly does one end up on the wrathful receiving end of one of America's most beloved (and disturbing) children's en-tertainers? The story begins in 1988 with Too Much Joy's song "Clowns," a ridiculously hummable slab of power pop that is about, as Quirk puts it, "how parents seem to think clowns are harmless even though all kids know that clowns are weird and evil."[1] A band member still had a Bozo the Clown LP from childhood, and when the group was in the recording studio, they excerpted a story recited by the happy/evil clown. In a voice that eerily resembled *The Simpsons's* Krusty the Clown, Quirk uttered something that can only be taken the wrong way: "I found something in one of my pockets. It was about as big as your shoe," Bozo declared on the scratchy piece of vinyl, "but it was *shaped like a rocket!*" This five-second sample served as the intro for "Clowns," a track off my favorite Too Much Joy album, *Son of Sam I Am*.

A clown was my boss at every job I ever had.
Clowns run all the record companies that ever said we're bad.
A clown pretended to be a girl who pretended to be my friend.
This world is run by clowns who can't wait for it to end.

Unfortunately for the band, Larry Harmon, who played Bozo and who owns the intellectual-property rights to the clown character, keeps track of the Bozo brand. He has a clipping service to monitor when Bozo is mentioned in newspapers. It was through this means that he discovered a review of *Son of Sam I Am* that described "Clowns," so Bozo's lawyers sent a cease-and-desist letter that claimed Too Much Joy's record infringed on Harmon's copyright. Above the dense legalese was a maniacal red-and-blue Bozo smiling in the upper right-hand corner. Too Much Joy was selling out and jumping from Alias Records—the independent label that originally released *Son of Sam I Am*—to Warner Records, one of the industry's largest major labels (which had recently signed R.E.M.). If Alias had pulled the record off the market because of Bozo's threats, it would have put this small label out of business, but because Warner paid Alias for the rights to re-release the album, this wasn't an issue.

The band felt there were bigger principles at stake, but no one had the money to defend themselves against the clown's copyright lawsuit. Alias agreed on a monetary settlement with Bozo, and Warner re-released the album, without the offending clown sample. In retrospect, the suit may have helped more than hurt, because Too Much Joy received some publicity and "Clowns," minus the sample, was used as the theme song to the 1992 cult-film classic *Shakes the Clown* (which was hailed by one reviewer as "the *Citizen Kane* of alcoholic clown films"). Despite the soothing waters of time, Quirk is still angry about the episode. "The goofiness of this incident obscures an important principle. Copyright can be used to prevent unflattering commentary on copyrighted works," says Tim, taking the words right out of my mouth. "That has more potential to suppress authors than it does to motivate them."

OVERZEALOUS COPYRIGHT BOZOS

"The impression I'm left with," says Quirk about Bozo's legal threats, "is that Larry Harmon didn't really care all that much about the sample, and just saw it as a way to make a quick buck." It may have also been true that Bozo felt he had the "moral right" to control his image. That's one way of looking at it, Quirk concedes. "But you know what I say to that? Tough shit, you fucking clown. *You said it!* All we did was remind the world." He adds, later, while sitting in his brick-walled Real Networks offices, "Just because Bozo had a copyright on that sound recording, copyright isn't a right to not look like an idiot." In tribute to Larry Harmon, I've coined the phrase "overzealous copyright bozos" to describe the overreaching actions of bullying intellectual-property owners.

Here's the rub: The original and re-released versions of *Son of Sam I Am* also sampled tiny fragments from the Clash, the Police, Gang of Four, Lou Reed, and many other artists, all without the band or the label worrying about these uncleared, unlicensed samples. What was a 1980s rock 'n' roll band doing using all those samples? Well, Quirk explains, it was 1988, "and if you're a music geek—and anyone in an indie-rock band in 1988 is a music geek—playing spot-that-sample is one of your new favorite pastimes." Not coincidentally, Too Much Joy was hopelessly addicted to Public Enemy's brand-new *It Takes a Nation of Millions to Hold Us Back.*

I myself wasn't prepared for this aural assault of a record, despite the fact that I was a record-store clerk/dork who had spent a year or two of his life in a supremely wack break-dancing crew of rhythmically challenged adolescents. We called ourselves the Virginia Beach Breakers. There was something in the music of Grandmaster Flash, Kurtis Blow, and the Fat Boys that moved me enough to do backspins on a cardboard box when most of the other neighborhood kids were listening to Van Halen or Duran Duran. This still didn't prepare me for the release of *It Takes a Nation*. This sonic space oddity came frontloaded with sirens, squeals, and squawks that augmented the chaotic, collaged backing tracks over which Public Enemy's Chuck D laid his revolutionary rhymes. He rapped about white supremacy, capitalism, the music industry, black nationalism, pop culture, and—in the case of "Caught, Can I Get a Witness?"—digital sampling. "Caught, now in court 'cause I stole a beat," Chuck D bragged. "This is a sampling sport."

"It's almost like 'Caught, Can I Get a Witness?' was a pre-Napster record," says Public Enemy member Harry Allen, talking with me years later in a friend's Manhattan apartment. "It's really speaking to the way the industry handles technological change." Just as there are now multitudes of panel discussions about digital downloading, which achieve little consensus, Allen vividly remembers that in the late 1980s sampling was the new music-industry boogeyman. "Even more than a prediction or looking forward to the controversies that would bloom around sampling," says Allen about Chuck D, "it was really more like looking forward to the controversies that would bloom around Napster."

"The first Public Enemy records are like the blueprint, technique-wise, for what I do," says Scott Herren, aka Prefuse 73, a key player in today's thriving underground hip-hop scene. "That was just the most powerful onslaught of sound that had been experienced, and it [was] all coming from, like, machines. When you heard it for the first time, back then, it's like"—cradling his temples with his fingertips—"whooooaaaa. It was inconceivable for me. Back then I didn't make music, and it sounded like science fiction, like, 'What the fuck?' " Mr. Lif—part of the Def Jux family, a popular independent hip-hop label—says that Public Enemy sounded "like they harnessed chaos, but somehow made it palatable." Nodding his dread-locked head, he grins and says, "They made chaos delicious."

I was destined to love Public Enemy's music because I'm the quintessential Bobo—"Bourgeois Bohemian"—and I loved the po-etry fired from these prophets of rage. As did Tim Quirk. "So," he remembers, "it's September 1988, and Too Much Joy are recording our second album. Our bass player loves Public Enemy as only a rich suburban white kid who's just graduated from Yale can, and we've been playing *It Takes a Nation* pretty much nonstop in the van for the last three months. . . . I think we loved that record the same way we'd loved the Clash's debut—because we were so re-moved from the social and political concerns that each addressed so aggressively, we could only appreciate that layer intellectually. On a gut level, we responded to both albums as pure music, sonic as-saults unlike anything we'd encountered previously."

They didn't really have the technical skills or even the knowledge to collage songs from the ground up as hip-hop artists did, but they wanted to honor and pay tribute to sampling. Sometimes their sonic quotations were relevant to the song itself. "In a tune about how the Clash broke our hearts, we drop Mick Jones saying, 'So hit it' from 'Hitsville U.K.,' " Quirk says. He mentions how they in-serted a sample of Chuck D shouting "BASS!" on *It Takes a Nation* right before Too Much Joy's bass player took a solo. "Other times," Tim explains, "we just liked the way the samples sounded." The band's guitar player had been imitating the "Sha Sha!" shout in a Big Country song. "We figure, 'What the hell?' and drop in the real thing."

In 1988 digital sampling was about three or four years young, and there were few legal precedents. It was a sort of Wild West, where there was a creative window that had been forced open by hip-hop artists, a magical time when surprises were abundant on records, the sort of moment that makes the sacrifices of obsessive music fandom worth it. But by the early 1990s, the free experimentation was over. The West was won by copyright lawyers and major labels who realized a whole new revenue stream could be opened up with a copyright-clearance bureaucracy.

You can hear the increasing limitations imposed on mainstream hip-hop stamped on Public Enemy's music. Between 1988 and 1990, Public Enemy released what are considered to be two of hip-hop's greatest albums, *It Takes a Nation* and *Fear of a Black Planet*. Public Enemy's production team, the Bomb Squad, took sampling to the level of high art while still keeping intact its populist heart. But by the time the group's *Apocalypse 91* came out, even the casual listener could hear a dramatic change. Gone were the manic collages that distinguished their previous two albums, where they fused dozens of fragments to create a single song. The new sample-licensing rules didn't differentiate between collaging small sonic chunks and using entire choruses, so by 1991 it became economically prohibitive to release a record such as *It Takes a Nation* or *Fear of a Black Planet*.

"That changed how we had to approach music," Chuck D tells me, "to the point where we couldn't use fragments in a song. That's what changed overnight. It would take maybe a hundred different artists to construct a Public Enemy song, though they are all unrecognizable." Tim Quirk concurs. "You can hear a difference from *Fear of a Black Planet* to *Apocalypse 91*," he says. "To me, it's the sound of the 1990s. The 1990s is just this big, hollow, empty period, where you are not hearing anything half as shocking, invigorating, creative, wonderful, and inspiring as you were at the end of the 1980s." By the turn of the decade, everyone had to pay for the sounds that they sampled or risk getting sued. For now, though, let's take a trip back in the day, before the copyright police came to Dodge.

KILLING THE AUTHOR SOFTLY WITH TWO TURNTABLES

Musical revolutions are often the result of the most mundane circumstances. Sometime in the mid-1970s at a housing project in the Bronx, a teenager was in his room blasting records. As parents are likely to do, his mom banged on his door, telling him to turn his music down. When she walked in, he stopped the record with his fingers, listening partially to what she was telling him while unconsciously moving the record back and forth over the same drumbeat. That teenaged boy morphed into Grand Wizard Theodore. "I wanted to get that same groove I was on," the veteran DJ explained in the documentary *Battle Sounds*. "So I was, like, back and forth and I said to myself, 'Hey, this sounds pretty good!' Ya know?" Whether this story is a fanciful bit of mythmaking or straight-up fact, it illustrates hip-hop's haphazard evolution—a series of events built around mistakes that sounded good, and which were further developed.

The DJs who inspired Grand Wizard Theodore—Kool DJ Herc, Afrika Bambaataa, and Grandmaster Flash—often plugged their massive sound systems into street-lamp outlets in local parks. They dug deep into their crates full of records and kept the party rocking till the cops quite literally came a-knocking. The earliest of these DJs to gain popularity was Kool DJ Herc, who had a habit of creating infectiously danceable collages with his two turntables. Herc was from Jamaica, and the music of his birthplace was extremely influential for him, especially the dub reggae records made by producer/engineers King Tubby and Lee "Scratch" Perry. These men turned the recording studio's mixing desk into a musical instrument. They altered the speed, equalization, and other elements of the recording—also dropping instruments in and out of the mix— to make multiple "versions" of one song.

The existence of these dub versions, British cultural studies scholar Dick Hebdige comments, demonstrates that "no one has the final say. Everybody has a chance to make a contribution. And no one's version is treated as Holy Writ."[2] In *Roland Barthes by Roland Barthes,* the French philosopher says something similar about his writing and his life: "What I write about myself is never *the last word.*"[3] He means that there's no way to permanently imprint his intentions in the words he types. Someone can always misinterpret his writing, or they can take a small fragment and put it in a new context—as I have just done with his words. Kool Herc brought from Jamaica the idea that the musicians no longer had the last word in their music, and when he arrived in the early 1970s, disco DJs had independently come to the same sonic conclusions.

With their two turntables and a mixer, early disco DJs stretched tunes from three minutes to twenty, crafting entirely new versions of songs—all without involving the original songwriters and musicians. Disco was primarily a downtown happening, while up in the Bronx hip-hop DJs such as Kool Herc were doing much the same thing in a different style. "I quickly realized that those breakbeats were making the crowd go crazy," Herc told me, speaking of the catchy and percussive breakdowns that make songs go BOOM. "As long as I kept the beat going with the best parts of those records, everybody would keep dancing, and the culture just evolved from that." Herc fused together the chunks of songs that were the most popular with dancers, segueing the instrumental and percussion breaks into one long musical collage.

Some of the better known hip-hop breakbeats came from the Incredible Bongo Band's "Apache," James Brown's "Funky Drummer," and even the opening bars of the Rolling Stones' "Honky Tonk Women" or Aerosmith's "Walk This Way." Afrika Bambaataa took a cue from Kool Herc's eclecticism, going a bit further by mixing in television commercials and the theme to *The Andy Griffith Show.* But in terms of sonic skills and agility, Grandmaster Flash left Kool Herc and other DJs in the proverbial dust. "Most great records had amazing parts," Flash told me. "You know, the percussive part that you wait for—before they called it 'the break' it was 'the get-down part.' What pissed me off was that part was so short, so I just extended it with two copies to five minutes."

The one thing Flash couldn't do was spit rhymes, which wasn't a big deal because in 1970s hip-hop culture the DJ was the star, not the MC. "I was like totally wack on the mic," said Flash, "so I had to find someone able to put a vocal entertainment on top of this re-arrangement of music."[4] From there, Grandmaster Flash and the Furious Five—best known for "The Message" and "White Lines"—were born. Herc, Flash, and Bambaataa inspired numerous up-and-coming Bronx DJs during the late 1970s, including Grand Wizard Theodore, Grandmaster D.S.T., and DJ Afrika Islam, among others.

Offering a window into that time is a rare taped performance by the Cold Crush Brothers that fell into my hands while writing this book. It was recorded over a quarter century ago, but something about it sounds fresh—funky fresh—because the music was created live with turntables, mixed by a deft (and def) DJ who might screw up and drop a beat at any moment. It's that sense of danger, the feeling that comes from live performances, that makes it so compelling. The same year of the Cold Crush Brothers recording, 1977, the French intellectual Jacques Attali published an important book, *Noise,* in which he unknowingly described (in the abstract) the turntable practices South Bronx hip-hop DJs had already perfected. In his book, Attali breaks up the history of music-making into four stages, with the fourth stage, *composition,* existing only in his imagination at the time, or so he thought.

"The listener is the operator," said Attali about this music-making method, where *anyone* could compose music, regardless of whether they fit the traditional category of "musicians" or not.[5] In the composition stage, the distinction between the worker and consumer, the musician and listener, was blurred—quite an advanced concept for the 1970s. Afrika Bambaataa's sonic collages echoed Attali's technique, in which the cultural *consumer*—the record buyer, the DJ—morphed into the cultural *producer.* The turntable is an object of consumption that was reimagined by DJs as a technology of production, and today's software programs now allow anyone with a computer to collage and compose.

This expansion of creative possibility has resulted in the MP3 "mash-ups" of today, where thousands of bedroom composers are creating new songs by smashing together two different songs and putting them on the Internet for free. One hilariously compelling mash-up I've downloaded crosses Eminem's "Without Me" with "Come On Eileen" by Dexy Midnight Runners, which—dare I say it?—aurally emasculates the posturing white rapper by placing him atop a goofy one-hit wonder of the 1980s. Another great one is Eminem's "The Real Slim Shady" set to a ragtime instrumental. At their best, mash-ups sound equally right and *wrong;* the fusion can be both seamless, but weird and jarring. Yet again, the original authors no longer have the last word.

This sensibility echoes philosopher Jacques Derrida's writings, in which he encouraged readers to play with the text—mocking, deconstructing, and reconstructing it. Derrida was publishing his writings on deconstruction roughly at the same time hip-hop DJs, disco DJs, and dub reggae producers developed their deconstructive music methods in the early 1970s. And his ideas were as revolutionary in the academy as hip-hop was in the South Bronx. There was a common impulse shared at the time by all sorts of people— whether they were working with typewriters or turntables, in the ivory tower or in the streets—to "break it down," so to speak. The deconstructive tactics these DJs used would have likely been approved of by Roland Barthes. He attempted a literary drive-by in his widely cited essay, "The Death of the Author," where he more or less blew away established assumptions about what authorship is.

For instance, in *Leviathan,* that influential Enlightenment artifact, Thomas Hobbes defined the author, first, as someone who is *responsible* for his writing and, second, one who *determines* the text's meaning after it circulates. For Barthes, the first definition doesn't stand up to scrutiny because it is the critical *reader* who determines the meaning of a text. Just ask that *Catcher in the Rye* fan and John Lennon assassin Mark David Chapman, or all the fans who misinterpreted Bruce Springsteen's anti-Vietnam anthem "Born in the U.S.A." as a jingoist ditty.[6] Barthes wanted to give more power to the people—the readers, in this case. This desire wasn't merely a theoretical exercise, because it was rooted in the very real fact that all readers have their own interpretations and can make their own meanings.

The attempt to eliminate the godlike power and influence of the author was only a reaction to the critical tenor of the times, when the author's intentions had previously eclipsed most everything in the field of literary criticism. One of Roland Barthes's motivations—which was shared by Michel Foucault in his essay "What Is an Author?"—was to undermine the overpowering influence of the author. The things that DJ Derrida, Funkmaster Foucault, and Roland 808 Barthes wrote about in the late 1960s and 1970s foreshadowed, in part, the way today's young adults have been brought up reading and playing with fragmented, hyperlinked texts and images. The manner in which my college students use the Internet and editing software has severely damaged the myth of the individual genius author, for it gives them the tools to freely collage image, music, and text.

OLD-SCHOOL SAMPLING

The reason these collage practices seem so natural and copyright industries have been unsuccessful in convincing people that it's wrong is that this kind of borrowing is a natural part of being a sentient being. The earliest example of "sampling" on the *Billboard* charts was Buchanan and Goodman's 1956 hit "The Flying Saucer." Bill Buchanan and Dickie Goodman composed this funny "break-in" record on a reel-to-reel magnetic tape recorder, creating a skit about an alien invasion—as told through then-current rock 'n' roll hits. Imitating the radio broadcasts of *War of the Worlds,* the songs break into the radio announcer's comments, creating a jarring, goofy collage of sound.

"Radio Announcer: The flying saucer has landed again. Washington: The Secretary of Defense has just said . . ." Then Fats Domino bursts in, singing, "Ain't that a shame." Elvis appears, as do many others, and the record sold over a million copies, inspiring a host of imitators. A few song publishers sued Goodman, which prompted these jokers to release the totally unauthorized "Buchanan & Goodman on Trial." The delirious 1956 single swiped the *Dragnet* theme, among many other songs, and Little Richard "played" their defense attorney—who argued in front of a jury of Martians. Four labels (Imperial, Aristocrat, Modern, and Chess) and two performers (Fats Domino and Smiley Lewis) filed for an injunction to prevent the sale of all Buchanan-and-Goodman recordings. They also asked for $130,000 in damages.

Judge Henry Clay Greenberg sided with Buchanan and Goodman, denying the injunction because he believed that the single was clearly a parody and not a violation of anyone's copyright. The judge stated that Goodman "had created a new work," rather than simply copying someone else's music.[7] Goodman had a long career, working into the 1970s ("Energy Crisis" and "Superfly Meets Shaft") and the 1980s ("Hey E.T." and "Safe Sex Report," which eclectically samples Michael Jackson, the Grateful Dead, L.L. Cool J, Huey Lewis, and Los Lobos!). To make his life easier, Goodman started working within the system—buying licenses for most of the songs he excerpted—but he never lost his subversive edge.

Igor Stravinsky once said, "A good composer does not imitate, he steals." He was one of many European composers who borrowed from folk melodies in composing their own works. Another notable appropriator was Johannes Brahms, who was quite obsessed with the songs of his youth. He arranged well over two hundred folk tunes in his lifetime, with some melodies finding their way into his art-song compositions such as *Sehnsucht*. But Brahms's most significant and highly regarded use of folk-song material was his *Deutsche Volkslieder* for voice and piano. He took as much pride in these works as his "original" compositions, perhaps more. Biographer Malcolm MacDonald wrote that Brahms's *Deutsche Volkslieder* are "a series of miniature masterpieces worthy to stand with any of his art songs of the same period."[8]

Although it is quite "original" in its own right, Brahms's First Symphony borrowed musical phrases from Beethoven's Ninth Symphony. And in composing the introduction to his Third Symphony, Mahler swiped a major theme from Brahms's Beethoven-biting symphony, converting it into minor mode but keeping the melodic structure intact. When someone pointed out to Mahler the fact that those two pieces were so similar, he snapped, "Any fool can hear that." Elements of Beethoven's Ninth can be heard in Mendelssohn's *Lobgesang*, as well as a great deal of Wagner's body of work. This kind of musical borrowing continued into the twentieth century and beyond. Woody Guthrie was inspired by and borrowed from all sorts of artifacts, including books. One such book is John Steinbeck's *The Grapes of Wrath*, which dealt with the plight of the dust-bowl victims during the Great Depression. Guthrie condensed much of the novel's action into his song "Tom Joad," down to Tom's last words to his mother, and he sang it to the tune of "John Hardy," an outlaw folk ballad Guthrie was familiar with.

Steinbeck later half-jokingly groused, "That little fuckin' bastard! In seventeen verses he got the entire story of a thing that took me two years to write!"[9] Rather than suing, the novelist was honored by the transformation of his work. Bruce Springsteen loved Guthrie's music, declaring during a concert that "This Land Is Your Land" was "one of the most beautiful songs ever written." And for the title track to his 1995 album, *The Ghost of Tom Joad,* Springsteen similarly transformed and drew inspiration from Steinbeck's novel. Bob Dylan also followed in Guthrie's footsteps. After reading Guthrie's autobiography *Bound for Glory* and mastering almost every song in his vast songbook, Dylan traveled from the Midwest to New York City to make his musical fortune.

One of his first compositions was, fittingly, "Hard Times in New York Town." Its melody borrows from an old folk song popular among white southern farmers. For his own song, Dylan took the verse structure, the opening two lines, and the primary melody from "Down on Penny's Farm." The one major difference is that he shifted the setting from the country to the city. The same is true of other early songs by Dylan, such as "Man on the Street," which borrows the melody of an American frontier song, "The Young Man Who Wouldn't Hoe Corn."[10] Like his mentor hero, Dylan pillaged and plundered from that which inspired him. Even the tune of "Blowin' in the Wind" was cribbed from an old freedom song sung by ex-slaves.

Although folkie Pete Seeger was the first to finger the Dylan song's original source, the enigmatic icon also admitted as much. " 'Blowin' in the Wind' has always been a spiritual," he said. "I took it off a song called 'No More Auction Block'—that's a spiritual, and 'Blowin' in the Wind' sorta follows the same feeling."[11] In a 1962 interview on the New York City independent radio station WBAI, Bob Dylan played his guitar, answered the DJ's questions, and gave a rare view into his early songwriting methods. WBAI: "That's a great song, how much of it is yours?" Dylan: "I don't know, I can't remember."

A minute later, he introduced another song, "I got a new one, it's called 'Emmett Till.' I stole the melody from Len Chandler. He's a folk singer, uses a lot of funny chords. He got me to using some of these funny chords, trying to teach me new chords. He played me these, said, 'Don't they sound nice?' So I said, 'They sure do.' So I stole it, the whole thing."[12] After Dylan released 2001's fittingly titled *Love and Theft,* reporters discovered that he directly lifted about a dozen passages scattered throughout the English translation of Junichi Saga's *Confessions of a Yakuza.* The author, rather than being incensed, was honored, telling the *Wall Street Journal,* "Please say hello to Bob Dylan for me because I am very flattered and very happy to hear this news."

ENTER THE SAMPLER: ART MEETS THE LAW

Once it was introduced in the mid-1980s, the digital sampler allowed for a new method of musical appropriation. Hip-hop producers could now manipulate recorded sound in a more complicated and sophisticated way, something Public Enemy took advantage of. Their songs contained dozens of fragmented noises, melodies, percussion, and spoken-word recordings from Malcolm X and others. Despite the fact that there had already been a tiny handful of copyright-infringement lawsuits against hip-hop artists, Chuck D and company didn't worry themselves with clearing samples, which gave them a huge amount of creative freedom. "The only time copyright was an issue was if you actually took the entire chunk of a song, as in looping a measure, which a lot of people are doing today," Public Enemy producer Hank Shocklee tells me.

"But the kind of things we were doing," says Shocklee, "we were just taking a horn hit here, a guitar riff there; we might take a little speech, part of a speech over here, a kick snare from somewhere else. It was all bits and pieces." At the time *It Takes a Nation* was released in 1988, hip-hop was largely an underground phenomenon and had yet to make inroads to pop radio or MTV. For a short time, hip-hop producers were getting away with the intellectual-property equivalent of murder, though many soon found themselves in court for their sampling sport. "We never really cleared the samples when we first did it," remembers Shocklee. "As a matter of fact, it didn't start catching up with us until the album afterwards, which was *Fear of a Black Planet,* in 1990. That's when the copyrights and everything started becoming stricter. . . . Usually you could put a record out there on the block and nobody would even think about it."

"The corporations found that hip-hop music was viable," Chuck D tells me. "It sold albums, which was the bread and butter of corporations. Therefore, lawyers felt that since the corporations owned all the sounds, people began to try to search out who had infringed upon their copyright." Record companies became stricter after an important 1991 copyright-infringement case that pitted sensitive 1970s singer-songwriter Gilbert O'Sullivan against Biz Markie, who used a twenty-second sample from O'Sullivan's most popular song, "Alone Again (Naturally)." Markie offered to pay for the sample but was denied permission, so he and his record company, Warner Records, put it out anyway.

The judge who presided over the case was not hip to these newly emerging sample practices, nor did he care about the culture from which the music emerged. Judge Kevin Thomas Duffy found the defendant guilty of copyright infringement *and* invoked the Seventh Commandment when suggesting Markie should be subject to criminal prosecution—for stealing. In order to remain consistent, though, that judge would also need to prosecute Igor Stravinsky, Gustav Mahler, William Shakespeare, Marianne Moore, T. S. Eliot, Bob Dylan, Muddy Waters, Woody Guthrie, and others, because they too were guilty of "blatant theft." To those who are skeptical of digital sampling as an art form, I say this: Even I, your author, the world's biggest spaz, can learn how to competently strum three guitar chords in three hours. Without much practice and with no previous musical training, almost anyone can play any number of songs on guitar, like "Louie, Louie" or "All Along the Watchtower."

It would take much more time for that same person to learn and become competent with the many technologies involved in sampling and collage. Public Enemy member Harry Allen puts it best when he explains to me that sampling is just a tool, like a paintbrush; it's a way of expressing yourself. There's nothing inherently creative *or* uncreative about the digital sampler. "Sampling is like the color red," Allen says. "Is the color red creative? Well, it is when it's used interestingly, and it isn't when it comes out of the can— just lying there, so to speak." The physicality of playing a musical instrument makes it seem to be a more "authentic" kind of musical expression than digital sampling. But I believe these notions of authenticity are more generational than inherent to the "pure" act of strumming a guitar itself; the distinctions are, in the end, arbitrary.

One of the more headache-inducing aspects of the way copyright law is interpreted is the seeming randomness of it all. When writing a book, quoting from another book is perfectly acceptable—for instance, Derrida's *Dissemination* and Kathy Acker's *Blood and Guts in High School* borrow large chunks from the prose writings of others. But quoting more than two lines from a song's lyrics in a book—even if it takes up only 0.001 percent of the book's total text—might get you and your publisher in trouble. As long as it's brief, singing a phrase from an old song and placing it in a new song probably won't get you sued, and a court likely wouldn't consider it an infringement. However, David Sanjek—director of the Broadcast Music Incorporated (BMI) Archives—is careful to point out to me that any copyright owner with an ax to grind *could* sue. There's nothing stopping them.

Fortunately for the irony-drenched metal band The Darkness, their fragmentary borrowing didn't provoke a lawsuit. On their 2004 hit, "I Believe in a Thing Called Love," the group lifted the line "touching me, touching you" from Neil Diamond's karaoke classic "Sweet Caroline" without asking. Although this wasn't a problem, if they digitally sampled those four words without permission, it surely would have instigated a lawsuit. More mind-numbing examples from other mediums: Referring to a trademarked good in everyday conversation will cause no problem, but movie directors often have to get permission from an intellectual-property owner to show it or even mention it in movie dialogue. Referring to trademarked brands in pop songs is okay. But creating satire on a Web site by using a company logo requires you to exactly duplicate a privately owned image, and this leaves you more vulnerable to a lawsuit.

Today's unrealistically high standards of originality don't reflect the way people have always made art and music. What's the difference, really, between T. S. Eliot invoking and *directly quoting from* the Bible, Greek myths, Dante, Shakespeare, Arthurian legend, and dozens of other cultural works, and Public Enemy doing the same sort of thing with sound? There is no convincing argument I have heard that justifies why it is fine in printed works to quote small fragments from books, poems, or plays, but quoting and collaging small fragments of sound is unacceptable. If T. S. Eliot were young and alive today, he would maybe, just maybe, use a computer and sampler to construct his cultural collages, rather than pen and paper. *The Waste Land Remixed?*

"With sampling, we took an arrangement and we was able to take an assortment of sounds and arrange it in our own way," Chuck D tells me. "We thought sampling was just a way of arranging sounds. Just like a musician would take the sounds off of an instrument and arrange it their own particular way. We thought we was quite crafty with it." The song "Don't Believe the Hype" from *It Takes a Nation* is an example of the kinds of aural experiments Chuck D and Hank Shocklee and the rest of the Bomb Squad were up to. "That's a song that's been basically played with the turntable and transformed and then sampled," says Shocklee. "Some of the manipulation we was doing was more on the turntable itself. Then there were certain things that was straight-up taking, and we applied multiple effects to it."

In the late 1980s, when they could still get away with it, Public Enemy collaged together hundreds of fragmentary samples to create an album. In some cases, the drum track alone was built from a dozen individually sampled and sliced beats. "The first thing we'd have is what is known as the beat, which is the skeleton of the track," remembers Shocklee. "The beat would actually have bits and pieces of samples already in it, but it would only be the rhythm sections—the thing that gives you some sort of idea or melody. Then the track goes through a writing process." They created new songs cobbled together from bits and pieces of old music, undermining dusty old romantic notions of originality and authorship with this crisp new digital technology.

Even though there was more freedom to sample and remix during this time, that doesn't mean people weren't paranoid. Coldcut is a British duo whose 1987 remix of Eric B. & Rakim's "Paid in Full" helped spread hip-hop outside the United States, and their copyright-violating debut record popularized the cut-and-paste aesthetic in the U.K. club scene. "John More and I," Matt Black tells me, sitting in Coldcut's overstuffed London recording studio, "when we made *Hey Kids, What Time is It?,* we sampled Kurtis Blow, and *The Jungle Book* [soundtrack], and a whole heap of stuff. We actually thought we might be arrested when we went down to the pressing plant, so we used false names." Black adds, "We went through each record and scratched out with a soldering iron the matrix number that identified it. We were aware that this was potentially litigious, but we thought we could probably get away with it with five hundred copies."

The $1.7 million lawsuit brought by the Turtles against De La Soul justified Coldcut's fears. "Sampling is just a longer term for theft," said an angry Mark Volman, a member of the Turtles. He complained about this after De La Soul used a relatively inconsequential song fragment in their 1989 album *3 Feet High and Rising.*[13] When sampling first started gaining attention in the late 1980s, this was the attitude of many aging rockers—and even some funksters. Protecting the individual artist is a large part of the rhetoric that props up the way copyright law is currently structured, even though in reality copyrights largely accrue capital for intellectual property–owning companies, not the artists themselves. Chuck D sums it up this way: "You might have some lawyers from Sony looking at some lawyers from BMG, and some lawyers from BMG saying, 'Your artist is doing this.' So it was a tit for tat that usually made money for the lawyers and garnered money for the corporations."

Most sampling cases were settled out of court, though one example that broke from this trend was the unanimous 1994 Supreme Court ruling that favored 2 Live Crew. The group, fronted by Luther Campbell, was sued for reworking Roy Orbison's hit "Pretty Woman" when they sampled the guitar, bass, and drums from the original song. Both songs begin, "Pretty woman, walking down the street," but after that, things go horribly awry on the 2 Live Crew version.

ORBISON LYRICS:

Pretty woman, walking down the street
Pretty woman, the kind I like to meet

2 LIVE CREW LYRICS:

Big hairy woman, all that hair ain't legit,
Cause you look like Cousin It.

Two Live Crew's lawyers argued that the song was a parody and it should have "fair use" protection, while Orbison's publishing company's lawyers claimed that the song violated their client's copyrights to the original song. The Court voted unanimously that this wasn't an infringement; instead, it qualified as fair use, even though the record was sold commercially. It also opened up the possibility that not all sonic quotations are automatically copyright infringements. Unfortunately, though, case law remains muddy when it comes to sampling. The Biz Markie and 2 Live Crew cases are the only two major rulings that have ended up guiding common practice. This is unfortunate because they both deal only with the song's main "hook," and don't deal with more fragmentary samples such as those used by Public Enemy. Therefore, the assumption is that any sampled sound of any length in any context is without doubt copyright infringement, unless it's a parody.

Two Live Crew's awful version of "Pretty Woman," by the way, is what fair use and free speech can sound like—sometimes it's not attractive at all. The fair-use statute was written into the 1976 Copyright Act to allow taking from a copyrighted work for the purposes of education, criticism, and parody, among many other things. Most copyright owners—corporate owners, especially—aren't very liberal in their interpretations of how their intellectual property is used by others (for them, *any* use is stealing). But for the most part, the law is not on their side; their only advantage is they have more money to devote to litigation than most individuals.

Although there's no hard and fast rule that allows us to instantly assess whether something is a fair use, the statute provides us with four factors to help us determine the legality of our borrowing. According to Section 107 of the 1976 Copyright Act, these include: "(1) the purpose and character of the use, including whether such use is of a commercial nature or is for nonprofit educational purposes; (2) the nature of the copyrighted work; (3) the amount and substantiality of the portion used in relation to the copyrighted work as a whole; (4) the effect of the use upon the potential market for or value of the copyrighted work." Fair use is an intuitively named statute, because it is designed to enable uses of copyrighted material that are considered, quite simply, fair.

Let's say a pop artist took a large chunk of "Pretty Woman" and only made slight alterations, essentially getting a free ride on Roy Orbison's creative labor. Such a use would seem unfair, especially because the updated version could replace the original in the market. In the 2 Live Crew case, it didn't unfairly step on the original's sales potential. Even though the amount taken was substantial, the Supreme Court recognized that parodies, by definition, require a relatively large amount to be taken. The Court's unanimous decision in the 2 Live Crew case stated that these four factors should not be seen as a rigid checklist—a yes/no binary. If you "fail" one (or even more) of the four tests, your borrowing still isn't necessarily a copyright infringement.

Instead, the Court ruled that these four factors should be seen as existing on a continuum, where an overall balance of fairness is struck between the old work and the new. In short, the high court argued that just because the new work is for profit doesn't mean it's not fair. It's a common misconception about the statute—that a commercial sale automatically disqualifies something from fair-use status. However, in drafting and interpreting copyright laws, the Supreme Court, lower courts, and Congress recognize that we live in a commercialized society. They have consistently acknowledged that if we make some things totally off-limits for comment, we undermine the founding principles of democracy.

COPYRIGHT CRIMINALS

Before the 1992 Biz Markie ruling, few record companies had internal rules about sampling, which explains why Warner Records allowed Too Much Joy to keep the U2 and Police samples on their record even after Bozo complained. In all likelihood, numerous record employees heard the Too Much Joy record, recognized the samples, but didn't think anything of it. But that was no longer true in 1992, when the band was trying to complete their next album, which was tentatively titled *Burn Down the Suburbs with Too Much Joy*, a reference to the song "Clash City Rockers." The band sampled Joe Strummer singing the line "Burn down the suburbs with . . . ," to which they appended with "Too Much Joy," itself a sample from one of the band's previous albums.

Because the tempos of the Clash and Too Much Joy songs were different, Tim Quirk and company had to slow Joe Strummer's voice down so much so that he became unrecognizable. You might think this would render the copyright issue moot, but that wasn't the case. For the first time, after recording three albums for the label, a "sample clearance report" landed in their laps, requiring them to divulge the sources of all samples so that the legal department could pursue licensing agreements with copyright holders. In 1992 this was a relatively new practice that was quickly institutionalized. "Some poor motherfucker in the legal department at Warner [Records] had to sit there with headphones," Quirk says, laughing, "pushing pause on our record any time they heard anything that they thought might be a sample." Sony wanted five thousand dollars for the Clash sample, which he points out is one thousand dollars a word. In retrospect, this was a bargain, given the skyrocketing costs of sampling throughout the 1990s. Too Much Joy also sampled their drummer's voice in his day job as an NYPD patrol officer, but their record-company lawyers told them that in all likelihood the NYPD owned the copyright to this recording.

"Now we're losing our patience," remembers Quirk. "The cost seems to have no relation to the use—if we have to pay five grand apiece for each sample, not to mention legal fees for getting all the paperwork signed, we'll end up spending more than ten percent of our recording budget for less than nine seconds of sound." Not caring much for legalities, the group signed a form stating there were no copyrighted sources on the album, an obvious lie, but one that lessened Too Much Joy's debt to their employer. They had to take off the Clash sample because the Warner Records lawyers were onto them, but the group claimed that the rest of the suspicious sounds were created by the band in the studio. This is a common escape hatch in the digital-sampling world.

The way copyright law was enforced helped turn on its head hip-hop's original creative method: reworking prerecorded sounds. For instance, when Public Enemy wanted to sample from Buffalo Springfield's "For What It's Worth" for the title song in Spike Lee's *He Got Game,* the fees were outrageous. Chuck D told me it was cheaper to mimic the song's instrumentation in the studio and to wheel in Stephen Stills, who originally wrote the song, and have him re-sing it. This way, they only had to pay royalties to Stills, the songwriter, and not deal with Atlantic Records, which released the Buffalo Springfield recording and demanded a steep price. This is how copyright law and the sample-licensing bureaucracy have forced hip-hop artists to bend and twist.

Today, hip-hop producers regularly hire studio musicians who are instructed to imitate a known song. This seemingly odd and irrational process is actually a very rational decision by producers who want to sidestep the often-expensive *mechanical* royalty fee, which pays for the right to sample a Buffalo Springfield record released by Atlantic. When using studio musicians, hip-hop artists still have to pay the *publishing* fee, which compensates a songwriter such as Stephen Stills. "Sampling a record violates both of these copyrights," said Hank Shocklee, explaining why he and other hip-hop producers changed their creative practices. "Whereas, if I record my own version of someone else's song, I only have to pay the publishing copyright."

As the nineties progressed, record companies began to more aggressively monitor the sampling practices of their artists, which helped create a new cottage industry, called sample-clearance houses. These are third-party companies that track down the original copyright holders and negotiate a license for a sampled sound. The director of a sample-clearance house estimated that the clearance fees for the average hip-hop album totaled about thirty thousand dollars in the early 1990s, and those rates dramatically rose over the decade.[14] Sometimes it can cost as much as one hundred thousand dollars for a single sample. Rapper/producer Kanye West—whose innovative production work on Jay-Z's records has been heard by millions—learned this licensing lesson when making his 2004 solo disc, *College Dropout.* He's on a label, Jay-Z's Roc-A-Fella Records, that can afford the ridiculously high prices companies charge, but West still had problems.

When Kanye wanted to include a brief sample taken from hip-hop artist Lauryn Hill's 2002 *MTV Unplugged* album, he encountered multiple obstacles. "The problem was it had to get cleared through MTV and also through Sony," says West, referring to the network that originally broadcast Hill's performance and the record company that owns her master tapes. "The sample was going to end up costing like around a hundred and fifty thousand dollars."[15] This is an extremely large amount of money, especially when it is added to the cost of recording, promotion, music videos, and the like. Even though Kanye and his record company were willing to pay for this very brief fragment of sound, the bureaucratic wheels turned so slowly that it would have significantly delayed the release of his long-anticipated record.

As a solution, West employed the services of R&B songstress Syleena Johnson, who sang Hill's part, legally bypassing the need to negotiate a mechanical license for the *MTV Unplugged* album. The rapper and producer Wyclef Jean, who has both sampled other people's records and used live instruments to closely mimic records, told me that copyright has played a part—on a subconscious level, at least—in his decision to use live instruments. "Yeah, it's a way of getting around that mechanical fee, so that has something to do with it," he tells me, shaking his head. "Licensing is expensive."

"Records like *It Takes a Nation of Millions* and *3 Feet High and*

Rising," Public Enemy's Harry Allen observes, "they're kind of like artifacts from an earlier time that couldn't exist today. They're just financially untenable, unworkable records. We would have to sell them for, I don't know, a hundred and fifty-nine dollars each just to pay all the royalties from publishers making claims for one hundred percent on your compositions." You can place the Beastie Boys' 1989 densely packed *Paul's Boutique* in the same category. "Ninety-five percent of the record was sampled," says engineer and producer Mario Caldato Jr., who worked on *Paul's Boutique*. "They spent over two hundred and fifty thousand dollars for sample clearances."[16] A quarter million turned out to be a bargain, because if those licenses were cleared today the album would be far too expensive to release. In an interview on his band's Web site, Beasties group member Adam Yauch agreed that "the hectic sampling laws are a bit of a deterrent from sampling."

These comments remind me of conversations I've had with researchers and businesspeople who deal with gene-patent licenses. Because many new drugs and therapies have to use multiple patented genes from many owners, the royalty costs can get very expensive. "I'm very much aware of how many patents that I've had to in-license to support one drug," Helena Chaye tells me, talking about her employer, MediGene. "It results in a stacking of royalties. It has to economically make sense to me, because if I have to pay royalties out to parties A, B, and C, you have to add it all up." She continues, "Oh, my God, this drug is going to bring in x number of dollars, but I have to pay out x percentage in royalties—that's not going to work." For the most part, in Chaye's experience, she's able to negotiate a price that makes it financially sensible for her company to release a drug.

However, the same isn't true of the music industry when it comes to reasonable royalty rates for samples, nor is it the case for documentary filmmakers. "I think of historical documentaries as being, in some ways, analogous to music that depends on sampling," documentary producer John Sorensen told the Center for Social Media, which has reported on the creative tensions surrounding copyright and filmmaking.

> It relies on earlier authors' work to provide the raw materials, but rearranges those images in a way that creates an entirely new creative work. As a producer who is primarily interested in historical documentaries, my concerns about copyright revolve around control of access to footage. Because of the increasing consolidation of private footage sources like Getty, it is becoming increasingly difficult for small independent producers to obtain any leverage in negotiating rates and rights for hard-to-find images. If corporations restrict access to our common cultural heritage, it makes it difficult (or at least expensive) for filmmakers like me to tell the stories that we want to.

In the world of music, some sampling artists have rebelled by cleverly altering the unauthorized samples through effects such as reverb, flange, distortion, or the limitless filters on editing software. DJ Muggs, the member of Cypress Hill who produces the group's instrumental tracks, tells me, "I don't worry much about copyrights. Yeah, I haven't been able to license some samples in the past, but the trick is to really fuck it up so that you don't even have to ask for permission." Sample clearance–business owner Hope Carr says that because the licensing fees are so high, "more people are doing songs without samples or trying to make songs where the samples are so obscure you don't hear them."[17]

DJ Spooky tells me that there's a generally recognized "four-second rule" concerning sampling in the underground and online DJ community. He doesn't literally mean four seconds can be lifted from another record without paying. It's about recognizability. Aesop Rock, another member of the Def Jux hip-hop collective, also thinks it's easier to sample if you're not selling a lot, though there are still risks. "The general rule of thumb is if you're not breaking ten thousand to fifteen thousand record sales then you should be okay," he says. "But of course," he adds, "you *could* be sued." In fact, friends of his on the Def Jux label have run afoul of copyright owners. "Any of these big labels can take us under if they find a sample, but we've been able to do the whole puppy-dog-eyes thing"—i.e., beg and explain that they're a tiny label—"and kind of get out of it." One way around getting sued, Aesop says, is "not to sample anything that's recognizable, or freak it, sample it and flip it so it doesn't sound like the original."

He's an MC, but he also produces his own tracks, and in answering my questions, Aesop gives us a peek into the way a sampler's mind works. "I can picture what that would sound like slowed down a lot," he says, speaking of what he looks for in sounds on records. "You don't listen to a song front to back. You'll hear a break in a song where maybe the drums cut out and it's just the instruments, or something, and you'll be able to picture hearing it slower or faster, or with something chopped out." He continues: "You'll find weird groups you've never heard of that may have been on some 1970s foreign independent label. If it's a major label, it's not the greatest idea to sample it. I do still, but only if I haven't heard of the group, or I know the group only put out one album. . . . A lot of producers will find a decade or a kind of music they like. You can literally look at the bands and the albums and buy stuff not based on the sound of the record, but based on what the record looks like. If they have cool instruments and [were] made in a weird year. Like, they're a rock band, and they're introducing synthesizers, whatever you want to look for."

Prefuse 73, who turns previously recognizable beats and melodies into mincemeat, explains, "If I take the perfect hook from the record, I'm basically doing a remix of that record, and I'm not interested in doing that. I'm more interested in using the sounds from that record and using it as a source, another source you throw into the mix." As the hip-hop genre continues to splinter and fragment, Prefuse 73 represents the avant point guard of the hip-hop team, regularly running circles around more traditional producers. "If someone's going to take something of mine—a sample of mine, a beat—and use it some different way," says Prefuse 73, "you know, do something creative with it, I'm not gonna trip. I'd be honored."

Mr. Lif, a kindred spirit in today's hip-hop underground, says much the same thing. "If someone uses my voice, I'm not coming after you," he says during an interview in *Copyright Criminals,* a documentary on sampling that I coproduced with Ben Franzen. "I remember the days when it was an honor to hear someone cut your voice on a chorus." As for the popular indie hip-hop artist Mr. Dibbs, you can call him a copyright criminal, because he just doesn't care. "Sampling, bottom line, it's stealing," the tattooed DJ says. "That's the nature of hip-hop." Near the end of Mr. Dibbs's interview, he gets worked up into a fever of bravado: "I will steal, I will jack, I will take whatever I motherfucking want to take—and fuck you, you'll never catch me." Staring into the camera, he adds, "Motherfucker, fuck you."

One of the only multiplatinum groups of the 1990s to match the chaotic sonic intensity of Public Enemy was the Wu-Tang Clan. This nine-member group was given to messing up song structures by nixing choruses, inexplicably changing tempos midsong, switching keys randomly and clogging the instrumental bed with an everything-*and*-the-kitchen-sink approach to sound design. The sonic architect behind the Wu-sound was RZA, who in 1998 released the soundtrack to a movie, *Bobby Digital,* which was never finished. At the time production on the straight-to-video movie was supposed to have begun, I spoke with the wizard of Wu about the soundtrack album.

I remember how RZA reacted when I went off the topic and asked him if he cleared all the samples on the records he produced. Through a haze of smoke, RZA locked me in a knowing, glassy gaze as he leaned into my tape recorder. "Well, yeah, all the sounds I lay down is shit I make myself. I don't sample anything, or else I get it cleared." He was shading the truth, I believe, but he was just protecting his neck while on record with a journalist. If you listen to the densely layered supersonic fifty-car (s)mash-up that is the Wu-Tang Clan's music, it's obvious that RZA plunders left and right from found sounds. But he does it in such a crafty way that the samples are next-to-impossible to identify.

PLAYING FAIR

Curtis Mayfield's 1970s funk records are sampled often, something that provides an ongoing stream of revenue for the deceased musician's widow and ten children. Mayfield—who wrote "People Get Ready," "Freddie's Dead," "Superfly," and other classics—received an expensive, paralyzing injury in 1990. Fortunately, this happened right around the time when his music started to be widely sampled. "Sampling let his family be financially secure," explains Marv Heiman, the executor of Mayfield's estate.[18] Who can argue with that? I certainly don't, because Snoop Dogg and others sampled significant elements of Mayfield's songs in ways that weren't especially transformative. The success of the derivative work, its funkiness or catchiness, depends on the power of the original Mayfield song. Although I'm quite critical of the way the current sample-licensing system works, I'm certainly not arguing that *no* payments should be made to the original artist at all.

"You couldn't just, like, go and sample an entire chorus of a Beatles record," Coldcut's Matt Black tells me, "and stick it on your track and go, 'Hey, I'm being totally original. I'm a collage artist, *man,* I don't owe you nothing.' It's bollocks." What's clear, though, is that sample fees need to be more reasonable, and should reflect the proportion of what was taken. This isn't the case with the present sample-licensing system, which is a very arbitrary arrangement that inhibits creativity more often than not. When copyright owners can demand a large percentage of the new song's royalties (Prince, for instance, requires 100 percent), it makes it impossible to legally release interesting collages.

Coldcut has been around since the mid-1980s, long enough to watch the sample-clearance system evolve into what it is today. Although Matt Black believes in paying artists, he feels the system has its problems, which he points out. "If you sample one snare drum off a Rolling Stones record," says Black, "and add ninety-nine percent of the song yourself, you shouldn't pay the Rolling Stones one hundred percent of the royalties—their lawyers notoriously insist on being very litigious." Most people would agree that if you take an entire hook or chorus, you should pay, but reasonable people (and judges) will disagree on how much you can use before it's copyright infringement. Those who sample and who have been sampled hold varying opinions about the subject.

De La Soul, which blames their record company for not clearing the Turtles sample, believes in compensating the original artist, especially when the borrowing is significant. "It's important to us that we clear samples, from day one to today," says group member David Jolicouer, aka Trugoy the Dove. "We definitely want people to be acknowledged and paid for what they've done."[19] When Robin Rimbaud—who records under the name "Scanner"—was sampled on a multimillion-selling record by Björk, he really didn't mind. However, Scanner's record company and the lawyers cared a lot, and insisted on suing. The polite Englishman describes how he was caught in a cauldron of lawyers, all while remaining apprehensive about what was going on, supposedly for his benefit.

"Morally, it felt wrong to be asking for money," Scanner tells me, "because this sound of mine is being introduced into another work, this popular piece of music, that took it in a completely different direction." Scanner eventually pulled the plug on the lawsuit, which frustrated the lawyers and his record company. In retribution, they terminated his contract and released his unfinished demos without his permission, which the record company advertised as a new Scanner album. Because of the terms of his contract, there was nothing he—the author and creator—could do about it.

The first time Tim Quirk thought about sampling as a moral issue was when he heard Grandmaster Flash and the Furious Five's "White Lines," which liberally borrows the bass line from "Cavern," by Liquid Liquid. "Since the hook from the new tune was pretty much the hook from the Liquid Liquid song, that felt like some kind of line had been crossed. Even then, I didn't think it was illegal—just lame." Liquid Liquid came out of the same genre-mixing downtown scene that was inspired by the hip-hop music of Grandmaster Flash and Afrika Bambaataa. "In the early 1980s," Public Enemy's Harry Allen tells me, "you had this mix of audiences around danceable music at clubs like Danceteria and the Funhouse. You'd have high-energy Latin 'freestyle' music, as it was called back then, and hip-hop and other kinds of dance music that are kind of intermingled."

The Funhouse's DJ, Jellybean Benitez, used "Cavern" as the last song of the evening, which helped it gain currency among downtown clubbers and hip-hop artists. The four white guys in Liquid Liquid were attracted to New York by the "no wave" punk scene, but were immediately sucked into the cacophonous collage of music that surrounded them. "We were listening to reggae and African stuff and picked up on stuff like merengue from the streets—you could hear it coming out of everywhere," remembers Richard McGuire, Liquid Liquid's bassist. "But it wasn't till I heard Grandmaster Flash's 'Wheels of Steel' for the first time, *that was the future*," a wide-eyed McGuire tells me while sitting in his spartan Manhattan studio, shortly before moving to France. "Later, when it turns out that Grandmaster Flash, of all people, ends up using my bass line, it was just an honor. It was this amazing thing at first, and then it got complicated with all the legal stuff later."

What Grandmaster Flash and Melle Mel borrowed from Liquid Liquid's song was not just the prominent bass line, but pretty much the whole song structure. This isn't to say they didn't transform it, but the element that makes Flash's "White Lines" so successful comes primarily from "Cavern." This prompted a lawsuit from Liquid Liquid's record company—a long, tangled litigation that wasn't resolved for a dozen years. "I'm totally for sampling. It's like any other art form," McGuire tells me. "And I don't think it's necessarily a given that the sources are more interesting than what the end result can be with a collage." He pauses. "But at the same time, I feel both ways about it. I mean, I'm always interested in how someone can reinvent something, but there has to be some sort of structure [for compensation, he means]."

When Afrika Bambaataa crafted one of old-school hip-hop's most important songs, "Planet Rock," he essentially created a mashup of two songs by Kraftwerk, a German electronic group. They were mad—less because they didn't get paid than because they weren't credited. "He knew perfectly well what he was doing," Kraftwerk associate Maxime Schmitt said. "He had not put the names of the authors and had not declared anything." Kraftwerk member Karl Bartos added, "It was completely the melody off 'Trans-Europe

Express' and the rhythm track from 'Numbers.' So we felt pissed off. If you read a book and you copy something out of it, you do it like a scientist, you have to quote where you took it from, what is the source of it."[20] Richard McGuire is a little more forgiving about the Grandmaster Flash experience. "I used to say it was my cross to bear," he says, half-joking. "It's the reverse of some black musician coming up with something and being stolen by a white performer. It's like, 'Hey, maybe I'm paying for the sins of my forefathers.' "

WHOM DO RECORD COMPANIES REALLY PROTECT?

Like Chuck D, when it comes to sampling, copyright law, and freedom of expression®, Tim Quirk has an almost inexhaustible supply of firsthand horror stories. "In 1996 something even more sinister happens when we try to clear one of the audio samples we're stupidly still trying to include in between songs for this record," Quirk says, referring to Too Much Joy's last album for Warner, *Finally.* "The sample comes from the movie *Simon,* starring Alan Arkin. At one point, Arkin's character says, 'Uh-oh, too much joy,' " says Tim. "The thing came out on Warner Video, and we were signed to a Warner company, so naive little me—still hadn't learned what I should have—I assumed that meant we would be able to use it for nothing. No. What it meant was Warner wanted five thousand dollars. Again, it was five words, five thousand dollars."

By now it's clear why Quirk is beginning to lose his hair—he must have started ripping it out after his major-label sampling ordeals. "My band would have been charged five thousand dollars by TimeWarner to use material controlled by TimeWarner," he says in a tone of bitterness laced with an appreciation for the absurdity of it all. "In other words, it was nothing more than a way for the company that controlled *our* sound recordings to put us five thousand dollars deeper in debt to them." With movies, it is the studio that owns the copyright. None of the many people who contributed to making the movie—the director, editor, actors, screenwriter, crew, etc.—sees any extra money. It all goes to Warner Video or to the parent company, TimeWarner.

So if Too Much Joy had agreed to the label's terms, they would have lost five thousand dollars from royalties that Warner Records owed them, and Warner Video would have received a five-thousand-dollar payment. No one except TimeWarner wins in this scenario, and when we pull back and examine the music industry as a whole, we see that this royalties drain happens on a grand scale. Multiply the samples found on the hundreds of albums released each year, multiplied by tens of thousands of dollars in licensing fees per album, and that's a *lot* of money that is deducted from artists' royalties. The original recording artists see only a fraction of that money, if they're paid at all.

Sample licensing is a shell game where money is split up and passed around among companies. When we look at it on the macrolevel, it becomes clear that the TimeWarners of the world benefit from copyright, not the musicians who are sampled. The process rarely involves the original musicians who wrote or recorded the music because, in many cases, they do not even own the songs' copyrights. For instance, George Clinton—the famous funkster who founded Parliament-Funkadelic—lost the copyrights for much of his catalog to a shady music-biz type. As alleged in Clinton's complaint, the man fabricated a cut-and-pasted document (the font and type size changed throughout) that transferred Clinton's pre-1983 copyrights to his ownership for a ridiculously small sum of money.

Clinton settled the case after the man hired the same lawyer George W. Bush used in 2000 to win the Florida election debacle. "He filed over eight hundred lawsuits against people, suing them for using George's work without his permission," says an exasperated Brian Zisk, cofounder of the Future of Music Coalition, a lobbying group focused on protecting artists' interests in the digital age. Public Enemy was sued as well, for using an extremely fragmentary P-Funk sample in their song "Bring the Noise."[21] Zisk is also a friend of Clinton's, which explains why he's so upset, especially when he tells me the following: "One of the people who got sued was George Clinton for using his own work."

These kinds of shenanigans are sadly common in the music industry. Oftentimes, however, it can pay to *not* back down from an overreaching lawsuit, as John Fogerty discovered in the 1980s. Fogerty—the lead singer, guitarist, and songwriter for Creedence Clearwater Revival—signed a bad contract that caused him to lose the copyrights to his old CCR songs. Adding insult to injury, when he released a new album in 1985, *Centerfield,* the copyright owner claimed that his new song "The Old Man Down the Road" sounded too much like his CCR song "Run Through the Jungle," and promptly sued him.

Fogerty allegedly infringed on the copyright of a song he himself had written, spending over three hundred thousand dollars to defend himself against those charges. Unlike many other casualties from the early rock 'n' roll era, this fortunate son actually had the money to defend himself, or else he would have had to accept an unfavorable settlement that would have reassigned the copyright to his new song to his old record company. Fogerty also won an important Supreme Court ruling in which he won back the legal fees he incurred, a precedent that made it easier to recover the money lost defending frivolous copyright lawsuits.

In 2003 Wu-Tang Clan member Ghostface Killah successfully claimed fair use in New York federal court for his marijuana-drenched parody of "What a Wonderful World," popularized by Louis Armstrong. "I see buds that are green, red roses too / I see the blunts for me and you / and I say to myself 'what a wonderful world,' " sang Raekwon, Ghostface's rhyming partner in the Wu-Tang Clan. "Where the original first three lines of 'Wonderful World' describe the beauty of nature," Justice Gerald Lynch drily wrote, the new song "reads more like an invitation to get high with the singer." Indeed, their song was named "Trees," hip-hop slang for a marijuana joint, and it also contained the line, "Goofy had kilos, big hole in his nose," one of many references to characters from children's stories engaged in unspeakable acts. Tom and Jerry, Porky Pig, Elmer Fudd, Peter Pan, Kermit the Frog, Miss Piggy, Snow White, Daffy Duck, and a couple dozen others make an appearance, but this parody was protected by the fair-use statute.[22]

By caving in to the demands of overzealous copyright bozos, you could end up like the Verve, a popular British band that scored a major worldwide hit in 1997 with "Bittersweet Symphony." The Verve negotiated a license to use a five-note sample from an orchestral version of one of the Rolling Stones' lesser hits, "The Last Time," and received clearance from Decca Records. After "Bittersweet Symphony" became a hit single, the group was sued by former Stones manager Allen Klein (who owns the copyrights to the band's pre-1970 songs because of aggressive business practices). He claimed the Verve broke the agreement when they supposedly used a larger portion than was covered in the license, something the group vehemently disputed.

The Verve layered nearly fifty tracks of instrumentation, including novel string arrangements, to create a distinctly new song. In fact, the song's signature swirling orchestral melody was recorded and arranged by the Verve; the sample from the instrumental record is largely buried under other tracks in the chorus. The band eventually settled out of court and handed over 100 percent of their songwriting royalties because it seemed cheaper than fighting for a legal ruling that might not end in their favor. As if things couldn't have gotten worse, they were then sued by *another* old Rolling Stones manager, Andrew Loog Oldham. Klein went after the Verve for infringing on the *songwriting* copyright, which he owned, but Oldham possessed the copyright on the sampled *sound recording.* They totally lost everything.

Not only couldn't the Verve earn money from their biggest hit, they were stripped of control of their song. For instance, after the group refused Nike's request to use "Bittersweet Symphony" in an ad, the shoe manufacturer aired the song after it purchased a license from Allen Klein. "The last thing in the world I wanted was for one of my songs to be used in a commercial," the despondent lead vo-calist Richard Ashcroft said. "I'm still sick about it." In one final kick in the groin, "Bittersweet Symphony" was nominated for a Grammy in the Best Song category, which honors songwriters. Because the unfavorable settlement transferred the Verve's copyright and song-writing credit to Klein and the Rolling Stones, the Grammy nomi-nation went to "Mick Jagger and Keith Richards."[23] Ashcroft quipped that it was "the best song Jagger and Richards have written in twenty years." He then suffered from a nervous breakdown and the group broke up.

When the Beastie Boys found themselves in a similar situation, they prevailed after not settling out of court, though they had to spend five hundred thousand dollars defending themselves. The veteran hip-hop group paid ECM Records to sample six seconds of a recorded flute melody played by James W. Newton Jr., but Newton claimed he should have been paid for his song-publishing rights. He said that those six seconds from his song "Choir"—repeatedly looped in "Pass the Mic" from 1992's *Check Your Head*—infringed on the "heart" of his composition. The court ruled that the Beastie Boys' use of the sample was minimal, and that "Newton is in a weak

position to argue that the similarities between the works are substantial, or that an average audience would recognize the appropriation."[24]

The way ownership is assigned in today's hip-hop songs highlights the absurd directions the law forces musicians to bend, a sort
of intellectual-property version of the game Twister. For instance,
Ma$e (the Puff Daddy / P. Diddy protégé who later quit the rap
game and found God) included a song on his second album that
listed *nine* people on the songwriting credits, six of whom never set
foot in the studio when Ma$e recorded "Stay out of My Way." The
interesting thing about this song is that it sampled Madonna's 1990
song "Justify My Love" (written by Madonna, Lenny Kravitz, and I.
Chavez), which in turn sampled and looped an entire measure from
Public Enemy's 1988 song "Security of the First World" (written by
J. Boxley, Chuck D, and Eric Sadler). In 1998 all of these people
were credited as writers on the Ma$e song.

In addition to the fact that it's excessive, this way of giving credit
for authorship is often unfair. It ignores some "authors" who contributed an important section of a song—for instance, a session
drummer or bassist who performed a funky breakbeat but didn't
get songwriting credit. It's the drumming of Clyde Stubblefield that
propels many James Brown samples, but the vast majority of James
Brown songs do not credit Stubblefield or his other backing musicians. "Anything they take off my record is mine," Brown once said
about sampling. "Can I take a button off your shirt and put it on
mine? Can I take a toenail off your foot—is that all right with you?"[25]
Yes, James Brown may have written the verse-chorus-bridge-verse-
chorus structure of a particular song. But the two-and-a-half-
second fragment that a hip-hop producer might sample has little to
do with what James Brown brought to the song and everything to
do with Stubblefield's amazing, influential drumming style.

This sample-clearance bureaucracy unjustly neglects the sampled authors who go uncredited, and it also unfairly treats those who sample by assuming that they are somehow being less creative than a traditional musician. Producers have to pay for the sin of importing a breakbeat or a horn hit into their digital sampler or Roland 808 drum machine because they weren't being "original." The idea of the "original genius" comes out of the early-nineteenth-century Romanticist movement, which put forth the notion that a great author creates something totally new from scratch. But the idea that an individual author is *solely* responsible for all aspects of a work is an ideological sleight of hand, a fiction that some philosophers and literary critics have tried to exterminate.

One of the themes of Jacques Derrida's scathingly sarcastic book *Limited, Inc.* focused on imploding conventional assumptions about authorship. He had previously written an important essay, "Signature Event Context," to which the scholar John R. Searle penned his very critical "Reply to Derrida." This prompted the philosopher-prankster to compose his own crafty comeback. Derrida begins by picking apart a brief passage from "Reply," "Copyright © 1977 by John R. Searle," riffing on it like a jazz musician—progressively reinterpreting and interrupting its intended meaning. In Searle's essay, he acknowledges "H. Dreyfus and D. Searle for discussion of these matters." Rather than being a lone author, Derrida suggests that this is "a Searle who is divided, multiplied, conjugated, shared. What a complicated signature!" The signature becomes ever more complex when Derrida points out that Dreyfus is an old friend with whom he has exchanged ideas.

Therefore, Derrida says that he, too, should control a share of Searle's essay, what he sardonically calls "the stocks and bonds" of "this holding company, the Copyright Trust." He goes on to refer to this corporation as "three + n authors," then dumps this ponderous expression, giving the "collective author" the French name "Société à Responsabilité Limitée"—literally "Society with Limited Responsibility." This is normally abbreviated as S.A.R.L., so for the rest of the book, Derrida mischievously refers to Searle as "Sarl," deadpanning, " 'I' therefore feel obliged to claim my share of the copyright of the 'Reply.' " With his linguistic gymnastics, he complicates the simple division of "author" and "nonauthor" and other false binaries, suggesting that this terrain "is slippery and shifting, mined and undermined."[26]

The questions about the nature of authorship make it all the more difficult to justify the current sample-licensing system. Take the case of the Funk Brothers, the talented and versatile session musicians who performed on most Motown hits—playing on more number-one songs than Elvis, the Beatles, and the Rolling Stones combined. The Funk Brothers played an important role in writing numerous songs, but they were never properly credited for their contributions. "The Funk Brothers were the main ones who pulled it off," says Martha Reeves, who, with the Vandellas, scored a massive hit on Motown with "Heatwave."

She says in the documentary *Standing in the Shadows of Motown* that Smokey Robinson would come into the studio with "maybe two bars or two verses of [a song] on some paper and say, 'What do you think of this?' " Reeves recounts how Funk Brother Joe Hunter would say, " 'This is what you're trying to play,' and give him the chord and full structure . . . and in a minute you'd have a song." In other words, creativity is far more collaborative than the myth of the original author lets on. Even when the copyright owner isn't a large corporation but an individual artist, sample licensing often works against the very people who intellectual-property lobbyists claim they are protecting: the artists themselves. It's the same old song (but with a different meaning).

In the end, everyone loses: the samplers, the samplees, the uncredited musicians, and the public, which has been denied the opportunity to hear the full creative potential that digital sampling once promised. Record companies have found yet another way to make millions more off the labor of underpaid or unpaid musicians such as the Funk Brothers. Some critics believe that sampling is just a way of piggybacking on the success of an earlier, popular song, but that's a very one-dimensional view of how people create art and music. Tim Quirk counters, "Assumptions like those use a businessman's logic, not an artist's," he says. "They assume the only reason to sample is to get a head start by stealing someone else's work. And ironically, rules based on those assumptions lead to unimaginative sampling becoming the norm, while making the kind of sampling I fell in love with virtually impossible."

He's talking about hip-hop songs that are dominated by one sampled hook, such as MC Hammer's "U Can't Touch This," Vanilla Ice's "Ice Ice Baby," or Puff Daddy's "I'll Be Missing You," which rewrites the Police's "Every Breath You Take." Built almost entirely around a looped measure of that Police song, it's the sort of unimaginative sampling that should have been left back in Hammer Time, or at least the Vanilla Ice Age. Sometimes an uninventive or obvious sample can make for a great song, but we need more possibilities, richer options. I want Mr. Daddy/Diddy's music to stand alongside heretofore unheard sounds and songs that are more sonically adventurous than the mainstream music of today. Given that hip-hop producers have had one hand tied in their creative process, it's amazing that so much first-rate and inventive commercial hip-hop music has been produced in the past ten years.

Take, for instance, Missy Elliot's "Work It"—with its played-in-reverse chorus and blippity-bloopity robot pop-rhythm track—or Mystikal's "Bouncin' Back"—a retro-futuristic take on New Orleans jazz. If there were fewer restrictions on licensing samples, can you imagine what those same producers would have accomplished with even more freedom? In early 2003 Tim Quirk and I had a long, beer-soaked conversation about sampling. Through the fog of alcohol, I recall his speaking about how he genuinely gets angry and depressed when he thinks about the incredible, mind-blowing music that *hasn't* been made or released since the Biz Markie ruling in 1991. Like Tim, I get depressed about the current state of sampling, too, though my spirits are raised by the handful of folks who have been willing to take risks, to possibly be sued for the sake of their art. But it's still not enough.

Just as rock-'n'-roll musicians of the 1950s and 1960s used the new technology of electric guitars as the primary way of expressing themselves, turntables and samplers are the dominant tools of musical expression today. "Anybody who can honestly say sampling is some sort of creativity has never done anything creative," insisted Mark Volman of the Turtles. Volman drew a line in the sand, but I choose to stand on the other side of that divide along with Igor Stravinsky, John Cage, T. S. Eliot, Buchanan and Goodman, De La Soul, and Public Enemy. I want to live in a creative universe where the aural equivalent of *Finnegans Wake* can exist.

We don't even need to imagine that other world, because we already live in it—at least those of us blessed with a computer and Internet access. Today, emerging technologies allow us to "write" in new ways. The rules of the game have changed, or, to put it more clearly, these technologies allow for *different* kinds of rules to develop. Many of us have the production tools that can create interesting and exciting works out of the old, discarded junk tossed into the garbage dumps of our consumer culture. "Tell the truth, James Brown was old until Eric and Rakim came out with 'I Got Soul,' " rapped Daddy-O in Stetsasonic's 1988 hit "Talkin' All That Jazz." Daddy-O was referring to the fact that few in the contemporary black music scene cared about James Brown until Eric B. & Rakim sampled him on their single "I Got Soul."

By the mid-1980s, the Soul Brother Number One's music was

considered so old school it was preschool; he had embarrassed himself with the wretched song "Living in America," the theme from *Rocky IV.* His records piled up in dusty cut-out bins and used-record racks throughout the country, ignored by the next generation of music consumers who rejected those albums as their parents' music. But when hip-hop artists began sampling Brown's 1960s gems "Give It Up or Turn It A-Loose," "Super Bad," and other funk jams, he sounded fresh again, and his music was given a new life. Hip-hop delivered James Brown's music to a new generation, just as Run-DMC revived Aerosmith's dead-end career when they appropriated "Walk This Way."

Revitalizing music from the past is one of the many ways sampling and collage help to refresh and reboot a shared popular culture. There are piles upon piles of ephemeral pop-culture rubbish that litter the information stupor-highways, pieces of trash that can be recycled and given new significance by deconstructing and re-working them. The mash-ups created by hundreds of amateur bedroom computer composers, the online distribution network of underground hip-hop music, and Internet itself are all positive signs of changing times. I don't buy into the utopian fantasies of certain cyber-geeks—computers will connect the global village and create a big happy family—but at least it's a start. It's time we began playing catch-up for a decade of lost music and suppressed art—overzealous copyright bozos be damned.

ART, COMMERCE, AND COPYRIGHT

Some may say that the creative restrictions I decry are an unfortunate but necessary consequence of making sure copyrighted goods are secure. Property, after all, should be protected. Although it's understandable that individuals and companies want to seek protection for their creations, there is nothing natural or inherent about the idea that copyright is a form of *private property*. Such a statement might appear to defy common sense. But copyright was conceived as a temporary, limited form of legal protection, and only recently has it been reconceived by some as an unbending law that protects private property. This protection, according to the U.S. Constitution, doesn't give the author *total* control over how it is distributed or consumed.

For nearly two centuries after the Constitution was adopted, courts interpreted copyright as a concept that encouraged authors to create new cultural goods that would benefit and eventually belong to our society. As I cited in the introduction, Thomas Jefferson argued that *"ideas should freely spread from one to another over the globe."* Jefferson's use of italics tells us this is something he felt strongly about, because for Jefferson and his contemporaries, the uninhibited spread of ideas, information, and culture was essential to a thriving democracy. Even though he was concerned that intellectual-property law could block the free flow of knowledge, Jefferson didn't argue against the existence of copyright. To the contrary, he stated, "Society may give an exclusive right to the profits arising from them, as an encouragement to men to pursue ideas which may produce utility."

The Constitution's framers wanted to avoid permanent monopolies over information and culture, so they took care to include the phrase "limited times" in the nation's founding document.[27] In the congressional testimony, legal briefs, law articles, and books from a quarter century ago and beyond, it was a widespread assumption that a balance between the author and the public good was the guiding principle of the law. "Copyright was a bargain between the public and the author," writes legal scholar Jessica Litman, "whereby the public bribed the author to create new works in return for *limited commercial control* [my italics] over the new expression the author brought to her works." Copyright was designed to be porous. It was meant to be full of holes that give some freedom and flexibility to the public and other creators.

The underlying premise of this theory of copyright was to create a balance that guaranteed that the author and the public both benefited from the creation of a new work. But by the early 1980s, the "balanced bargain" rhetoric of copyright began to change, as advocates for copyright holders began to rearticulate copyright's purpose by drawing from an *economic* analysis of the law.[28] Over the last quarter century, the dominant metaphor for copyright changed from a shared, balanced model to one of private property that needs to be protected, by any means necessary. This has done more to inhibit creativity and freedom of expression® than to encourage it. For most corporations, and the politicians whose campaign coffers they filled, this change in perspective was a very practical matter. There was no need for all that socialist-sounding nonsense about the public good, even if it did originate from James Madison, Thomas Jefferson, and other upstanding members of the white male property-owning elite.

The copyright owner, today's conventional wisdom says, is entitled to control all the contexts in which the work is used. It may seem that we have arrived at a permanent impasse over sampling. However, Congress successfully dealt with other copyright conflicts surrounding the emergence of the phonograph, radio, and cable television. In the early days of each industry, record companies, radio stations, and cable-television companies were the copyright criminals, because their existence relied on using others' copyrighted works. The copyright owners—threatened by new technologies and new business models—often refused to grant permission to use their property, or charged exorbitant prices to allow such a use. Congress stepped in and changed that.

Congress also made it possible for musicians to remake someone else's song. Otis Redding—the soul singer who wrote and originally recorded "Respect," which Aretha Franklin made famous—once mock-complained, "That little girl stole my song." In many ways, she did. Popular confusion over its authorship runs so deep that even Prince got his R&B music history wrong. During a rant about why lesser musicians shouldn't try to remake others' songs, including his, Prince asserted, "Have some respect, man. If anyone tried to cover 'Respect,' by Aretha? I would shoot them myself!"[29] Franklin's version of "Respect"—all cover versions, for that matter—exists because of legal freedoms granted since the Copyright Act of 1909.

The act established a "compulsory license" for sound recordings, which allows musicians to record copyrighted songs in whatever style they see fit, as long as they don't alter the lyrics and they pay the copyright owner a standardized fee set by Congress. Effective 2004, the statutory rate (which increases every two years) requires a payment of $0.085 per copy of songs under five minutes. For songs over five minutes, the rate is based on a per-minute fee. So, if you sell one thousand CDs that contain a four-minute cover of "Respect," you pay eighty-five dollars to the copyright owner. Radio stations, by purchasing another kind of compulsory license, also don't have to get consent from copyright owners to broadcast a song, even if it's in a context the copyright owners believe is negative. Instead, radio stations purchase a license, report what was played and pay a lump sum to ASCAP, BMI, and SESAC, the organizations that collect royalties for copyright owners.

In the case of digital sampling, the primary barriers to creativity revolve around the fact that copyright owners can: (1) censor the sampling of sounds they own; (2) demand prohibitively expensive fees; and (3) assert that *all* unauthorized sonic quotations are theft. Under the current copyright system, you can record a Beatles song without permission, but the surviving Beatles almost never allow sampled reinterpretations of their work. They make it clear that the

Beatles are not for sale when it comes to digital sampling, because it will damage the integrity of the original songs. There's a contradiction here. Hundreds of butchered cover versions of Beatles songs have been released that would probably make the Fab Four cringe (ever heard William Shatner's spoken word version of "Lucy in the Sky with Diamonds" from his 1968 *Transformed Man* album?).

Sampling a recording and playing someone's song with your own bass, drums, and guitar are indeed two different activities, and I'm not trying to conflate the two. However, you can denigrate the original meaning of the song both with traditional instruments and with samplers. Why should one form of creativity be free and another severely constrained? While it's extreme and irrational to say that people don't have to pay for *any* samples, it's equally absurd to claim that *all* kinds of sonic quotations are copyright infringement. Even though most copyright lawsuits settle out of court, a few recent court rulings have complicated the assumption that all unauthorized samples of copyrighted recordings are illegal.

In *Williams v. Broadus,* hip-hop producer Marley Marl sued Snoop Dogg for sampling his 1988 song "The Symphony." In a very ironic defense strategy, Snoop's lawyers argued the following: Because Marl's song contained an unlicensed sample of an Otis Redding song, "Hard to Handle," Snoop's borrowing wasn't an infringement. The court dismissed Snoop's lawyers' motion, stating that it was reasonable that a jury might think Marl's sample wasn't a violation of Redding's copyright. In his summary judgment, District Judge Michael Mukasey stated, "A work is not derivative simply because it borrows from a pre-existing work." He also stated that "a reasonable finder of fact could nonetheless conclude that the copied measures of 'Hard to Handle'—two measures that appear only in the opening of that composition—are not a substantial portion of the work."

In *Tuff v. Profile,* Tuff 'n' Rumble Management claimed that Run-

DMC sampled a drum break from the Honey Drippers' 1973 song "Impeach the President." District Judge Sidney Stein ruled against Tuff because the company couldn't prove that it was the actual copyright owner, and he went on to assert that Run-DMC's sample probably wasn't an infringement. The court said it would be difficult to demonstrate that the sample would rise to the level of "substantial similarity" needed to prove that the new recording infringed on the Honey Drippers' copyright. Having assessed the two songs, Judge Stein ruled that the Run-DMC song is not "substantially similar to 'Impeach the President.' "

The sampling morass got even messier when in late 2004 the Sixth Circuit Court of Appeals ruled on a significant case. It involved the new copyright owner of George Clinton's Parliament-Funkadelic recordings and N.W.A., who sampled a three-note P-Funk guitar riff, chopping it up and altering its pitch. The court asked, "If you cannot pirate the whole sound recording, can you 'lift' or 'sample' something less than the whole?" No, it said in the ruling. "Get a license or do not sample. We do not see this as stifling creativity in any significant way."

Another way out of this stagnant sampling cesspool is to begin acting as though fair use exists in reality, not just in theory. However, even though fair use protects *some* forms of audio sampling, primarily parody, as a solution it's too limited. This is why there needs to be some kind of compulsory-licensing system for digital sampling that eliminates the veto power of copyright holders or keeps them from charging one hundred thousand dollars for a sample. Because the standardized licensing fee for remaking others' songs is based on the length of a song, it seems reasonable the same could be true for a potentially similar system covering sampling. Some might argue that this sample-licensing system would dissuade artists from making something entirely new because they can easily recycle a proven hit. Just license two seconds of Prince, and—

bam!—instant hit. However, there are plenty of singles released every year that sample an old pop song but don't go anywhere.

Conversely, there are also hit songs that resurrect a brief musical or percussive moment that has little to do with "the heart" of the original song. Len's 1999 pop hit "Steal My Sunshine" uses as its main hook a part of the 1975 disco song "More, More, More" by the Andrea True Connection. This looped percussive piano break running through the entirety of "Steal My Sunshine"—which makes the Len song immediately identifiable—appears only momentarily in the 1970s disco song. In other words, Len found new "value" in "More, More, More" by extracting a small fragment and placing it in a new context. Some might argue that it's not fair to have a government-related body determine the market price of, for instance, a Beatles song. After all, it could be sampled for the same price per second as a relatively unknown act. However, Congress already regulates the fees that copyright holders can demand for cover songs and radio broadcasts—yet another example of how copyright has always been treated as a *limited* monopoly by courts and Congress.

Compulsory licenses ensure that no owner can price competitors out of the marketplace and prevent other musicians or radio stations from remaking or broadcasting a song. This system both promotes the creation and dissemination of new works *and* sets limits on the powers of copyright holders, while still respecting their rights. It's a win-win situation. However, at the present moment our copyright regime cultivates a situation where legitimate works of art can be banned, regardless of their merits, just because they quote and transform sounds. A version of a compulsory-licensing system for sampling could solve this problem. Record companies will certainly resist such a change, even though it's the right thing to do—but then again, when has the music industry ever done the right thing on its own?

CHAPTER THREE

ILLEGAL ART

when art gets in trouble with the law, and
art gives the law trouble back

I t was the first shot fired in the intellectual-property wars—the first one I heard, at least, back in 1991. During a skirmish between Island Records and the sound-collage collective Negativland, the corporate Goliath took aim at the group's record (titled simply *U2)* and blew it off the face of the earth. A nerdy, motley crew of San Francisco Bay Area artists, weirdos, and computer programmers, Negativland weren't even a blip on the pop-culture radar, an unlikely target for a major lawsuit. So what would prompt a huge record company to use its full legal and economic might against an insignificant band? As you may have guessed from Negativland's album title, they made the mistake of sampling U2's music, the crown jewel in Island Records' multiplatinum crown.

More troubling (to Island, at least) was that fragments of U2's music commingled with hilarious, gut-busting moments of tongue-tied obscenity by veteran DJ Casey Kasem. "This is *American Top 40,*" says the congenial-sounding Kasem, "right here on the radio station you grew up with. Pubic Radio 138— *OH, FUCK!*" The amazing thing about this recording—which was likely smuggled out of Kasem's studio by a disgruntled, abused staff member—is the weird cognitive dissonance it provokes. The same voice that warmly announces innocuous hits by Phil Collins also spews mouth-foaming, foul-mouthed rants such as "That's the last fucking time! I want someone to use his FUCKING brains and not come out of a record that's up-tempo every time I do a goddamn *death dedication!*"

Kasem also screwed up his lines in a segment about the Irish rock band. "That's the letter U and the numeral 2," says the host, starting off innocently enough. "The four-man band features Adam Clayton on bass, Larry Mullin on drums, Dave Evans, nicknamed 'The Edge'—" Kasem suddenly grew agitated. "Wait, this is bullshit. *Nobody cares!* These guys are from England and WHO GIVES A SHIT? Just a lot of wasted names that don't mean DIDDLEY SHIT!" To add insult to injury, Negativland also mixed in a speech by U2's lead singer, Bono, which made the self-important Nobel Peace Prize nominee sound pious and ridiculous. Public Enemy's Harry Allen remembers the first time he heard it. "I was stunned—amazed—it was *so* funny," Allen tells me. "They're the greatest. I love their political statement, the idea that information should be free and open."

"We were out on tour and this guy came up to us [after a show] and he handed us a cassette," Don Joyce tells me as he sits in the Negativland's studio in Berkeley, about a dozen years after the record's release. The Negativland workspace is a tangled mess of cables, audio cartridges and cassettes, analog soundboards, and old computers; it doubles as the sixty-year-old Joyce's home. The windows are covered to block out the sun so that the most visible things in the room are his silver hair, shaped in a bowl cut, fair skin, and the giant white CIA letters printed on his black T-shirt. "That night at the hotel we listened to it and sorta just fell over laughing. . . . We had never heard it before and it was amazingly funny, so immediately when we hear things like that we say we can make something out of this."

U2 was released with little fanfare on SST Records, a small independent punk-rock label. But within ten days of its release Island Records and U2's song publisher, Warner-Chappel, served Negativland with a lawsuit after R.E.M. manager Bertis Downs sent U2's management a copy of the single, a Negativland member later discovered. Recognizing that they were small fish compared to this oceanic multinational corporation, the group sent out a press release that stated, "Preferring retreat to total annihilation, Negativland and SST had no choice but to comply completely with these demands." They lost a lot of money. Even worse, their song's copyright was transferred to Island Records, much like what happened to the Verve when they handed over "Bittersweet Symphony" to former Rolling Stones manager Allen Klein.

Even though Negativland had a strong fair-use argument, primarily based around parody, the Supreme Court had not yet ruled in 2 Live Crew's favor regarding their spoof of "Pretty Woman." Negativland didn't have the resources to fight a prolonged court battle, and because of pressure from their record company, they agreed to a very unfavorable settlement. "Companies like Island depend on this kind of economic inevitability to bully their way over all lesser forms of opposition," the group stated in a 1991 press release. "Thus, Island easily wipes us off the face of their earth purely on the basis of how much more money they can afford to waste than we can. We think there are issues to stand up for here, but Island can spend their way out of ever having to face them in a court of law." Backed by litigation war chests of millions of dollars, intellectual-property owners can swat away and squash unflattering commentary by intimidating those who can't afford a lengthy court battle (which is most of us).

TRADEMARKING FREEDOM OF EXPRESSION®

If Negativland hadn't been sued, this book wouldn't exist. As a teenage hipster-doofus, I admired the group because they held up arty, funhouse mirrors to the media-saturated culture that surrounded me. Their collage aesthetic seemed a natural way of commenting on the world, especially since I had grown up listening to hip-hop. In titling their 1987 album *Escape from Noise* (the same year Public Enemy released "Bring the Noise"), they were referring to the ubiquitous pop-culture cacophony that blankets us. But instead of *literally* escaping—living off the grid, so to speak—the group engaged with the world by putting something new and subversive into the media mix.

They were also pranksters. When Negativland couldn't afford to take time off from their day jobs to tour in 1988, they put out a press release claiming that the FBI had asked them to remain in the Bay Area until an investigation of a multiple homicide was concluded. They claimed that the suspected cause of the murders, a Midwestern teenager's slaying of his family, was their song "Christianity Is Stupid" (which sampled from an evangelical preacher's sermon, who sarcastically shouted, now out of context, "Christianity is STUPID, Communism is GOOD!"). Although the murder was real—painfully real for the victims and extended family, something that makes the prank a bit tasteless—Negativland's involvement was completely fictitious. "One of the band members, Richard, came up with an excuse for why we couldn't do the tour," Don Joyce explains. "He found this article in the *New York Times* or someplace about a kid who had killed his parents in Minnesota with an ax."

If any media outlets had bothered to call the FBI or the small-town police department, they would have uncovered Negativland's prank. But local radio and television stations jumped on the story, sensationalizing it even further, until a media snowball formed. No longer in control of events they set in motion, the group sat back and recorded the broadcasts as things grew ever more tasteless, in a way that only an exploitative news media can achieve. Negativland remixed and reworked the news coverage to make a concept album, *Helter Stupid,* which scrutinized the same media that carelessly examined them. It was similar to what Public Enemy was doing around the same time—remixing media coverage about themselves on their own records. In both cases, it was a meta-commentary on the echo chamber we call mass media, calling into question the distinction between truth and fiction, information and sensationalism.

Negativland introduced me to two of the major tropes that have dominated my life—media pranks and copyright law—so it's fitting that the group's legal problems first inspired me to trademark freedom of expression® when I was an undergrad. A few years later, in 1998, the Patent and Trademark Office granted me my trademark, the same year that Fox News was awarded ownership of Fair and Balanced®. Like Fox's trademark, my registration doesn't actually give me full legal control over how freedom of expression® appears in all contexts, for my trademark was filed only under Class 16 of the international schedule of goods and services, which covers "printed matter"—pamphlets, magazines, newspapers, and the like. Even though I can't prevent, for instance, a phone company from using freedom of expression® as an advertising slogan, I could very well keep the American Civil Liberties Union from publishing a magazine with that title. However, I'd never do that to the ACLU.

In my application to the Patent and Trademark Office, I didn't write: "I want to trademark 'freedom of expression' as an ironic comment that demonstrates how our culture has become commodified and privately owned." I simply applied to register this trademark and let the government decide whether or not we should live in a world where someone can legally control freedom of expression®. In filing this application, I crossed the enemy line at the Patent and Trademark Office, feigning allegiance by speaking their slippery language of legalese, fooling them into saying what I hoped wasn't actually possible.

After I received my freedom of expression® trademark certificate, I wanted to publicize the event, and I knew just the way to gather a large audience: a media prank. Early in my life I learned how easy it was to manipulate the media into telling my strange little stories. When I was a junior at James Madison University, I gained local and national media attention when I attempted to change the school mascot to a three-eyed pig with antlers, a movement that culminated in a rally where I married one hundred people to bananas in front of TV news cameras on the JMU commons. A few years later, I got a lot of press coverage when I sold my soul in a glass jar on eBay, being quoted saying things such as "In America, you're rewarded for selling your soul and compromising your principles. I may not have a soul, but I have a new car, and I'm doing great."

Pranks, for me, aren't the same as hoaxes. Hoaxes are what they are: they use deception to make someone or something look foolish, and nothing more. Media pranks, on the other hand, involve cooking up a story or an event in order to make a larger, satirical point. For instance, 1960s radicals Abbie Hoffman and Jerry Rubin dumped hundreds of dollar bills from a balcony overlooking the New York Stock Exchange, causing trading to stop as brokers grabbed at the money that was falling from the sky. Hoffman and

Rubin invited reporters to cover the event, which was designed—ingeniously and hilariously—to peel back the Stock Exchange's blanket of respectability to reveal the naked greed that bubbled underneath.

I figured that the media wouldn't be able to pass up a story about someone threatening to sue another for the unauthorized use of freedom of expression®. The problem was I didn't really want to sue some innocent infringer who used my trademark. So I enlisted my high-school prankster friend, the Reverend Brendan Love, who posed as the publisher of a fictitious punk-rock magazine named *Freedom of Expression*. I hired a lawyer, who wrote Brendan a cease-and-desist letter, soberly stating, "Your company has been using the mark Freedom of Expression. . . . Such use creates a likelihood of confusion in the market and also creates substantial risk of harm to the reputation and goodwill of our client. This letter, therefore, constitutes formal notice of your infringement of our client's trademark rights and"—this is my favorite part—"a demand that you refrain from all further use of Freedom of Expression."

When talking to reporters who responded to a press release I sent out, I played the quasi-corporate asshole to Brendan's indignant anarchist underdog, spouting poker-faced lines such as "I didn't go to the trouble, the expense, and the time of trademarking freedom of expression® just to have someone else come along and think they can use it whenever they want." Brendan countered that I was an "opportunist." The venerable western Massachusetts newspaper the *Hampshire Gazette* published an article with a headline that read, "Freedom, and Expression of Speech"—a story that played up the inherent absurdity of someone successfully trademarking freedom of expression®. I wanted to reprint a chunk of the *Hampshire Gazette* article in the introduction to my first book so as to expose the purpose of my prank to more people. But when I explained in a letter that it was a "socially conscious media prank," the paper's editor wouldn't allow me to reprint the article. In fact, he didn't bother composing a letter, instead scrawling on my own dispatch, "Permission <u>Denied</u>," and mailed it back to me.

I was completely naive and perhaps more than a little stupid. I assumed the folks at the *Hampshire Gazette* would be irritated with my deception, but at the end of the day I honestly thought they would grant me permission, given the slant and the content of their own story. In my first book's introduction, however, I was able to point out the fact that the *Hampshire Gazette* used copyright law to prevent me from reprinting its own story that was about how intellectual-property law restricts freedom of expression®. But the little saga didn't end there. After my book, *Owning Culture,* came out in 2001, the publisher of a very smart magazine of cultural criticism called *Stay Free!* contacted me. Carrie McLaren was putting together an art show entitled Illegal Art: Freedom of Expression in the Corporate Age. She wanted to include my framed freedom of expression® certificate in an exhibit that featured art and ideas that pushed the envelope of intellectual-property law. I was flattered to discover that among the many great artists included in the show, Negativland was involved.

Serendipitously, at that time I was teaching an undergrad course on intellectual-property law. One of my students, Abby, brought in a copy of an AT&T ad from the *Daily Iowan* that used the slogan "Freedom of Expression"—WITHOUT MY PERMISSION—to lure college students into signing up for their long-distance plan. My class told me I should sue AT&T, and we all laughed, and I said, "Sure." Soon I realized that the synergy of the art show, the publicity it was generating, and my own freedom of expression® project was too perfect not to exploit. I hired a lawyer in Iowa City, gave him my government documents, and a copy of the ad, and he drafted a cease-and-desist letter addressed to AT&T (just as the company would've done to me if I stepped on their trademarked toes).

It's important to note that I had no real case. My trademark didn't protect the phrase in the context of advertising, just as Fox News wasn't able to prevent its trademarked slogan from being used as the title of Al Franken's book. I was overreaching, much as overzealous corporate bozos so often do when they try to muzzle freedom of expression®. Conspiring with the Chicago organizers of the Illegal Art show, the good folks at *In These Times* magazine, I used the show's opening as a press conference to publicly announce my scheme. The *New York Times* broke the story and others picked it up, including the U.S. government's overseas broadcasting arm, *Voice of America* (which allowed me to air my critiques of intellectual-property law all the way to Afghanistan). AT&T never did respond to, or worry about, my lawyer's cease-and-desist letter. Although I didn't prevent AT&T from using freedom of expression® without my permission, my media prank did succeed in broadcasting to millions a critique of intellectual-property law that wouldn't normally get national or international attention.

ART PRANKSTERS

Political and artistic pranks stretch back to the European Dada movement of the early twentieth century and beyond. In fact, Abbie Hoffman wasn't the first revolutionary American prankster; that title belongs to Ben Franklin. He was at his most clever and hilarious when he authored *Poor Richard's Almanac.* An unknown writer at the time, Franklin goaded a more established almanac writer, Titan Leeds, into a ridiculous public dispute that would anticipate the over-the-top pranks of the Dadaists. In his first almanac, published in 1732, Franklin created a fictitious "author" named Richard Saunders. The advertisement published in the *Pennsylvania Gazette* stated that *Poor Richard's Almanac* would announce "the predicted death of his friend Titan Leeds." Franklin/Saunders narrowed it down not just to the date, but to the exact second when three planets aligned ("October 17, 1733, 3 ho., 29 m., P.M. at the very instant of . . .").[1]

This enraged Leeds, who didn't take kindly to a prediction of his own death by someone who *wasn't* his friend. In next year's *Poor Richard's Almanac,* a bestseller because of this mini-scandal, Franklin/Saunders wrote that he had been "treated in a very gross and unhandsome manner" by Titan Leeds. "Mr. Leeds was too well bred to use any man so indecently and so scurrilously," he wrote, "and moreover, his esteem and affection for me was extraordinary." Franklin wouldn't let it go, writing in the 1735 edition of his almanac, "I say, having received much abuse from the ghost of Titan Leeds, who pretends to still be living . . . I cannot help but saying, that tho' I take it patiently, I take it very unkindly." He continued, arguing that because the *real* Leeds would never have treated him so poorly, this proved that in fact he was dead. "And whatever he may pretend, 'tis undoubtedly true that he is really defunct and dead."[2]

When Leeds finally did die in 1738, Franklin wouldn't throw in the towel. He printed a letter from Leeds's ghost admitting that "I did actually die at that moment, precisely at the hour you mentioned, with a variation of 5 minutes, 53 seconds." He then had Leeds's ghost issue one more prediction: John Jerman—another one of his competitors in the almanac market who had also hired Franklin as a printer—would convert to Catholicism. This was an outrageous claim, especially in a time of anti-Papist prejudice. After four years of Franklin needling him in print, Jerman took his business to another printer. Until his final breath, Franklin engaged in similar pranks. His last published piece was under an assumed persona, of which he had at least one hundred throughout his life. Under the pseudonym "Sidi Mehemet Ibrahim," he wrote letters to newspapers with an ironic, over-the-top zeal favoring slavery, letters meant to shame American slave owners.[3] Ben Franklin: American Hero? American Weirdo?

Many of the strategies Franklin used—humor, irony, scandal—were shared over a century later by a European group of political artist-pranksters, the Dadaists. These early-twentieth-century aesthetic anarchists aimed to destroy both bourgeois capitalism and Romantic ideas about art—and had a good time trying. They celebrated the liberating potential of "chance" as an artistic method, which was a direct reaction to the "civilized rationality" that resulted in World War I. From chance emerged collage. "They cut up photographs," wrote early Dadaist Hans Richter in a lively first-person account of early Dada, "stuck them together in provocative ways . . . to confront a crazy world with its own image."[4]

The way he talks about the emergence of photomontage echoes the way Negativland describe their sound collages. "One of Negativland's artistic obsessions," said the group in their book *Fair Use,* "involves the media, itself, as a source and subject for much of our work. We respond (as artists always have) to our environment, an environment increasingly filled with artificial ideas, images, and sounds." Just as Negativland liberated their sound sources from a fixed context, the Dadaists gave letters, words, and sentences a new kind of freedom. These activities were similar to a critical practice that French theorist Jacques Derrida would call *deconstruction* fifty years later. This strategy is carried out by an active reader/writer who disobeys the wishes of, as Derrida slyly puts it, "those authors whose death does not await their demise."[5]

Dadaists were passionately devoted to turning artistic ideas into action, and wanted their art to impact the social, economic, and political world. They hated and endlessly ridiculed the idea that the artist should be detached from daily life, which was promoted by the Romantic movement. The collage method was an excellent tool that undercut the Romantic ideal of originality, a weapon that also quite easily lent itself to the prankish nature of the Dadaists. Tristan Tzara, a principle Dadaist provocateur, gave instructions on how "to make a Dadaist poem" in which the creator takes a newspaper, cuts out words from an article and places them in a bag only to be randomly pulled out. It was a humorous polemic that made fun of high-minded Romantic notions of originality and creativity. Tzara sarcastically concluded:

> *The poem will resemble you.*
> *And there you are—an infinitely original author of charming*
> *sensibility even though unappreciated by the vulgar herd.*[6]

The Futurists, another group of European artist madmen who preceded the Dadaists by a few years, were also interested in the possibilities of textual collage, particularly in its potential for delivering their pro-war propaganda. Conversely, the Dadaists used collage as a political and artistic tool that broadcasted their leftist antiwar views. Although there were aesthetic similarities between the Dadaists and the Futurists, they had very different worldviews, which was perhaps best summarized in the *Futurist Manifesto*: "We will glorify war—the world's only hygiene—militarism, patriotism, the destructive gesture of freedom-bringers, beautiful ideas worth dying for, and . . . will fight moralism, feminism, every opportunistic or utilitarian cowardice."[7]

Where the Futurists were artsy, chest-beating libertarian yahoos with paintbrushes *and* guns, the Dadaists reacted against the ravages of the war that the Futurists promoted. As was to be expected of a group that embraced chaos, Dadaism imploded by the early 1920s. Surrealism arose from Dada's ashes with the printing in 1924 of *La revolution surrealiste,* published by Surrealist figurehead André Breton. Surrealism embraced the subconscious, privileging it as an irrational road away from a "rational" civilization that had almost slaughtered itself. This movement brought a new interest in collage, in part because Breton saw these techniques as opening up new sources of "unreal reality" for art.[8]

More than anything else, the Dadaists were serious jokers (and perhaps even midnight tokers). "We destroyed, we insulted, we despised—and we laughed," reminisced Richter. "We laughed at everything. We laughed at ourselves just as we laughed at Emperor, King and Country, fat bellies and baby-pacifiers. We took our laughter seriously." This laser-guided hilarity, which was aimed directly at, to use the 1960s counterculture term, "the establishment," was a reaction to the bloody times. "Pandemonium, destruction, anarchy, anti-everything," Richter wrote, "why should we hold it in check? What of the pandemonium, destruction, anarchy, anti-everything of the World War? How could Dada have been anything but destructive, aggressive, insolent, on principle and with gusto?"[9]

The Dadaists reveled in their twisted media pranks. For instance, Tristan Tzara and Jean Arp were at the center of a scandal that rocked Swiss newspapers when they convinced reporters that they fought each other in a duel. Numerous members of Swiss society surely would have been happy if they had both Dadaists died, so that part of the story wasn't scandalous. The fury came from the fiction that the "universally popular sentimental poet" J. C. Heer was involved. Many, wrote Hans Richter, "wondered how a sedate figure like J. C. Heer, who was not in the least eccentric, could possibly have become involved in such goings-on." Just as Titan Leeds did when Ben Franklin goaded him into a public row in the papers, Heer approached the papers with a furious disclaimer, stating that he had never been involved in such nefarious activities. Richter sets the scene:

> On the evening of the same day there was a disclaimer of the disclaimer. Its first paragraph caused a sigh of disappointment to be heard all over Zurich; neither of the combatants had been hurt (the report said that they had both fired in the same direction—away from each other). The second paragraph plunged the reader into total confusion. Two witnesses (both Dadaists, it is true) announced that they understood of course that a respected figure like J. C. Heer did not wish to be associated with the stormy quarrels of youth, but that respect for the truth forced them to say (with a polite bow in the direction of the revered poet) that he *had* been there.[10]

Dadaists' art was in the act of living, and so was their revolution. They mocked and molested bourgeois society with prankish acts that knocked art off its pedestal; they wanted to dismantle the museums and turn the streets into galleries.

ART AND EVERYDAY LIFE

Marcel Duchamp, while widely remembered as a pioneering artist, was equally a prankster—the two couldn't be disentangled. In 1913 he left the painting world behind after displaying his *Nude Descending a Staircase,* which was alternately referred to as a "masterpiece" or, more derisively, an "explosion in a shingle factory." That year, Duchamp displayed his first ready-made, *Bicycle Wheel;* it was the culmination of Dada's anti-art aesthetic. A ready-made, according to Duchamp, is something torn from daily life and turned into art by the artist's simply being audacious enough to call it that. "As early as 1913," Duchamp deadpans, "I had the happy idea to fasten a bicycle wheel to a kitchen stool and watch it turn." A couple of years later, in another example of found and self-defined art, he bought a shovel at a New York City hardware store and wrote "in advance of the broken arm" on it.[11]

With *Fountain,* his most famous ready-made, Duchamp bought a mass-produced urinal and signed on its white porcelain surface the name "R. Mutt" (the name of a sanitation company). He also famously drew a mustache and goatee on a store-bought reproduction of Da Vinci's *Mona Lisa,* naming it *LHOOQ.* When the letters in Duchamp's title are read aloud in French—*"Elle a chaud au cul"*—it's a pun on a phrase that translates colloquially as "She is hot in the ass." Not only were these works clever pranks that sent up the sober art world, they also directly attacked Romantic notions of originality and authorship that are central to copyright. Ready-mades were also among the first works of art that incorporated everyday, mass-produced objects. Although Duchamp was never mentioned in Walter Benjamin's 1935 essay "The Work of Art in the Mechanical Age of Reproduction," this influential cultural critic wrestled with many similar ideas.

Benjamin argued that mechanical reproduction undermines traditional ideas of originality because it overwhelms the "aura" of the original work. The aura decays and the distance between the work and the audience shrinks, allowing art to be absorbed into everyday life instead of being fenced off in a museum or gallery. Tradition called for the work of art to be unique. However, the development of photography, motion pictures, and the popularity of socialism created a crisis in art. The ritual of art for art's sake was, in part, a reaction to this crisis, where "pure art" was conceived as being disconnected from daily life and having no social function. Artists associated with Romanticism cultivated this kind of antisocial ritual, but Dada celebrated the death of the original genius and they danced on its grave. "Another aspect of the 'ready-made' is its lack of uniqueness," wrote Duchamp approvingly.[12]

Years later, beginning in the early 1980s, artist Sherrie Levine pushed these artistic boundaries by photographing famous works of art and displaying them. Levine's work had political and feminist undercurrents because she chose to solely re-create the work of "seminal" male artists associated with a masculine style. Working in the 1960s, Elaine Sturtevant produced paintings that were clearly identical to Andy Warhol's paintings and silkscreen prints. Sturtevant was even applauded by pop artist Claes Oldenburg, though he grew irritated when she slyly began making replicas of *his* work.[13] Notably, I have found no documentation before the 1960s of any American or European artists who were threatened or prosecuted for intellectual-property "theft" when they appropriated from the commercial world, even in the most brazen way.

The advent of reproduction opened up room for art to be based on politics. Duchamp's ready-mades were less "unique works of art" than provocative, physical reminders that the separation between art and everyday life was an artificial one. When authenticity ceases to be an important part of making art, Benjamin wrote, "the total function of art is reversed. Instead of being based on ritual it begins to be based on another practice, politics." In other words, the decay of the aura is connected to the democratization of art. This is how art (traditionally associated with the upper class) could realize its progressive potential and get "the masses" involved. Art became political.

In the hands of Dadaists, the mixing of art and life took a political turn, something that left an imprint on the primary inheritor of the Dada flame: Situationism. This anti-art movement emerged in 1957, and its key members, particularly *Society of the Spectacle* author Guy Debord, played an instrumental role in the May 1968 uprising in Paris. The events of the revolt, which began after scuffles broke out between government police forces and student radicals, nearly brought the French government to its knees. Unrest quickly spread across Paris, manifesting in such forms as looting, graffiti slogans adorning the walls, and students occupying universities. Workers showed their solidarity by enacting a general strike, closing down the country's major industries, and on Monday, May 13, one million protesters marched through the streets of Paris. Situationists were in the thick of these events.

The Situationists wanted to abolish art and replace it with what they called "play," creating "situations" that they theorized would set the sun on the old world and create a brand-new liberated day. An example of a *major* situation was the chaos of May 1968, when the following words were attached to the Sorbonne's entrance: "We are inventing a new and original world. Imagination is seizing power." Arguing for the relevance of Situationism, Debord believed Surrealism didn't live up to its revolutionary pretensions: "The whole genre of ostentatious Surrealist 'weirdness' has ceased to be very surprising." He claimed that the Surrealists were theoretically incompetent and, more troubling, unwilling to align themselves with the working class, which meant the Surrealists had "joined the camp of mystical idealism."[14] The term "mystical idealism," of course, was a potshot.

"Surrealist dreams correspond to bourgeois weakness, to artistic nostalgia, and to the refusal to envision the emancipatory use of the superior technical means of our times," he said, speaking of mass media. Debord said that the masses should seize the means of media production and experiment with new ways of being and understanding, creating new "situations" that would help usher in an "authentic revolutionary culture." In an example of *literally* controlling the means of production, during the May riots the Situationists and forty others formed the CMDO (Council for Maintaining the Occupations), which occupied print shops. They produced major tracts and broadsides in print runs of up to a quarter million. Songs were included in these tracts, including the CMDO–written "The Commune is Not Dead," which went, in part:

> *One match and, Forward!*
> *Poetry written in petrol . . .*
> *While waiting for self-management,*
> *We'll apply the critique of the brick.*

Although the Situationists weren't the primary driving force behind the Paris uprising—it was very decentralized, involving workers, students, and other sympathizers—they contributed to the tone and the tactics of the movement. Debord, who applied the critique of the brick, was deeply influenced by Henri Lefebvre, a Marxist philosopher of the post–World War II period who ran in French bohemian circles. Lefebvre also had an impact on the 1968 Paris uprising, going so far as to suggest slogans that were adopted by the student revolters such as, "Let everyday life become a work of art!" The Situationists took the pop culture that surrounded them and remixed it to include a critique of the dominant culture.

They called this technique *détournement,* and it was, for instance, manifested in the act of altering copyrighted comic-strip speech balloons to undermine the original message. It's also a method used today by the artists/activists who modify the trademarked logos and ad copy on roadside billboards that use the image of, for instance, the Dalai Lama. In the late 1990s the Billboard

Liberation Front altered the headline of an Apple ad from the grammatically challenged "Think Different" to the more appropriate "Think Disillusioned." The closest English translation of *détournement* falls somewhere between "diversion" and "subversion." Another translation might be "un-turning" or "de-turning"—where culture is turned back on itself, against itself.

Détournement is a plagiaristic act that, like a martial-arts move, shifts the strength and weight of the dominant culture against itself with some fancy linguistic and intellectual footwork. Debord insisted that a "Dadaist-type negation" must be deployed against the language of the dominant culture. He claimed that it is "impossible to get rid of a world without getting rid of the language that conceals and protects it, without laying bare its true nature." The Situationists believed that the truths revealed by *détournement,* the lifting of "the ideological veils that cover reality," were central to its revolutionary project.[15] While deconstruction and *détournement* aren't exactly the same, their overall strategy is shared: juxtaposition as an act of literary and cultural subversion.

Echoing the Situationist and Dadaist spirit of engagement, Derrida argues that deconstruction doesn't want to "remain enclosed in purely speculative, theoretical, academic discourses." It wants to "aspire to something more consequential, to *change* things," he argues, "in what one calls the city, the *pólis,* and more generally the world." Deconstruction can't really be understood in the abstract because it is first and foremost an *activity.* Nor should it be considered simply textual vandalism, for the word "deconstruction" is a close linguistic cousin of the word "analysis," rather than "destruction." The origins of the word "analysis" means "to undo," which is pretty much a synonym for "to deconstruct."[16]

The deconstructionist is a revolutionary reader, one who targets society's old, taken-for-granted meanings—waging a civil war of words that pits differing philosophies against one another until ink is spilled. This strategy looks for little slips—slipups—in texts that on the surface seem "natural," self-evident, or undeconstructable. A deconstructive reading of the Declaration of Independence (if it had been done over two hundred years ago, at least) would have found a bloody battleground in the phrase "all men are created equal." Today, it's an obvious contradiction, though years ago such a phrase more easily escaped scrutiny. "The deconstructive double agent feigns alliance and conducts clandestine operations behind the enemy's line," writes my former adviser at the University of Massachusetts, Briankle Chang. "The feigned alliance enables him to move freely across the war zone. . . . Freely crossing the war zone, the deconstructive mole traverses the lines separating the self from the other, friend from foe; he becomes a wartime nomad."[17]

Public Enemy used these deconstructive techniques when creating their own world of sound on records like *It Takes a Nation* and *Fear of a Black Planet.* This isn't to say that the strategies adopted by Public Enemy and others *exactly* mimic Derrida's deconstructive writings. Nevertheless, there's a common impulse occasionally shared by the operators of typewriters and turntables. Chuck D and company cut up and inserted into their records speeches by black leaders, media commentary about the group, and other such material to slash through hypocritical American ideologies. Harry Allen, for instance, was the group's "media assassin." The title was a conscious attempt to integrate a journalist into a hip-hop crew—to fight media misinformation campaigns on its own turf.

" 'Media assassin,' " Allen tells me, "makes an allusion to the notion of warfare, of weaponry. It naturally fits with a group for whom these were ideas through which to make music and statements—the ideas of violence and language and history." Harry Allen, who met up with me during a visit to Manhattan, turns my attention to a track from *Nation,* "Show 'Em Whatcha Got," where the group sampled a lecture by Sister Ava Muhammad of the Nation of Islam. Her voice was placed atop a mournful horn and a slow, hypnotic drum and bass line—a warm, booming track constructed from cold, digital 1's and 0's. "What you get," Allen says, "is something that has even more pathos and a kind of sadness—but yet defiance—that I think was in her voice. However, Public Enemy found and accentuated what was already there by sampling her voice and putting it in this new context.

"Public Enemy re-edited screams and hollers and grunts and moans, bringing together this orchestra of human passion, you might say. And the interesting thing is that Public Enemy used something as cold and brittle as computer chips and samplers to give this kind of resurrection and life to the voices of black people as uttered in song and voice." African American musician, filmmaker, and spoken-word poet Saul Williams points out that powerful men have regularly used similar strategies throughout history. "The remix, I believe, has always taken place," he says in his thoughtful, easygoing way. "The Bible itself is a remix. You have King James or a Pope who would take all these books—all of these religious texts—and say, 'Use this. Take Woman out of that story and replace that with Spirit. Don't say Woman, say Holy Spirit for Trinity.' It's a remix of ancient folklore from Egypt and what have you.

"So remixes have always happened," says Williams. "Unfortunately, they've happened *under the table* quite often and have been presented as the original mix." He adds, speaking of this deconstructive strategy, "The remix is perhaps the most sincere approach to looking at history and revisiting it, because it's done *on top of the table*—in fact, sometimes on turntables themselves." Deconstruction, *détournement,* and pranks all use deception to reveal that all "truths" are tricks, frauds. It's a seeming contradiction, but not a real one. Derrida's primary target was Western philosophy, so it's no surprise that the translator's introduction to Derrida's *Dissemination* colorfully characterizes one of his acts of deconstruction as "shortsheeting Plato's bed." "To laugh at philosophy," Derrida argues, is a form of awakening that calls for an activity that "acknowledges the philosopher's byways, understands his techniques, makes use of his ruses, manipulates his cards, lets him deploy his strategy, appropriates his texts."[18]

In a clever little prank, when U2 guitarist, the Edge, was interviewed via phone by the hip cyber-geek magazine *Mondo 2000,* he unwittingly ended up speaking to Negativland members Mark Hosler and Don Joyce. At first, the two remained unidentified, allowing themselves as wartime moles into a culture-industry machine that makes and breaks the careers of superstars. This was a year or so after the lawsuit in which Negativland was sued by Island Records and Warner-Chappell. At the time, the Edge was trying to bolster U2's credibility among the magazine's techno-literate readers to promote their media-savvy Zoo TV tour.

MARK HOSLER: I wanted to ask you something more about the Zoo TV tour. One thing that wasn't really clear to me—you have a satellite dish so that you can take stuff down live off of various TV transmissions around the world?

THE EDGE: Yeah, essentially the system is, like, we've got the big screens on the stage, which are the final image that's created. Down by the mixing board we've got a vision mixer which mixes in, blends the images from live cameras, from optical disks, and from live satellite transmissions that are taken in from a dish outside the venue. So the combination of images can be any of those sources. . . .

DON JOYCE: So you can kind of sample whatever's out there on the airwaves. . . .

THE EDGE: Yeah, it's kind of like information central.

MARK HOSLER: One thing I'm curious about—there's been more and more controversy over copyright issues and sampling, and I thought that one thing you're doing in the Zoo TV tour is that you were taking these TV broadcasts—copyrighted material that you are then rebroadcasting right there in the venue where people paid for a ticket—and I wondered what you thought about that.

DON JOYCE: And whether you had any problem, whether it ever came up that that was illegal.

THE EDGE: No, I mean, I asked the question early on—Is this going to be a problem?—and apparently it . . . I don't think there *is* a problem. I mean, in theory, I don't have a problem with sampling. I suppose when a sample becomes just part of another work then it's no problem. If sampling is, you know, stealing an idea and replaying the same idea, changing it very slightly, that's different. We're using the visual and images in a completely different context. If it's a live broadcast, it's like a few seconds at the most. I don't think, in spirit there's any . . .

DON JOYCE: So you think the fragmentary approach is the way to go?

THE EDGE: Yeah. You know, like in music terms, we've sampled things, people sample us all the time, you know, I hear the odd U2 drum loop in a dance record or whatever. You know, I don't have a problem with that.

DON JOYCE: Well, this is interesting because we've been involved in a similar situation along these lines. . . .[19]

Doh! Joyce and Hosler then revealed their ruse, one of those fantasy moments of intellectual revenge that one waits a lifetime for, and Negativland only had to wait a year. "I think at the end of it," Joyce recalls, "we asked for some money, and then he hung up." After all the bad publicity, U2 paid lip service to the collage artists, claiming they tried to have Island Records return to Negativland the copyrights of their record. However, Kasem and his attorneys made it clear that if that ever happened, Negativland *and* Island Records would be sued. As if to say, "Screw it," in 2001 Negativland re-released the *U2* record on their own label, gave it a new title, added multiple bonus tracks, and never heard a peep from another lawyer. They called the new record *These Guys Are from England and Who Gives a Shit.*

INAPPROPRIATE APPROPRIATIONS

The images produced by television, comics, and motion pictures created a new kind of vocabulary that artists used to comment on the world. However, by the 1960s, the rise of pop art, typified by Andy Warhol's Campbell's Soup cans and Roy Lichtenstein's comic-strip paintings, demonstrated that this language was privately owned. Pop artists became the first copyright criminals—which is ironic because, unlike Dadaists and Situationists, they were largely apolitical. "Look, we live in a world filled with products!" they essentially said while they sampled from existing commodities, but there was little to no critical impulse behind their work.

Because Andy Warhol's creations so heavily appropriated from pop-culture images, it's not that surprising that he was sued a number of times for copyright infringement. Warhol freely took images from magazines, such as the time when he based a number of pieces on a photograph of four poppies found in an issue of *Modern Photography.* He called the series simply *Flowers.* Warhol enlarged and silk-screened the image—originally photographed by Patricia Caulfield—and painted the flowers in bright colors. His studio, "the Factory," produced nearly one thousand prints of the transformed image, and he eventually licensed *Flowers* as posters (which is how Caulfield eventually discovered Warhol's appropriation). Warhol settled with the photographer and her attorney, handing over two of his paintings and agreeing to pay her a royalty in the future.

Despite the settlement, Caulfield remained unsatisfied because Warhol's appropriations disturbed her on a more fundamental level. "The reason there's a legal issue here is because there's a moral one," Caulfield said. "What's irritating is to have someone like an image enough to use it, but then denigrate the original intent."[20] The fact that Warhol clipped out Caulfield's photograph and used it in his own work was, to her, inherently problematic and morally wrong. This is how some musicians who have been sampled felt, and Caulfield's use of the term "original intent" in conjunction with her other statements underscores how pre-Dada notions of originality and creativity are still quite popular.

Similarly, photojournalist Charles Moore discovered that Warhol used—in a series called *Red Race Riot*—his pictures of three men who were attacked by police dogs in Birmingham. They were originally published in *Life* magazine. This upset Moore, who told Warhol, "I want it settled so you know, and other artists know, you can't just rip off a photographer's work."[21] The case was settled out of court, with Warhol handing over to Moore a number of prints from the *Flowers* series (something that's ironic and funny, given the story behind that series). Robert Rauschenberg also found himself in hot legal water when he collaged a photograph taken by Morton Beebe into a print titled *Pull,* one of Rauschenberg's most important pieces. Beebe's photograph of a man diving into a swimming pool was widely reprinted in the early 1970s and was used in an ad campaign for the Nikon camera company. Its very ubiquity contributed to Rauschenberg's desire to use it.

The angry photographer sent Rauschenberg a letter, and the artist responded with surprise. "I have received many letters from people expressing their happiness and pride in seeing their images incorporated and transformed in my work." Rauschenberg continued: "Having used collage in my work since 1949, I have never felt that I was infringing on anyone's rights as I have consistently transformed these images sympathetically . . . to give the work the possibility of being reconsidered and viewed in a totally new context."[22] In mid-1977 Beebe retained a lawyer, suing Rauschenberg for copyright infringement and asking for a minimum of ten thousand dollars in damages plus attorney and court fees, and profits from the sale of *Pull*. In 1980 Beebe and Rauschenberg settled, with Beebe receiving a copy of *Pull*, three thousand dollars, and a promise that Beebe would be attributed whenever the work was displayed in the future.

The Beebe-Rauschenberg case was yet another copyright-infringement lawsuit in the art world that was settled out of court, and which never set a legal precedent. Rauschenberg's attorney argued that his client admitted no wrongdoing in the settlement, adding that a collage artist "has the right to make fair use of prior printed and published materials in the creation of an original collage, including such preexisting elements as a part thereof and that such right is guaranteed to the artist as a fundamental right of Freedom of Expression under the First Amendment of the Constitution."

Pop art defanged the political and aesthetic tactics of Dada, and no one represents this mainstreaming more than the monster that pop art wrought: Jeff Koons. Koons's credibility and integrity as an artist has been challenged because of his showboating and his very public marriage to Italian ex–porn star and politician Ilona Staller (aka La Cicciolina). While a number of art critics write favorably of

Koons, many don't. Harvard University professor of modern art Yve-Alain Bois argues, "His work is totally trivial and a pure product of the market. He's considered to be an heir to Duchamp, but I think it's a trivialization of all that. I think he's kind of a commercial artist."[23] Koons first drew attention to himself with an exhibit that included a display of a series of ordinary, brand-new vacuum cleaners that were neatly arranged and presented within shiny, clear Plexiglas cases.

After his career took off, in 1988 Koons mounted his Banality show, a kitsch-filled exploration of "bad taste" that was as controversial as it was financially successful. The show displayed *String of Puppies,* a carved wooden statue depicting a middle-aged couple holding a string of German shepherd dogs. A total of three identical statues were produced, and this work was based on a cutesy mass-produced postcard that Koons bought at a gift shop. He took the postcard and sent it to his Italian studio to be made into a painted sculpture, resulting in the 42″ × 6″ × 37″ work *String of Puppies.* The photographer who shot the postcard picture, Art Rogers, discovered *String of Puppies* when he opened a copy of the *Los Angeles Times* and read a story about how "Manhattan millionaire Jeff Koons has once again shocked the world with the extremity of his kitsch vision." Soon after, Rogers sued Koons (who had also been sued for his appropriation of copyrighted cartoon characters the Pink Panther and Odie from the comic strip *Garfield).*

Rogers was understandably mad because, first, his work had been used without permission; second, Koons made a significant amount of money from the sales of his derivative work; and third, as one newspaper wrote, his "heart-warming snap was apparently viewed by swanky Manhattan as a hilarious piece of crud."[24] A federal court ruled in 1991 that Koons was guilty of copyright infringement, and in 1992 the U.S. Court of Appeals in New York upheld the lower court's ruling. Further setting a precedent, the Supreme Court refused to hear Koons's appeal, upholding the original ruling. Koons's attorney, John Koegel, claimed that *String of Puppies* was protected by the fair-use provision of the copyright statute, but Koons's appropriation was too obvious and not transformative enough for the court to rule that it was used as parody or critique. In *Rogers v. Koons*, the judge did not believe that Koons's appropriation could be considered fair use. "No copier may defend the act of plagiarism by pointing out how much of the copy he has not pirated," wrote the judge, adding, "there is no case here."

Because *String of Puppies* wasn't a blatant parody, the court didn't care that Koons's sculpture twisted many of the original photo's elements. The sculpture added color to the black-and-white photograph—the puppies were rendered an unnatural bright blue—and was three-dimensional. Art critic Martha Buskirk noted that the postcard photograph and Koons's work differ dramatically in medium, size, and certainly in contexts where they might be appreciated, i.e., a tourist-postcard shop versus a SoHo gallery. Also, Koons's piece undermines the sentimental cuddliness of Rogers's photograph, replacing it with a tacky, slightly disturbing, and subtly hilarious image. Subtlety, unfortunately, can work against an artist in the legal arena. "Art has a real problem when it gets in court," says Negativland's Don Joyce. "The law isn't written to accommodate the vagaries and varieties of artistic expression. They just don't mix."

Copyright protection should not allow an author to have *total* control over his or her published work, a position the Supreme Court has forcefully argued on numerous occasions. This is a simple fact of the U.S. copyright regime. That doesn't mean, however, that fair use opens up an avenue for artists and other creators to be unfairly ripped off. There are times when appropriations cross the line and get a free ride on someone else's creative labor; clearly, there are going to be moments when derivative uses are "unfair." Koons made the mistake of doing very little to Art Rogers's photograph beyond changing the medium (and with it, certain other details of the image). Put side by side with collages by Rauschenberg, Negativland, and, more generally, the Dadaists and Situationists, Koons's creative transformation pales in comparison. In other words, fair use doesn't mean that people have a free pass to pillage from others' work, though many scholars and artists argue *String of Puppies* is a legitimate and legal work of art.

ILLEGAL ART

It isn't only artists who sue artists. It has become increasingly common for corporations to file lawsuits, and in these cases it's a far more one-sided contest. Even though the artists who use iconic trademarks (Mickey Mouse or Barbie) might be legally in the right, Disney, Mattel, and other corporations can outspend them in court. Companies want to saturate us with their trademarks and their brands, but only to the point where they don't lose control of them. In effect, they want it both ways. In 1998 Mattel went after the Swedish pop group Aqua, which had an international hit with the satirical "Barbie Girl" (sample lyrics: "I'm a Barbie Girl in a Barbie world / Life in plastic, it's fantastic"). Mattel claimed that the song debased their brand by, according to the lawsuit, associating "sexual and other unsavory themes with Mattel's Barbie products." Because the group's major label, MCA, was also sued, Aqua had the financial muscle of a multinational corporation behind them.

Fortunately for the group, the court ruled in its favor. The Ninth Circuit's ruling began with the line, "If this were a sci-fi melodrama, it might be called Speech-Zilla meets Trademark Kong." In the closing line of the *Mattel v. MCA Records* decision, the judge stated, "The parties are advised to chill." Unfortunately for Utah-based artist Tom Forsythe, he didn't have a big company to protect him. Commenting on the unrealistic beauty myth and consumer culture, Forsythe jammed nude Barbie dolls in kitchen appliances and photographed them, calling the series *Food Chain Barbie*. "I put them in a blender," said Forsythe, "with the implication they're going to get chewed up, but no matter what, they just kept smiling. That became an interesting commentary on how false that image is." Mattel sued Forsythe, and after five months of looking, the ACLU and the San Francisco law firm of Howard Rice Nemerovski Canady Falk & Rabkin defended him *pro bono*. This meant he wasn't billed for his lawyer's time, though the process is far from free. It takes lots of money to hire expert witnesses, file court documents, and do the extensive legal searches necessary to defend oneself against a trademark lawsuit.

As more and more of what we look at, the physical space where we stand, and what we hear becomes privatized, it becomes increasingly difficult for artists to reflect on and interpret our world. "We're living in this commercial culture," curator Carrie McLaren tells me. It was a few hours before her traveling Illegal Art Show opened at San Francisco MOMA's Artist Gallery, which featured Forsythe's Barbie photographs as well as my freedom of expression® certificate from the Patent and Trademark Office. "It's all privatized. It really hampers your ability to be able to talk about what's going on in the world if you can't talk about things that are privately owned because, well, that's just about all there is." Before the twentieth century, she points out, "Corporations weren't the central institutions that they are now. So people would make art about religion and whatnot, things that were more central to culture."

In the early 1990s, the Berkeley Pop Culture Project documented that Mickey Mouse's image was the number-one most-reproduced in the world, Jesus was number two, and Elvis had the number-three spot. Only one of these guys isn't fiercely protected by an intellectual-property owning juggernaut, and that's because the Son of God had the unfortunate timing to be born long before such laws existed. Artists have always based their art on the things that dominate the popular consciousness, and it just so happens that Elvis, Barbie, Ronald McDonald, and others are the ubiquitous icons of our time. When John Lennon infamously declared at the height of Beatlemania that they were bigger than Jesus, he wasn't saying they were better or more important. He was just stating a fact.

Todd Haynes's first movie, *Superstar: The Karen Carpenter Story*, appropriated the easy-listening music of the Carpenters (as well as Mattel's most prized trademark, Barbie). The director, who went on to make *Safe* and *Far from Heaven*, cast the doll in the leading role for his short student film about the tragic pop star who died of anorexia. "There were a lot of connections," Todd Haynes told *Graffiti Magazine*, "like the idea of the Barbie doll as this kind of icon of femininity that seemed very fitting." Rather than being a smirky, ironic take on Karen Carpenter's sad story, it's a moving human drama that critiques our obsessive culture of thinness. Unsurprisingly, both Mattel and Richard Carpenter (her brother, who was unsympathetically represented as a Ken doll) made it impossible for the 1987 film to be legally distributed. "Richard in particular has a lot of stake in controlling the way people look at the story," Haynes said.[25]

"Intellectual-property lawsuits limit the scope of artistic expression in such a way these days because everything's branded," Forsythe points out. "If you want to comment on society today, you're using somebody's brand if you're at all in touch with reality."

In the end, Forsythe's lawyers spent almost $2 million defending him, reminding us that freedom of expression® can come with a hefty price tag. "I knew for a fact that I was protected under the fair use doctrine," Forsythe told the *Boston Globe*. "What I didn't know was just how difficult it would be to press that case."

"A lot of people have asked us," Carrie McLaren tells me, " 'Oh, are you trying to get sued by doing this exhibit?' And nothing could really be further from the truth." Carrie can't afford a lawsuit. She's a high-school teacher in Brooklyn and the publisher of *Stay Free!* magazine, a small respected publication that is done more for love than profit. "I mean, the last thing I want to do is get sued." It's this fear of legal retribution that creates a chilling effect that can lead to self-censorship. Jessica Clark, the managing editor of *In These Times*, a political magazine whose offices provided the site for the Illegal Art show in Chicago before its visit to San Francisco, vividly described her uneasiness as a host. Clark wrote:

> Could we get sued? That was my first reaction when I read a recent *New York Times* report on *Illegal Art: Freedom of Expression in the Corporate Age*, the art exhibit coming to the *In These Times* offices. Law professor Edward Samuels claims that "half the exhibition is in violation" of copyright law. Paul McCartney's spokesman, meanwhile, suggests that the show's organizers are akin to media pirates. I could already envision the cease-and-desist letters, the harassment, the headaches . . . in a word, I was chilled.

Chilled, but not deterred; the show went on without incurring a lawsuit. As a kind of prank—showing politicized art in the Dada tradition—the Illegal Art show won a small victory for freedom of expression® by committing repeated acts of copyright civil disobedience. It provoked a lot of media attention but no lawsuits because it forced copyright-owning companies into a catch-22 situation. If they tolerated the existence of the show, it would set an important precedent that demonstrates that fair use *does* exist in practice, that artists and musicians shouldn't be scared of overzealous copyright bozos. Or at least should be less scared. If anyone tried to sue the show's artists, organizers, or venues, it would have generated a bevy of bad publicity for them.

Today, the show's contents are archived on the Web—at illegal -art.org—offering free MP3 downloads of Negativland's *U2* single and other banned works discussed in this book. As a multimedia clearinghouse of outlaw sound and video collages, the Illegal Art site's continuing presence on the Web is very much a political act, a kind of virtual sit-in. I hesitate to even use the terms "copyright civil disobedience" or even "illegal art" for the following reason: The show's contents are perfectly legal and protected by fair use. Rather than being an evaluation of their legal status, the term "illegal art" is really just a provocative rhetorical device. In a *New York Times* article about the exhibit, Jane C. Ginsburg—professor of literary and artistic property law at Columbia Law School, and daughter of Supreme Court Justice Ruth Bader Ginsburg—stated, "The irony is that most of the stuff that I see on the Web site wouldn't be considered illegal."

When the Supreme Court unanimously found 2 Live Crew not guilty of copyright infringement, it unambiguously strengthened the fair-use doctrine by establishing case law that many lower-court decisions have cited. "The fair use doctrine," the high court stated, "permits and requires courts to avoid rigid application of the Copyright Act of 1976 when, on occasion, such application would stifle the very creativity which the act is designed to foster." Repeatedly, the Supreme Court and lower courts have emphasized that copyright's primary purpose is to promote creativity, and they have consistently upheld and expanded the fair-use doctrine. In theory, then, all is fine. The real-world problems occur when institutions that actually have the resources to defend themselves against unwarranted or frivolous lawsuits choose to take the safe route, thus eroding fair use.

In suggesting a remedy for the kinds of horror stories contained in this book, I need to reiterate that, for the most part, we don't need any new legislation. Fair use is a great solution in the United States, but for it to have any real impact in our culture we need to vigorously and confidently (though not carelessly) employ this legal doctrine in daily life. It's too bad that a schoolteacher with few material resources should be the one to risk taking a fall, rather than those institutions that can afford it. It's a sad commentary on our culture. Despite Illegal Art's small scale and infinitesimal budget, the world is arguably a safer place for collage artists because Carrie McLaren mounted this show.

And in mid-2004 it became even more secure when a federal judge awarded $1.8 million in legal fees to Tom Forsythe, who could now pay back his lawyers after a lengthy and costly battle against Mattel. The court called Mattel's case "objectively unreasonable" and "frivolous." The day after the ruling, Forsythe told me, "The fee award promises to have real implications for artists who may now be more willing to critique brands and feel more confident that they will have an easier time finding attorneys to represent them. Maybe it will even keep these brand bullies from filing the lawsuits in the first place."

MIXING IT UP WITH THE SOUND COLLAGISTS

When they first started out, some of the members of Negativland had little knowledge of the rich history of avant-garde sound collage. They were just teenagers making noise. "When we were doing early Negativland recordings," Mark Hosler tells me, "the television set was mixed in, we played tapes from game shows and interview talk shows, and I'd have a mike outside recording what was going on in our neighborhood." He elaborates, "You see, I'm a kid, I've grown up in a media-saturated environment, and I'm just tuned in to it. I was born in 1962; I grew up watching *Captain Kangaroo*, moon landings, zillions of TV ads, the Banana Splits, *M*A*S*H*, and *The Mary Tyler Moore Show*. When I started messing around with sounds, there was no conceptual pretense at all."

This reflects the attitude of a great many artists who use collage as a tool to create their art. Not many people consciously say to themselves, "I'm going to deconstruct texts from the media barrage in order to undermine the dominant culture's ideology." They just do it because it feels natural. Negativland's Don Joyce, on the other hand, knew his art-music history. He says from his darkened recording studio, "I went to art school, studied painting, so that's my whole background. I'm thinking musique concrète, John Cage, those kinds of people." Vicki Bennett, who performs under the name People Like Us, is one of the few women who work in the male-dominated world of sound collage. She also came to the appropriation method through art school, where she made the transition from cutting up photos to collaging sound and video in the late 1980s.

As a young woman in the United Kingdom, Bennett largely lived in an isolated cultural vacuum. "That was before the days of the Internet," she says, sitting in the sun by the river Thames, "when it's so easy to do a search for things." When Mark Hosler came around Vicki's house in Brighton (looking for someone else), she didn't know of his group, so he gave her a copy of *Escape from Noise*. The fact that others were crafting collages legitimized what she was doing, and from there, there was no turning back. Also aware of the avant-garde collage tradition are Iowa City–bred sound collagists the Tape-beatles—whose logo is the AT&T "globe" trademark with Mickey Mouse ears. "We were influenced by the French [musique] concrète musicians," says Lloyd Dunn, "such as Pierre Henri and Pierre Schaeffer, and a few other modernist composers like Edgar Varese and John Cage."

In 1952 the incorrigibly experimental Cage composed *Imaginary Landscape No. 5*, a sound collage he scored specifically for magnetic tape. Earlier, he was interested in the turntable. In his 1937 essay "The Future of Music: Credo," Cage argued that we could manipulate the sounds of a record and "give to it rhythms within or beyond the reach of imagination." Cage was as important as a composer as he was as a theorist, and his contemptuous sneering at Art—with a capital *A*—made him a worthy successor of the Dadaists. In the same ways Roland Barthes and Jacques Derrida wove into their theorizing a certain rascally subversive edge, John Cage was the master of the straight-faced jeer. His ultimate prank-as-art piece was *4'33"*, in which he instructed the "musician" to sit quietly at the piano bench for four minutes and thirty-three seconds. The ensuing uncomfortable rustling and impatient chatter *is* the music, something that illustrates Cage's commitment to the notion of chance, a method the Dadaists pioneered.

The late John Cage used Western classical instruments in ways they weren't intended, similar to the way 1970s hip-hop DJ Grandmaster Flash redefined what the turntable could do. He blew open the doors of the highbrow art-music world, letting in the noise of the outside, blurring art and everyday life. Fittingly, *4'33"* was itself the subject of a prank. Mike Batt made headlines in 2002 for supposedly violating Cage's copyright when his group the Wombles placed a minute of silence on their latest CD.[26] In the press, Batt was indignant, firing off nuggets such as "I certainly wasn't quoting his silence. I claim my silence is *original* silence." He added, "Mine is a much better silent piece. I have been able to say in one minute what Cage could only say in four minutes and thirty-three seconds." He pulled the Cage estate into the fracas when he credited the minute of silence to Batt/Cage and paid a part of the royalties to ASCAP, which collects money for the composer's song catalog. Newspapers picked up the story after the wheels of bureaucracy began to blindly turn and the payment was forwarded to Cage's estate, which cashed the check.

Amazingly, Cage representatives aggressively defended themselves. "We had been prepared to make our point more strongly," the managing director of Cage's publishing company told CNN, "because we do feel that the concept of a silent piece—particularly as it was credited by Mr. Batt as being cowritten by 'Cage'—is a valuable artistic concept in which there is a copyright." Most every media outlet took this case at face value, never investigating it as the prank that it obviously was, despite the fact that Batt was clearly using it as a platform to comment on the actions of overzealous copyright bozos. Later, Batt claimed to have registered hundreds of other silent compositions, from one second to ten minutes, including $4'32''$ and $4'34''$. "I couldn't get four minutes and thirty-three seconds, obviously, but I got everything else," said Batt. "If there's ever a Cage performance where they come in a second shorter or longer, then it's mine." Cage obviously would have appreciated Batt's statement, though he might have smacked his representatives upside the head for being so oblivious.

Heavily influenced by twentieth-century experimental music, avant-noise-rockers Sonic Youth (under the pseudonym "Ciccone Youth") also "covered" a John Cage song on their 1988 *Whitey* album, a side project. It was only a minute of silence, so they jokingly said that it was a "sped up" version of $4'33''$. (Today, you can buy this bit of silence on iTunes for ninety-nine cents.) Without asking permission, they also sampled Madonna's "Into the Groove" back when, as group member Thurston Moore put it, "the idea of sampling and its legalities was just brewing." Ciccone is Madonna's given last name—hence the band's alias Ciccone Youth—and the album cover "sampled" Madonna's face, blown up as a crude fifth-generation photocopy.

"It was all about sampling her celebrity," Moore tells me in an e-mail exchange. "We were playing with the idea of sampling in the sense [that] we were already interested in it from an art-world [perspective]." Guitarist Lee Ranaldo tells me, "The art-world history of it—from Warhol to Sherrie Levine and many others—made it clear, if not legal, that it was a valid form of investigation." Madonna was of particular interest to Sonic Youth because they came out of the same neighborhood and performed in the same downtown Manhattan clubs in the early 1980s. Moore self-deprecatingly described his band as being "too cool for school" at the time, but they were nevertheless "somewhat giddy liking her music." He adds that their being Madonna fans "was a turnabout, as we had always ditched out of the club before she would perform" because "we always thought she was corny in her disco b-girl routines."

Given that Ms. Ciccone went from making out with one of Sonic Youth's friends to being, well, *Madonna,* she was a fitting target for commentary. "The stuff spewed out by the media—in this case, Madonna—was something we felt free to use," Ranaldo says. The media that surrounds us, he says, "becomes your mind's property as much as anybody's, I figure." The *Whitey* album, which also sampled from L.L. Cool J and other sources, was an underground record, Moore says, so they didn't think anyone would notice. And no one did, especially Madonna's lawyers. When it was re-released a few years later by a major label, Madonna quietly granted permission.

As a student in 1950s Paris, Sonic Youth–favorite Karlheinz

Stockhausen was introduced to musique concrète, a technique whereby fragments of industrial noises, voices, music, and other sounds are edited together on magnetic tape. One of Stockhausen's strangest (or at least most playful) compositions was *Stimmung*. In this piece, six vocalists sang a text that was based on erotic poems penned by Stockhausen mixed in with the names of gods and deities. Soon, these advanced ideas about sound seeped into the world of rock; fittingly, Stockhausen was one of the icons featured on the Beatles' *Sgt. Pepper's Lonely Hearts Club Band* album cover.

On the group's "I Am the Walrus," they added a segment of a radio broadcast of *King Lear* to the collaged layers of sound. Though the play is in the public domain, the performance of the play was copyrighted, but the Beatles were never sued. During this time, and after, Miles Davis applied tape-collage methods to his radical jazz records, particularly *In a Silent Way* and *Bitches Brew*. He and his producer at Columbia, Teo Macero, would record jam sessions, then cut up the tapes and create new compositions, kind of like Stockhausen did.

The most famous example of musique concrète was the Beatles' "Revolution #9," the song on the White Album that was voted the worst Beatles song in a *Village Voice* poll. Yoko Ono introduced John Lennon to magnetic-tape sound collage, and their collaborative piece used dozens of unauthorized fragments from radio, television, and other sources, including sports cheers, screams, baby gurgles, and sirens. Ono wasn't the grasping groupie that many people thought she was, but rather an artist who was well established long before she met Lennon (they met when he came to *her* art show). Ono had previously collaborated with Ornette Coleman and John Cage, among others, and she had deep ties with the Fluxus art movement, which was inspired in part by Dadaism.[27]

The basic rhythm for "Revolution #9" was built from the sound

of twenty tape loops pillaged from the archives of EMI, the Beatles' record label. "We were cutting up classical music and making different size loops, and then I got an engineer tape on which some test engineer was saying, 'Number nine,' " John Lennon recalled.[28] Included in "Revolution #9" was a fragment from Sibelius's Symphony No. 7, and a moment from a performance of Beethoven's Opus 80. While the Beatles obviously had the implicit approval to chop up EMI's material, it's highly unlikely that the Beatles paid any "sampling" royalties or got permission from the original performers.

Thirty-six years later, in 2004, underground hip-hop artist Danger Mouse produced the *Grey Album*. He spent over one hundred hours chopping up instrumental fragments from the Beatles' White Album, matching them with rapped vocals from Jay-Z's recently released *Black Album*. Earlier, Jay-Z had released his a capella tracks to the world and challenged DJs to "remix the shit out of it." Conceptually, the *Grey Album* is a great idea, but it's also a fine, listenable record. "I stuck to those two [the White Album and *Black Album*] because I thought it would be more challenging and more fun and more of a statement on what you could do with sampling alone," Danger Mouse told MTV. "It is an art form. It is music. You can do different things, it doesn't have to be just what some people call stealing."

Danger Mouse only pressed a limited edition of three thousand copies, but it spread like digital wildfire on file-sharing networks, receiving praise from *The New Yorker*, *The New York Times*, and *Rolling Stone*. College radio stations, such as the University of Iowa's KRUI, added it to their playlists. Then EMI/Capitol, which owns the copyrights to the White Album, began sending out cease-and-desist letters. In response, the music-industry activists at downhillbattle.org coordinated a major online protest, dubbed "Grey

Tuesday," where at least 170 Web sites risked a lawsuit by hosting the album. That day, nineteen thousand anonymous individuals hosted the entire album on various file-sharing networks such as KaZaA, and by day's end another million tracks were downloaded—setting it on par with multiplatinum-selling artists.

Island's lawsuit against Negativland succeeded in suppressing their *U2* record in the pre-Internet days, but EMI/Capitol's attempt to squelch the *Grey Album* only made it more broadly available. "It became probably the most widely downloaded, underground indie record," said Fred E. Goldring, a music-industry lawyer, "without radio or TV coverage, ever. I think it's a watershed event."[29] Within a couple weeks, the "Jay-Z Construction Set" was available on file-sharing networks, demonstrating it had taken on a life of its own. The downloadable CD-Rom included Jay-Z's a capella vocals, instrumental samples, drum breakbeats, and software to mix it all up. It also included a couple dozen more *Black Album* remixes (in addition to *The Black and Tan Album,* someone created *The Double Black Album,* mixing Jay-Z's and Metallica's *Black Album*).

Even a nation of a million lawyers couldn't hold these copyright activists back. I was one of the many who received a cease-and-desist letter from EMI/Capitol after I posted the album on my Web site, kembrew.com and refused to take it down. (Oddly enough, minutes after I got the letter, UPS delivered to me a package of free CDs that EMI/Capitol sent me, because I'm a music critic.) One Web-site operator replied to EMI/Capitol's legal threats by quoting the entirety of the Beatles' "Piggies," which goes, in part: "Have you seen the bigger piggies in their starched white shirts" and "In their eyes there's something lacking / what they need's a damn good whacking." In my response, I posted on my Web site an essay about the matter. Later, I added a photograph of me standing in front of the famous rounded Capitol Records building—while giving it

the middle finger—taken during a trip to L.A. soon after "Grey Tuesday."

I never removed the *Grey Album* from kembrew.com, nor did I ever hear from EMI again, which came as a relief to me. I didn't feel like an "outlaw," nor was there anything particularly sexy about fretting over a lawsuit. I took that risk because I felt a responsibility to show that fair use exists in practice, not just in theory. For me, it would have been ethically wrong to act as a detached academic while others took the fall, because if anyone could make a fair-use case, it's me. As a professor who regularly teaches undergraduate and graduate courses on copyright, popular music, and pop culture, it's important to make some copyrighted materials available without worrying about getting sued. It was in the spirit of promoting conversation and debate about an "illegal" artwork that I engaged in this act of copyright civil disobedience.

The *Grey Album* was of interest to many journalists, law professors, and media scholars because it is an example of a work that does not fit into an outdated copyright regime. By "outdated," I mean that there exists no kind of compulsory-licensing system for sampling. Such a system would allow artists to collage fragments of sounds without fear, as long as they pay the copyright owner a statutory fee set by Congress. Art that relies on literal quotation is still at the mercy of the original artist, or, more likely, a layer of managers, lawyers, and accountants. As a result, the *Grey Album* was yet another example of a creative work that literally had no place in this world; it was stillborn legally, even if it's very much alive creatively.

Also, when discussing collage, we should not forget fair use. This statute opens a space for artists to freely use elements of copyrighted works as long as the derivative work is transformative or doesn't freely ride on the presence of the original. If Negativland had the resources to fight the lawsuit brought against them, it's likely they would have won based on a parody–fair use defense. When thinking about fair use and the need for a type of compulsory license that regulates sampling discussed in the last chapter, the *Grey Album* is a rich source for discussion. The amount of material taken from Jay-Z and the Beatles is so large that it seems reasonable that Danger Mouse should pay for his use of it, especially if the CD were commercially available on a wide scale. It's very hard to convincingly claim that this kind of borrowing is "fair," so works such as the *Grey Album* will always fall through the cracks until we modify copyright law.

The Tape-beatles, whose name is a partial nod to the Beatles' tape experiments, formed in the 1980s and adopted the phrase "Plagiarism: A Collective Vision" as their motto. It was an attempt to call attention to how the group's appropriation activities are viewed by some as morally suspect at best, and illegal at worst. The motto also contains an implicit cultural and political argument that culture should be a "collective," shared thing. Canadian composer John Oswald goes even further than the Tape-beatles and Negativland in his sonic borrowings. He combines obvious, recognizable segments of well-known songs in an unapologetic manner, referring to his method as "plunderphonics." Oswald's intention is to create some sort of recognition in the listener, as well as cognitive dissonance.

Since the mid-1980s, Oswald has released a series of plunderphonic works. The most interesting one is his 1993 release, *Plexure.* The nineteen-minute CD consists of twelve musical movements that are titled by playfully stringing together pop-star names such as "Bing Stingspreen," "Marianne Faith No Morrissey," and "Sinead O'Connick Jr." Hundreds of 1980s and 1990s Top 40 songs have been "plundered" and squeezed into the CD by overlapping a second, and sometimes only a split second, of musical fragments that are marginally recognizable. Like a mad pop professor, Oswald constructs these compositions on his computer, piecing them together like an electrified jigsaw puzzle. It produces a jarring but also oddly flowing piece (when I played an Oswald CD in class, a student with a hangover held his hands to his head and moaned, "Oh, God, *please* shut it off!" Others loved it).

On *Plexure*, Whitney Houston bounces off Fine Young Cannibals and crashes into Peter Gabriel, rebounding into Metallica and off Edie Brickell, crash-landing on top of Nirvana's screeching guitars. It's like hearing a decade's worth of pop music during a perilous car chase with a drugged-out James Brown behind the wheel while randomly listening to radio stations that only play skipping CDs. Then you crash into a satellite dish.

In 1989 Oswald produced and distributed a plunderphonics record similar in content to *Plexure*. It contained twenty-four "plundered" compositions that reworked the songs of Michael Jackson, Elvis Presley, Public Enemy, Dolly Parton, Metallica, and other musicians. He sent one thousand copies to libraries, radio, and press on a strictly nonprofit basis, and a "shareright" notice on the CD stated that it could be copied, but not sold. Oswald quickly received a cease-and-desist letter from the Canadian Recording Industry Association (CRIA), which believed he was infringing on musicians' copyrights. The CRIA forced him to hand over all remaining copies of the CD, to be destroyed. "If creativity is a field," quipped Oswald, "copyright is the fence."[30] It's a fence that copyright activists are trying to tear down, or at least replace with a more porous barrier that embraces more kinds of creativity.

Copyright activism comes in all shapes, sizes, and sounds—the weirder and funnier, the better. The British prank-pop group KLF (Kopyright Liberation Front) used avant-garde sound-collage techniques to fuel a briefly successful career in a music industry that they despised. Under the moniker the Timelords, they had a number-one hit in the United Kingdom, "Doctorin' the Tardis," which was subsequently used as a vehicle for a satirical book titled *The Manual (How to Have a Number One Hit the Easy Way)*. KLF's debut album, *1987 (What the Fuck's Going On?)*, made extensive and provocative use of samples from the Monkees, the Beatles, and ABBA, with the album's liner notes claiming that all sounds were liberated "from all copyright restrictions."

After ABBA's song publishers (Polar Music) demanded that the samples be removed, KLF quickly released—almost as if the whole affair was planned from the beginning, which it probably was—an edited version of the album. It deleted all offending samples and included instructions for how consumers could re-create the original version of *1987* using their old records. In response to Polar Music's role in suppressing their album, the members of KLF took a trip to Sweden. While KLF's song "The Queen and I" played in the background, the group had a prostitute dressed as one of the women in ABBA receive a fake gold album that contained the inscription "For sales in excess of zero" outside Polar Music's offices.

Clearly Dada-inspired, when the KLF were voted Best British Group by the Brit Awards, the British version of the Grammys, they bit hard into the hand that fed it. During a 1992 awards ceremony, they performed (jointly with the accurately named band Extreme Noise Terror) an ear-bleeding rendition of one of their biggest pop hits, "3 A.M. Eternal," then fired on the audience with an automatic rifle filled with blanks. "The KLF have left the music industry," went the post-performance intercom announcement—and with that, they retired the band forever.

MASH IT UP

In 2001 a new kind of pop-music genre emerged. Some people called these songs bootlegs, some named them mash-ups. The first mash-up that got major media attention was Freelance Hellraiser's "A Stroke of Genie-us," a shotgun wedding where pop diva Christina Aguilera sings atop the music of New York garage band the Strokes. Even Aguilera, trying to gather as much street credibility as possible, said, "It's cool." One of the finest mash-up masterpieces is Soulwax's "Smells Like Teen Booty," a smirky track that hammers Nirvana's "Smells Like Teen Spirit" into "Bootilicious," by Destiny's Child. Everything is business as usual when Nirvana kicks off with that familiar riff, until you hear the voices of Destiny's Child coo over Kurt Cobain's guitar. It's a marriage made in hell, and it sounds heavenly.

The mash-up phenomena couldn't have happened without the simple programs that allow amateur bedroom composers to juxtapose two or more songs in interesting ways. "Today, algorithms have been written that will do things like time-stretch it perfectly for you," says Scanner, who both has been sampled and samples in his own work. "So you can take a Christina Aguilera track with a Nirvana track and pitch it so it fits perfectly. You can take two beats that would never, ever match and throw them in a piece of software and time-match them so they fit like a perfect puzzle." Mash-ups also couldn't have happened without the digital distribution power of the Internet. The millions of MP3s on file-sharing networks such as KaZaA provide the materials for mash-up artists, and these networks also make it possible for their new creations to circulate across the globe.

"There's a phenomenal availability of material," says Ian, a member of the London-based Eclectic Method. Performing live in clubs behind a bank of computers and mixing equipment, the three members of Eclectic Method draw from a hard drive full of sampled audio and video loops. Using the VJam software developed by Coldcut—the godfathers of the British cut-and-paste aesthetic— Eclectic Method make mixes live on the spot. For instance, they might drop the rhymes of hardcore rapper DMX on top of a groove from a 1960s easy-listening track, all while chopping up one of his videos, in real time. Ian says that without file-trading networks, "what we do would be absolutely impossible, because it would cost too much. You can't buy all of these tunes you're going to DJ, and you can't buy all of these videos. They're transmitted on TV, someone encodes them, they go out on KaZaA, and it's rich pickings."

The Internet is a Wild West of today, sort of like hip-hop in the late 1980s before laws and bureaucracies limited its creative potential, at least as a mainstream art form. I hope the creative door won't slam shut on the Internet, though alternatives always seem to pop up, like a crazy sociological version of that Whack-a-Mole carnival game. Long after Grandmaster Flash used his bass line for "White Lines," Liquid Liquid's Richard McGuire still keeps track of sampling's evolution. "You can't keep creativity down. There will always be new ways, combinations of things that come out," he says, speaking about mash-ups. "It can sometimes be miraculous how they fit, and it knocks me out," McGuire tells me. "This is the same kind of thrilling thing. Every time there's new stuff like that, it's so simple. It's like, 'Why didn't *I* think of that?' "

With mash-ups, one of the underlying motivations of bedroom computer composers is to undermine the arbitrary hierarchies of taste that rule pop music. Those hierarchies are often gendered, with the "raw," "real" rock representing the masculine and the "soft," "plastic" pop representing the feminine. By blurring high and low pop culture (Nirvana representing the high; and Destiny's Child, the low), these mash-ups demolish the elitist pop-cultural hierarchy that rock critics and music-collecting snobs perpetuate. With mash-ups, Nirvana and Destiny's Child can sit comfortably at the same cafeteria table, perhaps showing holier-than-thou arbiters of cool that legitimate pleasures can be found in both varieties of popular music. "I think mixing Busta Rhymes with a House tune will make people dance," says Jonny, of Eclectic Method. "But mixing Britney Spears with N.W.A [Niggas Wit Attitude] will make people dance *and* laugh."

When you take the bad-boy rhymes of Eminem and force him to rap over "Come on Eileen" by Dexy's Midnight Runners, you've engaged in an act of trickery. The humorless white rapper takes himself far too seriously, which at times reduces his image to self-parody. This is ironic because at the same time that Eminem makes fun of "boy bands" and other targets in his videos, Eminem doesn't like it when others satirize him. (At his most pathetic and defensive, he once got really mad at Triumph the Insult Comic Dog, a puppet that mocked him during an MTV awards show skit.) I can guarantee you that Marshall Mathers isn't too happy about having his rap on top of the "gay-sounding" (to him) Dexy's Midnight Runners, but there's nothing he can do about it. His powerlessness illustrates how he, as an author, has little control over how his music is received and understood—that he literally doesn't have the final word, as Roland Barthes would say—no matter how many sock puppets he tries to beat down.

The origins of the mash-up can be heard in the medleys found on disco twelve-inch singles, where a mixer would seamlessly segue from one song to the other. Sometimes these were unlikely medleys, like Donna Summer's eighteen-minute dance masterpiece that effortlessly fused her versions of "Heaven Knows," "One of a Kind," and "MacArthur Park." As far back as the 1910s, record companies were making megamixes—of opera. Because the 78 rpm record could only hold a few minutes per side, CUNY professor Wayne Koestenbaum notes tempos had to be quickened and episodes trimmed, even for arias. In a 1911 catalog, the Victor Company boasted about a *Carmen* medley, "An amazing number of the most popular bits of Bizet's masterpiece have been crowded into this attractively arranged potpourri."[31] Although this was close to the spirit of mash-ups, they were medleys, rather than the laying of vocals from one song atop a different song's instrumental.

The earliest example I've found of such pop-music surgical grafting is television-theme composer Alan Copeland's "Mission: Impossible Theme/Norwegian Wood," from 1968. Just what gave him the idea to plop the vocal melody of the Beatles' "Norwegian Wood" (originally in a ¾ waltz time signature) on top of the *Mission Impossible* theme song (in jazzy ¾ time) is a complete mystery, but somehow it works. Even more remarkable, it won a Grammy for "Best Contemporary Pop Performance by a Chorus." The rather arbitrary legal difference between medleys and mash-ups is that the former doesn't require permission from the copyright owner but the latter does. This is because medleys are essentially mixed horizontally and composed of discreet songs that don't overlap, rather than vertically stacking one composition on top of another. Under the present compulsory-licensing system, permission doesn't have to be sought for the first kind of alteration, but because mash-ups intertwine both compositions, the copyright owner has veto power.

Mash-ups are an extension of the experimental spirit of hip-hop, before it was co-opted and lost that loving feeling. "My audience was the most progressive of all," Afrika Bambaataa said about hip-hop in the 1970s, "because they knew I was playing all types of weird records for them. I even played commercials that I taped off the television shows, from Andy Griffith to the Pink Panther, and people looked at me like I was crazy."[32] Mash-ups allow people to participate in—to make and remake—the pop culture that surrounds them, just as Bambaataa did. Despite my appreciation of them, I don't mean to idealize mash-ups, because as a form of creativity, they're quite limited, and limiting. First off, because they depend on the recognizability of the original songs, mash-ups are circumscribed to a relatively narrow repertoire of Top 40 pop tunes.

Mash-ups also demonstrate that Theodore Adorno, the notoriously cranky Frankfurt School critic of pop culture, was right about at least one key point. In arguing for the superiority of European art music, Adorno claimed that pop songs were simplistic and merely made from easily interchangeable modular components. After hearing half a dozen mash-ups, it's hard to deny that he's correct about that particular issue. If pop songs *weren't* simple and formulaic, it would be much harder for mash-up bedroom auteurs to do their job. From this point of view, it would be quite easy to see mash-ups as proof that our culture has withered and run out of ideas. Yes, it would be cause for alarm if mash-ups were the *only* form of creativity that uses the collage method, but they're not.

Some forward-looking copyright owners are realizing that they ought to embrace these kinds of unauthorized acts, because it's free advertising. Instead of attacking these bastard pop confections—fruitlessly trying to track down the anonymous infringers—some record companies are appropriating the appropriations. They also realize that they can capitalize on these active audiences, expropriate this creative labor and make it theirs. Increasingly frequent in Europe is what Freelance Hellraiser calls a "lawyer's mix," where an already existing mash-up is legally released by a record company. He bitterly writes on his Web site that this is done "without giving credit to the people who came up with the original idea." In Freelance Hellraiser's case, the Aguilera/Strokes mash-up was released two years later as a legitimate single, and a lot of money was made, though not by him.

It's an unusual thing for him to complain about—the idea that someone is ripping off his own rip-offs. But he does raise an interesting point. In collage, the author is somewhat absent from the new work of art, a kind of meta-author or even a curator. What sort of protections should he or she have, if any? In another instance of mining creative labor, David Bowie sponsored a "mash-up contest," which encouraged fans to mix the vocals from Bowie's then-current *Reality* album with the instrumental of one of his classic songs. It was a way of promoting his new album—not to mention Bowie himself—and one such mash-up was used in a car commercial for Audi's TT coupe, which was also the grand prize. The most interesting thing about the contest is the fine print:

> Each entrant into the Contest hereby irrevocably grants . . . all copyrights, all music and music publishing rights, and all rights incidental, subsidiary, ancillary or allied thereto (including, without limitation, all derivative rights) in and to the Mash-Up(s) *for exploitation throughout the universe* [my emphasis], in perpetuity, by means of any and all media and devices whether now known or hereafter devised.

ETHICS 101: WHAT'S (COPY)RIGHT AND (COPY)WRONG?

Although I have little sympathy for the plight of Eminem, I can't dismiss artists' discomfort about their work being chopped up out of hand. One should not call them naive romanticists who don't realize that "our realities are socially constructed" and that "the author is dead" and no longer has the final word. My friend Claudia Gonson—who performs in the erudite pop group the Magnetic Fields, which she also manages—is one musician who feels uneasy about the sound-collage process. "This way anyone today can rearrange song structures," she tells me, "make mash-ups, add beats, change the song structure—it feels kind of weird. . . . There are all sorts of authorial issues at stake." The creative act produces a real emotional connection to that work, which makes it all the more difficult to look artists in the eye and tell them to lighten up.

Nevertheless, in an environment where copies are being shared with the world, it's hard to defend the position that an author can (or should) have *total* control over his or her creation. Even though Congress has regularly created compromises that address how copyrighted materials can be used by others, there are also philosophical and moral principles that can't be ignored. As far back as 1878, Thomas Edison anticipated the death of the author in the recorded world. In his ghostwritten essay, he observed that sounds can be captured, preserved, and multiplied "with or without the knowledge or consent of the source of origin."[33] Even Matt Black— one of the members of the British duo Coldcut, who have sampled *lots* throughout their twenty-year career—has worried about how digital-editing technologies can misrepresent him.

Perhaps this was because we had just been talking about Coldcut's recent "Re:volution (featuring G. W. Bush)" and other politically motivated collages. After the interview, he grew concerned when I asked him to sign a standard release form permitting us to reproduce our footage of him for a documentary. Mr. Black had been lovingly described to me by someone who knew him as "an old hippie," and he lived up to that description, in the best possible way. In a burst of half-joking lefty paranoia, he added to the contractual agreement that my documentary coproducer and I could use his words as long as we "reflect the spirit in which they were intended." The irony was duly noted.

Communication historian John Peters points out that this anxiety is hardly new. More than two thousand years ago, Socrates watched as the spoken word gave way to the technology of the alphabet, something he viewed with skepticism. For this philosopher, the new medium of writing scattered stray messages and had unintended effects. "When it has once been written down, every discourse rolls about everywhere, reaching indiscriminately," argued Socrates, via Plato's writing.[34] His critique of writing was concerned with the fact that the voice, once captured on paper, could then be forced into conversations the author never intended.

Socrates said that written text, as opposed to direct face-to-face oral communication, "doesn't know to whom it should speak and to whom it should not. And when it is faulted and attacked unfairly"—such as the violence done by a deconstructive collage—"it always needs its father's support; alone it can neither defend itself nor come to its own support."[35] Fittingly, the word "plagiarism" is derived from the Latin term for "kidnapping." Daniel Defoe, back in 1710, referred to literary theft as a kind of child-snatching: "A Book is the Author's Property, 'tis the Child of his Inventions, the Brat of his Brain; if he sells his property, it then becomes the Right of the Purchaser; if not, 'tis as much his own as his Wife and Children are his own."[36]

In early eighteenth-century England, the notion of the author was still an unstable marriage of two different concepts inherited from the Renaissance: a "craftsman" who followed rules, manipulating words and grammar to satisfy tradition for patrons in the court, or, in some cases, the author might produce something "higher," more "transcendent." That "something" was attributed to a muse or to God. But as the century wore on, the craftsman model was played down and the source of inspiration shifted from the external (the muse or God) to the internal, where a great poem was seen as coming from the *original genius* of the author. Because the existence of the new poem could now be attributed to the writer, the author, this justified the idea that the poem was the property of the person who wrote it.[37] A new paradigm of authorship was born.

There were economic reasons for this shift. Writers in England—and a few decades later, in Germany—found it increasingly difficult to make a living because the patronage system was breaking down and no copyright protection existed to help them in the market-place of words. Reacting to these economic realities, writers and other Enlightenment-era philosophers attempted to redefine the nature of writing. Many of the legal battles within eighteenth-century Britain that led to copyright law were informed by emerging Enlightenment- and Romantic-period notions of originality, authorship, and ownership—including, but not limited to, John Locke's notion of individual property. Just as Locke understood property as being created when a person mixes his labor with materials found in nature, the author's "property" became "his" own when he stamps his personality on the work, doing this in an "original" manner.[38]

Recording technologies complicate issues of ownership. They also give the "death of the author" a new meaning, especially when authors really do die but are then resurrected in advertisements and songs. I wonder if John Lennon rolled in his grave when he was posthumously forced to rejoin the Beatles, a group he hated by the time of their bitter breakup. To promote *The Beatles Anthology* documentary miniseries, Yoko Ono unearthed demo tapes of Lennon singing and playing piano. The other three-fourths of the Fab Four polished one of those demo tapes into "Free as a Bird," the "new" single by the "reunited" Beatles. In 2004, Jimi Hendrix's estate sold his image and music to be used in a Pepsi ad that showed how its product made the young Jimi switch from accordion to guitar.

At the end of their lives, Tupac Shakur and the Notorious B.I.G. had a very antagonistic relationship; Tupac even released a track that viciously eviscerated Biggie, bragging that he had slept with Biggie's wife. But to promote the release of a family-sanctioned documentary about Tupac—who was shot down six months before the murder of Biggie—the two men ended up trading verses on a new track, "Runnin' (Dying to Live)," produced by Eminem. Perhaps they reconciled in the afterlife, but who knows? Following Natalie Cole's hit duet with her dead dad, the histrionic French Canadian singer Celine Dion dueted with the deceased Frank Sinatra. He very well could have been a Celine Dion fan, but the leader of the Rat Pack still had no choice in the matter; as with Lennon, Nat Cole, Hendrix, Tupac, Biggie, and others, the decision wasn't theirs, it was up to the heirs. This situation echoes Thomas Edison's earlier comment that recording technology allows anything to be done with sound without the "consent of the original source."

On a related note, early writings about the phonograph framed it as a device that could cheat death and open the door to the spirit world. It's no wonder, then, that one of the music industry's most enduring trademarked logos is the RCA-Victor dog, "Nipper," who is pictured obediently listening to "his master's voice." Supposedly, his master was dead, but little Nipper couldn't tell the difference—that's how great this new phonograph technology was supposed to be. Years later, an audiotape manufacturer would ask, "Is it live or is it Memorex?" The shift from the phonograph to magnetic tape—then to digital technologies—made it easier to chop up sounds and recontextualize them.

Collage tools make it possible for the African American sound and video artist Paul Miller, or DJ Spooky, to remix the film *Birth of a Nation*. This ugly, racist "cinematic classic" portrays blacks as little more than animals, so Spooky deconstructed the film in multimedia live performances. It's another example of how appropriation can be a form of political speech, free speech. The fact that the 1915 film is now in the public domain—it barely escaped being saved by the Sonny Bono Copyright Term Extension Act—makes some of the legal and ethical questions evaporate. But when the source material is still copyrighted, as is true of most collages today, the legal questions get more complicated, not to mention the ethical issues. What if, for instance, a member of the KKK took Spooky's remixed art and reworked it in a way that's offensive to Mr. Miller and others?

You hear "What if?" questions all the time in the debates about free speech. The Supreme Court has addressed many of these concerns, and it has replied that the First Amendment exists to protect even offensive speech, as long as it doesn't cross the line into provoking violence. Democracy should be offensive. It should tolerate uncomfortable ideas—or sounds or images—and if someone is insulted, then they have the right to speak back. It's true that those with more power can often shout louder; however, no one should be muzzled by copyright law when it comes to political speech or social critique, in any medium. The Supreme Court has reiterated this. Today, oral forms of communication aren't the only kinds of "speech" out there. Sounds and images can often be more persuasive than the spoken word, but intellectual-property laws can also forcefully control them when wielded by overzealous copyright bozos.

We live in a consumer culture, which sometimes obscures the fact that we first and foremost live in a democratic society. Giving up control is part of the democratic bargain, and it's also part of the copyright bargain written into the U.S. Constitution. Some of my examples of this principle will understandably make certain authors cringe, and I can sympathize. I've had my own work, a documentary, excerpted and shown in a context that made me squirm, but I didn't prevent it from happening. After all, I had already put it out into the world. Perhaps if someone took unpublished excerpts from my diary I would have objected, but works that have already been published are quite a different matter, both legally and ethically.

Because of the compulsory music-licensing system that has been in place since the Copyright Act of 1909, musicians can bypass the wishes of an artist such as Prince, who has said, "I don't like anyone covering my work. Write your own tunes!" This system makes it possible for the all-female grunge band Dickless to do a "straight" cover of "I'm a Man" by Bo Diddley, undermining the song's macho swagger. Diddley might not have appreciated their intentions—who knows?—but he did make his song publicly available, so it seems reasonable that others should have the right to comment on or reinterpret it. No doubt the world is a better place because Aretha Franklin's version of "Respect" exists, but that also means tolerating the possibility of aberrant readings that are far less appealing. This might create discomfort among some artists and authors, but it's better than choosing the other, less culturally vibrant option.

CHAPTER FOUR

CULTURE, INC.

our hyper-referential, branded culture

Multiplatinum rapper and MTV mainstay Missy Elliot comes from the same place I do: the southeastern corner of Virginia, called Tidewater. We're even the same age. "There's nothing in particular there," Missy says about the place. "We'd sit on the beach, go in different stores. We didn't come from a place like New York or L.A., where there are big events in a club. A lot of music we made was just done in the house, and it kind of circulated through friends on the block, on tapes."[1] We went to different schools, but sometimes I imagine we crossed paths at the record store I worked at or on the Virginia Beach boardwalk, a popular hangout. There, Missy could have good-naturedly cheered on my lame backspins on a flattened cardboard box—my break-dancing tag was Cold Crush Kembrew—or my arhythmic popping and locking. I might have even watched her rap over "Jam on It" during a "break-dancing festival" I attended at the Virginia Beach Civic Center, by the ocean.

The first time I heard her retro-futuristic hip-hop, I had no clue about any of these connections; there was no hometown pride. I only knew that her music dropped from nowhere. "Work It"—her

ubiquitous 2003 single, the masterpiece of her career, thus far—
pushed all the right avant-pop buttons with its can't-get-it-out-of-
your-head hook and back-masked chorus: "Is it worth it, can I work
it? I put my bang down, flip it and reverse it / ti esrever dna ti pilf
nwod gnab ym tup-i." It's like Stockhausen's musique concrète tape
experiments put to a beat you can dance to. About two-thirds the
way through the song, the instrumental track abruptly switches
gears as Missy and her coproducer Timbaland drop in a percussive
loop from Run-DMC's 1986 classic, "Peter Piper."

Jam Master Jay was Run-DMC's DJ, but he was murdered soon
after the release of Missy's "Work It." The irony was that the album
from which her song came, *Under Construction,* was a tribute to the
simplicity of less violent times—the old-school days of hip-hop
that were the soundtrack to her youth. On this album, Missy
doesn't just produce a verbal snapshot of that era (name-checking
Public Enemy, Salt 'n' Pepa, Big Daddy Kane, Slick Rick, and other
1980s hip-hop icons). She also samples the music of that time, with
each track unfolding like pages of a musical history book. Or, to use
a more appropriate metaphor, it's akin to a *hyper*-hyperlinked Web
page that sends you zooming from one clickable reference to the
next, a groove-y kind of pop-culture collage.

T. S. ELIOT, MISSY ELLIOT, AND MISS-Y MOORE

Missy Elliot's *Under Construction* may be a quilted musical bed of
virtual citation marks, but T. S. Eliot's modernist masterpiece *The
Waste Land* is quite literally loaded with footnotes. Eliot's mosaic
method was also used by modernist contemporaries such as Marianne Moore and *Finnegans Wake* author James Joyce. Joyce used literature like a library, periodically checking out and inserting into
his writing ideas, words, and sentences that interested him. Actually, he was less like a respectable library patron and more like a

Dumpster diver who found interesting things to recycle. The screaming irony in all this is that Stephen Joyce, the beneficiary of his grandfather's copyrights, regularly uses copyright to prevent his ancestor's words from being quoted in films, plays, and even scholarly works.

When Stanford University professor Carol Loeb Shloss wrote a book about Joyce's troubled daughter, Lucia, she encountered tremendous obstacles that almost stopped her book from being published. "The process of deleting things that had taken years to find out was just excruciating." She added, "The ability of people to use quotes from Joyce has ground to a standstill." Robert Spoo—the former editor of *James Joyce Quarterly*, who also happens to be an intellectual-property lawyer—said, "There is a climate of concern bordering on fear among Joyce scholars that their work may suddenly come under copyright scrutiny."[2] Unlike the scholars who study him, the quote-happy James Joyce collaged at will, creating a kind of "recirculation"—his word—of cultural history. "The letter! The litter!" Joyce wrote in the *Wake*, wordplay that reminds me of Chuck D's opening lines, "The rhythm! The rebel!" from "Rebel Without a Pause." Like Missy Elliot, Joyce put his bang down, flipped it, and reversed it.

Missy samples Public Enemy in two of *Under Construction*'s songs, but the aural and verbal nods to the old school are at their most dense on the track "Funky Fresh Dressed." It features a sampled hook by the influential female rapper MC Lyte, and begins with the line, "Here's a little story that must be told." It's from Rodney Cee's "Stoop Rap," a track from the 1982 hip-hop flick *Wild Style*, and it is followed by another sample, "and it goes a little something like this," culled from Run-DMC's "Here We Go."

Throughout the song, Missy evokes another old-school classic, U.T.F.O.'s "Roxanne, Roxanne," by exactly imitating its cadence and rhyme scheme, which went: "She said she'd love to marry, my baby she would carry / And if she had a baby, she'd name the baby Harry." The song branded itself on the DNA of most everyone who grew up on hip-hop in the 1980s and was a standard of amateur MC competitions in cafeterias throughout the nation. Elliot's homage is unmistakably obvious, even when transcribed onto the page. "My flow is legendary, and your style is temporary / Yeah, you need to worry, like Jason, it gets scary."

Like "Work It," the beat takes a ninety-degree turn two-thirds of the way through the song, this time sampling an instrumental loop from the Beastie Boys' 1986 story rap, "Paul Revere." (True to the connect-the-dot nature of Missy's song, "Paul Revere" similarly begins with the line, "Here's a little story I've got to tell.") The Beasties themselves are hyper-referential: The opening song on their first album is named "Rhymin' and Stealin'," and it plods along over a blatant Led Zeppelin sample, from "When the Levee Breaks." The "stealing" reference is a direct nod to sampling, and the song's rhymes also pillage from *Moby Dick*, KFC's Colonel Sanders, *Mutiny on the Bounty,* and Betty Crocker. The Beasties' twenty-years-plus lyrical oeuvre contains around one thousand refrences to high, low, and pop culture, from Pablo Picasso to Budweiser to *Dirty Harry.*

It's clear that Missy Elliot's referencing of old-school staples was purposeful; there's nothing random about the complicated web that makes up the deceptively simple party jam. Hip-hop artists often weave pop-culture references into their critiques of the dominant culture by using metaphors their audiences can relate to. Cultural critic Todd Boyd argues that hip-hop connects with so many because it is "at once humorous *and* a weapon of guerrilla warfare" against the powers that be. He writes in *The New H.N.I.C.,* "Hip-hop speaks in a code that allows us to communicate with one another beyond the eavesdropping that those in power often engage in." The cloaked nature of hip-hop's very public mode of communication was amusingly illustrated in 2003 when three British judges were forced to rule on a copyright battle between competing groups. The case revolved around the nature of the Heartless Crew's lyrics, but Judge Kim Lewison admitted that the job was made more difficult because those hip-hop lyrics were "for all practical purposes a foreign language."

The judge went on to comment on the "faintly surreal experience of three gentlemen in horsehair wigs" examining the meaning of such phrases as "shizzle my nizzle."[3] Hip-hop broadcasts its message far and wide, but in code. It's in this way that Chuck D can rightly claim that hip-hop is black America's CNN, while Boyd accurately refers to it as a lyrical tower of Babel barely decipherable to its ideological foes. Hip-hop has been around long enough for it to seep into every area of American life, every imaginable demographic. For instance, the white, all-female Long Island crew called Northern State—featuring an MC named Hesta Prynne—represents the brainy wing of the hip-hop party. Her moniker, of course, is a nod to Nathaniel Hawthorne's *Scarlet Letter,* and she even refers to herself in verse as having a "liberal-arts-college academic-literary-kinda-name."

If Marianne Moore were alive today, she might have written rhymes for Northern State. The Missy Elliot of the twentieth-century poetry world, she staked herself out in a male-dominated territory, earning the respect of peers such as T. S. Eliot and Ezra Pound. (Moore was so hip she even penned the liner notes for a Muhammad Ali album.) The hyper-referential remixes of Marianne Moore, who began publishing in the early twentieth century, were perhaps more subversive than those of other modernist writers. She absorbed the politicized spirit of Dada, particularly in her 1923 poem "Marriage," which reworked fragments from history, literature, newspapers, and her own memory.

For Moore, who never married, matrimony was the wasteland. Her collage style smashed familiar ideas and phrases against one another, breaking them apart and putting them back together in disorienting ways, shaking up a sacred institution in the process. Her departure point is the Bible—specifically Adam and Eve—though she also uses many mundane sources from daily life, such as an article from *Scientific American* magazine. Moore also samples from a review in *The New Republic,* reworking and recontextualizing the words to make Adam a bit androgynous in the poem. At another point she quotes a lengthy passage from Edward Thomas's *Feminine Influence on the Poets.* It describes King James I's love for the daughter of the Earl of Somerset, Joan Beaufort, whom the king sees through his prison window, having no access to her. Thomas compares Beaufort to a bird that is made to sing sweet songs of love, though Moore tweaks this interpretation. Almost word for word, Moore appropriates Thomas's written text into her own verse, but with a major alteration: "He dares not clap his hands . . . lest it should fly off."

Thomas *intended* it to be a sweet passage about love at first sight, but Marianne Moore flipped and reversed it so that the suitor was unable to make his bird sing. "Just by being married," explained Elizabeth Joyce, a Moore scholar, "the husband assumes that he can control the wife, the bird, and decide when and how she should give him pleasure. Instead, he looks merely foolish in his failure to manipulate her."[4] By reworking these sources with her own hand, Moore achieves a powerful and subversive layering of texts. This ironic and, at times, quite sarcastic poem was also radical because of its unconventional shifts in tone, vocabulary, rhythm, and point of view.

In "Marriage," Moore also manipulated her sources to release meanings never intended by the original authors, such as Shakespeare (whose play *The Tempest* was cut up in this proto-feminist poetic manifesto). Soon after the Shakespeare quote is the line "Men are monopolists," from a 1921 founder's address at Mount

Holyoke College, along with a charming line by Ezra Pound, "A wife is a coffin." She sometimes changed the phrasing of the original sources to fit their placement in the poem, because fidelity to her own unconventional aesthetic trumped the academic desire to quote exactly. Moore wrote a species of anti-poetry at times, much like the Dadaists practiced anti-art. Her cut-up method, where she plopped matter-of-fact advertising copy into a new context, mirrored Duchamp's ready-mades.

Despite her cavalier attitude toward authors' intentions, Moore felt a responsibility to acknowledge her stolen sources—even going so far as putting entire borrowed sentences or phrases in quotes, which were then cited in the appendix to *The Complete Poems of Marianne Moore*. It creates a strange sight on the page, a smattering of quotation marks that disturb the flow of the poetry. Moore confessed her penchant for incorporating lines from others' work into her own verse in *Complete Poems*' oddly titled passage, "A Note on the Notes," which introduces the appendix of citations. Moore explains, "I have not yet been able to outgrow this hybrid method of composition, [so] acknowledgements seem only honest." Kenneth Burke, an influential literary critic and early communication scholar, says of Moore's appropriation method, "Since the quotation marks escape notice when such writing is read aloud, the page becomes wholly an act of collaboration, a good thing that seems to transcend any one person's ownership."[5]

In an interview, Moore further explained her use of quotation marks: "I was just trying to be honorable and not to steal things. I've always felt that if a thing has been said in the very best way, how can you say it better? If I wanted to say something and somebody had said it ideally, then I'd take it but give the personal credit for it"—an interesting statement on the morality of borrowing.[6] Sometimes Moore's quotation and citation methods seem overly scrupulous, as when she identifies a quotation that was "overheard at the circus." But Moore had manners, so she acknowledged what she took, after which she would do with it what she wanted.

BRANDING EVERYDAY LIFE

From Marianne Moore to Missy Elliot, pop culture provides artists—and everybody else—with a kind of shorthand, a tool for expressing ourselves. By choosing our media-culled words wisely, we can convey a wide range of meanings and emotions, sometimes with only one monosyllabic utterance (i.e., "Doh!"). In titling his book *Sex, Drugs, and Cocoa Puffs*, the goofy, gonzo cultural critic Chuck Klosterman speaks to this tendency. The point of living, Klosterman argued in his "low culture manifesto," is to understand what it means to be alive, or at least try to. This is something that philosophers have done for thousands of years. He admitted there are many respectable ways of deducing the answer to that question, but, he says, "I just happen to prefer examining the question through the context of Pamela Anderson and *The Real World* and Frosted Flakes. It's certainly no less plausible than trying to understand Kant or Wittgenstein."

In the writings of many philosophers, religion provided a common reference point for their big questions, but today the media has become our lingua franca. The average American college student is more likely to recognize a line from *The Simpsons*, for instance, than an allusion to a story from the Old Testament. Referencing pop culture helps define our identities and cultural preferences. It also provides us with a kind of grammar and syntax that structures our everyday talk. In face-to-face interactions we can still refer to these intellectual properties, and we will continue to without inhibition. We can invoke popular (or unpopular) intellectual properties like, say, *The Phantom Menace*'s Jar Jar Binks—one of the most hated cinematic figures of the 1990s. More important, we can do it in satirical ways that his owner (the extremely litigious Lucasfilm, Inc.) doesn't approve of without worrying about it. In the multimedia space that is the Web, however, the metaphorical intellectual-property police can (and do) invade our homes in the form of cease-and-desist e-mails.

While much of popular culture is vapid—it's a form of escapism, after all—it does impact our consciousness powerfully. As a social theorist, Karl Marx offered us a way of understanding our place in the world by explaining that we are born into conditions "not of our own choosing." If the world is like a home (one littered with pop-culture products), the social conditions Marx describes are like the walls. We know our houses have been constructed, *socially* constructed, and we are free to roam around within rooms and halls that already exist. But those walls are very real. We can walk through them only if we take a hammer and knock them down, or blow the walls up. If we want to dismantle that house—or merely remodel the home—it is necessary for us to manipulate and transform the language of popular culture that surrounds us.

In recent years, it has been difficult to do so because federal law protects trademarks from being portrayed in an "unwholesome or unsavory context." Some courts have suppressed unauthorized uses of famous cultural icons, even when there is no reasonable possibility of confusion in the marketplace. For example, when an environmental group used a caricature of the Reddy Kilowatt trademark in literature that was critical of the electric-utility industry, the company responded by filing an injunction for the unauthorized use of their mark. The U.S. District Court for the District of Columbia upheld this injunction. It essentially ruled that you cannot use a trademarked property to express yourself—it constitutes a type of trespassing. The Manitoba Court of Appeal similarly ruled that striking Safeway workers could not appropriate the Safeway trademark in their union literature. The court stated that, "there is no right under the guise of free speech to take or use what does not belong to [you]."[7]

Ironically enough, recently retired MPAA CEO Jack Valenti once alliteratively quipped that digital downloading gives movie producers "multiple Maalox moments." Unlike Hollywood directors—who usually are required to secure permission when they reference a trademarked product in their movies—Valenti didn't have to confer with Maalox's lawyers. Nor was Valenti paid to do a product placement for Maalox.

Companies want us to feel comfortable with their intellectual properties and their brands, for them to feel like our "friends." But they are extremely needy, attention-seeking, and money-draining friends. For instance, here's an excerpt from an internal McDonald's memo, which promoted the idea that customers should feel that the company "cares about me": "The essence McDonald's is embracing is 'Trusted Friend' [which] captures all the goodwill and the unique emotional connection customers have with their McDonald's experience," the memo states. "Note: this should be done without using the words 'Trusted Friend.' "[8]

The friends that corporate marketers desire most are young ones. "You'll agree that the youth market is an untapped wellspring of new revenue," reads an enthusiastic brochure from the Fourth Annual Kid Power Marketing Conference. "You'll also agree that the youth market spends the majority of each day inside the schoolhouse. Now the problem is, how do you reach that market?"[9] Companies have solved that dilemma with creative tactics, such as corporate-subsidized textbooks that contain math problems with Nike logos or that regularly mention Oreo cookies. "The bestselling packaged cookie in the world is the Oreo cookie," reads the 1999 edition of a McGraw-Hill math textbook. "The diameter of an Oreo cookie is 1.75 inches. Express the diameter of an Oreo cookie as a fraction in simplest form."

America's largest producer of corporate-sponsored teaching aids, Lifetime Learning Systems, said in one of its pitches to potential sponsors: "Now you can enter the classroom through custom-made learning materials created with your specific marketing objectives in mind. . . . Through these materials, your product or point of view becomes the focus of discussions in the classrooms."[10] Some cash-strapped schools turn to Coke and Pepsi, which pay very little (in relation to the exposure their products receive) in exchange for exclusive contracts that place their goods in cafeterias, halls, and locker rooms. Companies can also transform the crisis in education into free advertising masked as tax-deductible public service.

In 2004 schools in sixteen states participated in McDonald's "McTeacher's Night," where principals and teachers were reduced to flipping burgers in exchange for a fraction of the evening's sales. More than one thousand schools split the proceeds, earning less than seven hundred dollars apiece. Sadder still, parents and friends of a public school in Eugene, Oregon, held a *blood-plasma drive* to save one of five threatened teaching positions (they raised only fifteen hundred dollars).[11] This makes me want to cry. With the governmental defunding of education, many schools believe they have no other choice than to accept deals with devils such as Coke. There's a depressing irony here. The massive funding cuts in American education made it possible for these companies to prey on kids by distributing their nominally educational materials.

Because of the supposed educational value of their propaganda—such as Oreo-centric math problems—the money that the corporations spend on these materials is fully tax-deductible. This kind of thinly veiled advertising can then be written off as money they don't have to pay the government, further reducing the pool of tax money that can go to education. Not only have we undermined the quality of education by stretching resources to the breaking point, but in doing so we have opened the window for marketers to crawl into schools. The branding and commercialization of education stretches from universities to elementary and high schools. Sometimes students strike back in creative ways, such as clever *détournements* of ads on bathroom-stall billboards. Other times, protests take a subtler form, such as wearing a Pepsi shirt to school when your principle has orchestrated a "Coke Day."

When Greenbrier High School student Mike Cameron did just this, he was suspended. The Evans, Georgia, school was trying to win a five-hundred-dollar "Coke in Education" prize, awarded to schools that came up with creative ways of distributing discount Coke cards. During the Coke rally—which was held in lieu of the unprofitable act of learning, I assume—Cameron revealed his Pepsi T-shirt during a group photo. This sent the administration into a tizzy. Defending her tactics, principal Gloria Hamilton said, "These students knew we had guests. We had the regional president here, and people flew in from Atlanta to do us the honor of being re-source speakers." As an act of protest, wearing a Pepsi T-shirt is awfully mild, hardly as in-your-face as the "détourned" "Starfucks" shirts some kids have made guerilla-style.

When simply wearing a competitor's logo to a corporate-sanctioned school event is considered a subversive act, it's much harder for freedom of expression® to be a tenable concept. Schools are no longer the oasis free of aggressive marketers they once were, so it's no wonder that kids start thinking early about brands. "It helps our work that teens define themselves by their possessions," says Amanda Freeman, formerly the director of research and trends at the teen-marketing firm Youth Intelligence. "They will say, 'I am Sony, not Panasonic.' Their favorite question is, 'If Coke were a person, who would it be?' I thought that was a stupid question, but they loved it."[12] It's in this way that media and brand references embedded in everyday talk become something darker. It's something that reduces us—in part, no matter how imaginative we're being—to walking commercials who are literally working to keep consumer culture alive.

The intellectual properties sold by lifestyle companies provide the foundation for much of our economy and culture. For instance, Nike is less a shoe company than a conceptual house of cards built around the strength of its trademarks—a remarkably sturdy house of cards that is supported by the policing powers of the state. Nike's massive profits stem not only from outsourcing its factory labor, legal scholar Rosemary Coombe points out, but also from its ability to successfully herd the migration of its trademarked brands into everyday life. Its CEO, Philip Knight, makes it clear that his company is not in the business of manufacturing shoes, but in the business of branding—connecting lifestyles to cheap pieces of plastic, leather, and rubber. This means that Nike must spend huge amounts on advertising and promotion in order to keep the Nike brand at the center of the popular cultural imagination.

Just as patents protect the research-and-development costs for pharmaceutical companies, trademarks protect the investments of companies such as Nike or the Gap or Tommy Hilfiger or any other company for whom people serve as walking billboards. Coombe, who has written extensively about the cultural life of intellectual properties, notes that the Nike logo "now marks sports teams, all clothing, and athletic equipment, colonizing the gymnasiums, classrooms, and washrooms of our schools and is even cut into the designs of people's hair and voluntarily branded onto the flesh of many North Americans who have marked their own bodies with swoosh tattoos to proclaim their brand loyalty."[13] Companies such as Nike *want* fans to use their trademarks, but in approved ways. As soon as critically minded citizens subvert those uses, the corporations lash back in the form of cease-and-desist letters.

The few places where biting satire is safe from the threat of intellectual-property litigation are areas clearly marked off as such. Two of these places are *The Daily Show with Jon Stewart,* a fake news show, and *The Onion,* a fake newspaper (both of which, interestingly, tend to be more influential and pointed than many legitimate news sources). *The Daily Show,* for instance, can get away with manipulating Mickey Mouse in ways that independent satirists who aren't backed by Comedy Central and its lawyers can't. For instance, it reported on a cutesy segment that occurred on the 2003 Academy Awards, which took place the week Gulf War 2.0 started. As blood flowed overseas, an actor on the Oscar stage traded innocuous dialogue with a computer-generated version of the rodent. The original dialogue on the awards show was no doubt approved by Disney; *The Daily Show*'s newly dubbed dialogue definitely wasn't. "Regime change begins at home!" ranted the high-pitched voice of Mickey. "Bush is the real dictator!"

Satire like this can still occur because overbearing assertions of intellectual-property rights would be PR suicide for Disney and would likely stoke public indignation. But it's far more risky for such satirical commentary to be produced by guerrilla satirists or, for that matter, by mainstream media that isn't designated as an "Official Source of Humor" for our hyper-commercial culture. Otherwise, they might get ruinously sued. One of the problems lies in trademark law itself, which is interpreted as requiring these companies to go after any and all unauthorized uses, even if they are obviously meant to be parodic social commentary. The law is written in such a way that if companies don't show a good-faith effort to prevent unauthorized uses, their trademark will suffer from "dilution." This is why Xerox lawyers constantly remind newspapers that its branded name isn't a generic term for photocopying, and why Jell-O does the same thing. When a trademarked product loses its specific meaning, its economic value dies, suffering from what is called, fittingly, "genericide."

Companies need to have it both ways, because if they are to remain profitable and relevant, they need to saturate us with their logos, brands, and services. But these companies don't want us to become *so* familiar and comfortable with their trademarks that we feel free to do with them what we will.[14] If trademarked goods are really our friends, it's a very one-sided, selfish relationship. Activist-journalist Naomi Klein notes that logos have become the lingua franca of the global village, and these trademarked properties are often used by antiglobalization activists as a site for their protests. If public spaces are disappearing—being replaced by branded environments—then activists have come to see logos as a new kind of public square they can occupy.

To use Missy Elliot–speak, these activists take a logo's corporate-sanctioned meaning, flip it, and reverse it; MIT grad student Jonah Peretti did just this in a humorous encounter with Nike. Peretti tried to order from its online customized shoe department a pair of ZOOM XC USA sneakers with the word "sweatshop" on them. As you might guess, Nike refused his request. The following is an exchange between the grad student and Customer Service, which became one of the most forwarded e-mail memes of 2001, reaching tens of thousands.

From: "Jonah H. Peretti" <peretti@media.mit.edu>
To: "Personalize, NIKE iD" <nikeid_personalize@nike.com>
Subject: RE: Your NIKE iD order o16468000

Greetings,
My order was canceled but my personal NIKE iD does not violate any of the criteria outlined in your message. The Personal iD on

my custom ZOOM XC USA running shoes was the word "sweat-shop." Sweatshop is not: 1) another's party's trademark, 2) the name of an athlete, 3) blank, or 4) profanity. I choose the iD because I wanted to remember the toil and labor of the children that made my shoes. Could you please ship them to me immediately.

Thanks and Happy New Year,

Jonah Peretti

From: "Personalize, NIKE iD" <nikeid_personalize@nike.com>
To: "Jonah H. Peretti" <peretti@media.mit.edu>
Subject: RE: Your NIKE iD order o16468000

Dear NIKE iD Customer,

Your NIKE iD order was cancelled because the iD you have chosen contains, as stated in the previous e-mail correspondence, "inappropriate slang. . . . "

Thank you, NIKE iD

From: "Jonah H. Peretti" <peretti@media.mit.edu>
To: "Personalize, NIKE iD" <nikeid_personalize@nike.com>
Subject: RE: Your NIKE iD order o16468000

Dear NIKE iD,

Thank you for your quick response to my inquiry about my custom ZOOM XC USA running shoes. Although I commend you for your prompt customer service, I disagree with the claim that my personal iD was inappropriate slang. After consulting Webster's Dictionary, I discovered that "sweatshop" is in fact part of standard English, and not slang. The word means: "a shop or factory in which workers are employed for long hours at low wages and under unhealthy conditions" and its origin dates from 1892. So my personal iD does meet the criteria detailed in your first email.

Your web site advertises that the NIKE iD program is "about

freedom to choose and freedom to express who you are." I share Nike's love of freedom and personal expression. The site also says that "If you want it done right . . . build it yourself." I was thrilled to be able to build my own shoes, and my personal iD was offered as a small token of appreciation for the sweatshop workers poised to help me realize my vision. I hope that you will value my freedom of expression[®] and reconsider your decision to reject my order. Thank you, Jonah Peretti

From: "Personalize, NIKE iD" <nikeid_personalize@nike.com>
To: "Jonah H. Peretti" <peretti@media.mit.edu>
Subject: RE: Your NIKE iD order o16468000

Dear NIKE iD Customer,
Regarding the rules for personalization it also states on the NIKE iD web site that "Nike reserves the right to cancel any Personal iD up to 24 hours after it has been submitted." . . .
Thank you, NIKE iD

From: "Jonah H. Peretti" <peretti@media.mit.edu>
To: "Personalize, NIKE iD" <nikeid_personalize@nike.com>
Subject: RE: Your NIKE iD order o16468000

Dear NIKE iD,
Thank you for the time and energy you have spent on my request. I have decided to order the shoes with a different iD, but I would like to make one small request. Could you please send me a color snapshot of the ten-year-old Vietnamese girl who makes my shoes?
Thanks,
Jonah Peretti

[no response]

PRODUCT PLACEMENT AND THE "REAL WORLD"

Because our world is saturated with commodities, advertisers argue that product placements in movies and television shows add realism to the production. Compared to our daily lives, though, there's nothing realistic about the way directors place products in the frame or, for that matter, the way products are spoken about. "I was talking to my friend Jason," says Illegal Art show curator Carrie McLaren. "He's a comic, and he sent Comedy Central about seven minutes of him just doing a stand-up routine. And in the stand-up routine he just happens to name a couple of brands, just like it would come up in conversation. And Comedy Central called him back and said, 'We like your stuff, it's really funny, but can you send us something that doesn't have any reference to brands in it, because we can't air it.'

"And that's the thing," she says. "We live in a very commercialized, privatized society, and sometimes brand names come up in conversation." But in a mass media with highly bureaucratized rules of internal conduct, the same kind of talk can't occur without significant editing. "When you go to make a film, you have to clear any product placement—or any cultural reference," says *Donnie Darko* director Richard Kelly. "I mean, there's attorneys that you hire specifically to protect yourself from getting sued. It's a very long and arduous process."[15]

On a cold Iowa winter day in 2004, I found myself eating at the Hamburg Inn diner with famed gross-out director John Waters—whose trademark pencil-thin mustache, I discovered when I sat across from him, is quite real. Waters is responsible for the arthouse classics *Pink Flamingos* and *Female Trouble,* as well as the PG crowd-pleaser *Hairspray.* He has worked in both the film underground and the mainstream, and now feels the power that intellectual-property owners exercise over their products. Upon broaching the subject of Hollywood filmmaking and intellectual property, I opened up a torrent of stories and opinions about the "incredibly stupid" rules he has to deal with. For instance, Waters told me that when filming the 1988 version of *Hairspray,* Aqua Net refused to allow him to use its hairspray cans in his film. He said to me, "I always tell young filmmakers, don't ask, because to seek permission is to seek denial." Conventional companies almost always tell John Waters no, though one of the few corporations that has granted him permission, Waters proudly told me, is *Hustler* magazine.

It's in these permission refusals that advertisers lie when they claim product placements reflect the real world, because the media world adheres to legal-gravitational laws that are anything but natural, that is, unless they are literally referring to MTV's *The Real World,* which is one of the most heavily product-placed shows on television. Reality television turned out to be an incredibly important vehicle for placement; indeed, *Survivor* producer Mark Burnett described his show as being "as much a marketing vehicle as it is a television show." On *Survivor,* the contestants will compete for bags of Doritos or an SUV that will be waiting for them when they leave their "exotic" set location. Burnett continues, "My shows create an interest, and people will look at them [brands], but the endgame here is selling products in stores—a car, deodorant, running shoes. It's the future of television."[16]

Product placement has also crept into MTV videos; for instance, Apple paid to have an iPod prominently framed at the beginning of Mary J. Blige's "Love @ 1st Sight," as well as other videos. Music videos now drown in a sea of placements, where advertisers such as Mazda pay to put its new car in a Britney Spears video. Another attractive thing for advertisers is that the production-turnaround time for music videos is much shorter than movies, so they can be more reactive to the marketplace. For the most part, the trademarked and copyrighted goods that appear in the fake world do so with the explicit permission (and often payment) of the intellectual-property owners. This is ironic, because in the non-*Real World* real world, *we* aren't given the choice of controlling which advertised intellectual properties are shoved in our face when we walk out our doors.

Product placement is everywhere in Hollywood films. This practice was kicked off when Reese's Pieces saw a dramatic 66 percent rise in sales after the candy was featured in Steven Spielberg's 1982 film *E.T.* Following that was the 1983 Tom Cruise vehicle, *Risky Business,* which set off an explosion in the sale of Ray-Ban sunglasses. Even a movie that makes fun of product placements— *Wayne's World,* starring Mike Myers and directed by Penelope Spheeris—was shaped by a legal-gravitational pull that is more powerful than the filmmaker. "We had to go through hell to get all the product-placement clearances," said Spheeris. She was referring to the multitude of products that appear in the movie in ironic ways, such as a scene that parodies a popular mustard commercial from the early 1990s. "It was so nerve-racking as a director to be like, okay, this is the day we have to shoot the Grey Poupon part. 'Do we have clearance yet, or should we change it to French's mustard?' We were skating by the seat of our pants."

Most of us associate satire with, well, freedom of expression®; genuine satire doesn't require permission from trademark lawyers. *Wayne's World* was lauded for its ironic, satirical take on consumer culture, but it is satire without any real bite, with no venom. For instance, there's one memorable segment where—wink-wink— Myers's character refuses to shill products in his show-within-the-film, *Wayne's World.* "Contract or no, I will not bow to any sponsor," he says as he opens a Pizza Hut box lid, then drinks from a prominently framed can of Pepsi.[17] While the gag is funny and *seemingly* subversive, the companies get to have their cake and eat it, too. Pizza Hut and Pepsi don't mind being included in this parody of product placement because their products have been very notably placed in a "cool" movie.

If the companies didn't like it, they would have sent their trademark-lawyer attack dogs to stop Spheeris and Myers. The barking of these dogs has made studios overly cautious, something that leads to self-censorship. Such was the case with *Raw Deal*, a documentary about rape that contained a scene shot at a frat-house party that had music playing. Artisan, the distributor, dropped the project because of music-licensing problems. Joe Gibbons's short film *Barbie's Audition* is a darkly comic retelling of the age-old Hollywood casting-couch story, and it stars a Barbie doll. The short was originally selected to screen at the Sundance Film Festival, but festival lawyers grew concerned and excluded it from the final festival line-up. In both cases, direct censorship didn't come from intellectual-property owners, but was the result of internal decisions and policies crafted by overcautious organizations.

In mass-media art such as motion pictures, a lot of content is dictated by forces external to the production of the art. Associated Film Productions, an agency that helps companies place intellectual properties in movies, brags that it "carefully controls the appearance of the client's product in films." For instance, Adidas got what amounted to a commercial shoehorned into Orion's *Johnny Be Good.* "It tied in visually so well," said Orion executive Jan Kean, "you didn't even know you were seeing a commercial."[18] Product placement can result in terrible, stilted dialogue, such as the following excerpt from *Who's Harry Crumb?*, where John Candy's character plugs Cherry Coke in a scene with Jim Belushi:

CANDY: Cherry?

BELUSHI: No fruit, thank you.

CANDY: Coke?

BELUSHI: No, thank you.

CANDY: Mix 'em together, ya got a Cherry Coke. Ah ha ha ha ha ha! A Cherry Coke, ha ha ha ha!

The film *You've Got Mail* seems completely constructed around its cross-marketing tie-ins with AOL and Starbucks. Written by the formerly respected journalist and essayist Nora Ephron, the film was in fact a remake of Ernst Lubitsch's product-free *The Little Shop Around the Corner,* a sharp and witty romantic comedy of the classic Hollywood era. In Ephron's highly commercialized cinematic remix, the relationship between Tom Hanks and Meg Ryan primarily takes place on their AOL e-mail accounts and during their encounters at one of the coffee chain's stores. In one memorable (though completely gratuitous) voice-over, Hanks comments, "The whole purpose of places like Starbucks is for people with no decision-making ability whatsoever to make six decisions just to buy one cup of coffee: Short, tall, light, dark, caf, decaf, low fat, non fat. . . ."

With its light, incidental music, the whole scene looks and sounds like a commercial for Starbucks. And it is. In terms of plot, however, the most obvious trademarked name—Barnes & Noble— was absent. Hanks's character played the owner of a large corporate bookstore chain that put Ryan's family-owned bookstore out of business. In a motion picture that owed its very existence to recognizable trademarks, wouldn't the obvious name of Hanks's store be Barnes & Noble, especially since Starbucks has partnered with the bookseller in the real world? To use the discourse of product-placing advertisers, wouldn't it add to the film's realism? Of course it would, but I'm sure Barnes & Noble had no desire to be placed in such a negative context.

Then again, *You've Got Mail* ended up asking the audience to sympathize with Hanks and accept the inevitability of the independent bookstore's death. This is how awful and insidious that film is: Near the end, Ryan discovered that Hanks knew her AOL identity, which meant he had been manipulating her in their cuddly online relationship and in their antagonistic business liaisons. On top of that, his faux Barnes & Noble drove her bookstore out of business, which had been in the family for generations. So what does Ryan do before the credits roll? Melt into Hanks's arms. Why audiences didn't riot at the end is completely beyond me; if ever there was a film that deserved the "critique of the brick," it's *You've Got Mail.*

Wayne's World made product placement (or at least "ironic product placement") cool. By the end of the 1990s, another Mike Myers–helmed blockbuster, *Austin Powers: The Spy Who Shagged Me,* epitomized the new consumer-culture zeitgeist. In this hyper-referential, hyper-commercial movie, Dr. Evil's world headquarters is located atop the Seattle Space Needle, which has been branded with the Starbucks logo. Myers was playing off the widespread idea that the coffee-shop chain is an evil empire that colonizes everything, so it's fitting that Dr. Evil is behind this operation. "Dr. Evil, several years ago we invested in a small Seattle-based coffee company," says Robert Wagner's character, Number Two. "Today, Starbucks offers premium quality coffee at affordable prices. *Delish!*" The humor here is toothless and faux-subversive, and required the permission of Starbucks.

The release of *The Spy Who Shagged Me* came bundled in so many cross-marketing tie-ins, it turned the film into little more than a series of vignettes tied together with quasi-commercials for Heineken, Virgin, and other companies. Since *Wayne's World,* other films have followed its product-saturated lead—from playful, knowing movies such as *Charlie's Angels* to so-totally-*not*-ironic films such as the Michael Jordan–Warner Brothers brand explosion that was *Space Jam*. Or somewhere in between, like the second *Matrix* film, where the Wachowski brothers' publicist claimed they clamped down on merchandising to avoid any negative *Star Wars* comparisons. "Thus they strictly limited the sequel's ancillary products," Frank Rich sarcastically wrote, "to an *Enter the Matrix* video game, action figures, sunglasses (featured in another TimeWarner magazine, *People*) and an animated DVD. They kept the movie's product tie-ins to a bare minimum as well: Powerade drinks, Cadillac, Ducati motorcycles and Heineken."[19]

Although lots of attention gets paid to product placement in film and television, video games occupy the imagination of just as many teens and twentysomethings. These games are important because they seamlessly integrate leisure activity, consumption, and everyday life. This industry did $9.4 billion in business in 2001, and its market share continues to grow, making it a lucrative site to place trademarked products. In her book *Branded*, Alissa Quart describes the action in *Tony Hawk's Pro Skater 3*, part of a series of Hawk games that has approached $1 billion in sales since 1999.

> Skateboarder Tony Hawk maneuvers near a Quiksilver sign. When Hawk melons or lipslides on a thin ramp, the Quiksilver logo is visible again, on his T-shirt. The action moves to Tokyo. When Hawk and his skater pals perform airwalks, they flash past the ubiquitous Quiksilver logo, which is nestled among all the other stickers and bright neon lights and the signs blaring brands such as Nokia and Jeep.[20]

Unlike most movies, people play video games multiple times and, by definition, they require the close attention of the viewer.

This makes it a product placer's dream. Activision, the company that produces the Hawk game, claims that advertisers who place their logo in a Tony Hawk game get one billion "quality brand impressions" from the millions of teen and twentysomething gamers. It allows players to outfit their virtual characters from a selection of brand-name shirts, shoes, and other gear. The branding virus has infected popular music as well. A study of 2003 Top 20 radio hits found hundreds of brand-name references littered throughout the songs. "It's about using brands as metaphors," San Francisco marketing expert Lucian James told *Billboard.* "Globally, when you say Gucci, people know exactly what you mean."

While companies don't mind the often-free advertising provided by pop-music artists, they don't like it when their trademarks are used for satirical purposes. But as I mentioned in the last chapter, a court ruled in favor of the Swedish pop group Aqua when Mattel sued over their song "Barbie Girl." Mercedes, the most popular trademark in the 2003 popscape, had 112 references in the *Billboard* Top 20, while Cadillac and Lexus were mentioned 46 and 48 times, respectively. (An inspired lyric from R. Kelly: "The way you do the things you do / reminds me of my Lexus, cool / That's why I'm all up in your grill.") In just one song by Lil' Kim, "The Jump Off," she mentions Bacardi, Barbie, Bulgari, Ferrari, Bentleys, Hummers, Cadillac, Escalade, Jaguar, Timberland, Sprite, *Playboy,* Range Rover, and Brooklyn Mint.

After Busta Rhymes's song "Pass the Courvoisier" spent twenty weeks on the charts, worldwide sales of Courvoisier rose 20 percent. Lucian James said that there are generally three reasons why artists mention a particular brand: They actually like the product; they hope to get free goods; or, increasingly, they have struck a strategic deal. Unlike Hollywood, the authenticity-obsessed world of music—especially hip-hop—remains tight-lipped about this issue.[21] All this isn't to say that youth marketers are abandoning movie product placements; it's just that they are now considered to be but one component in a larger attempt to colonize the consciousness of kids. *Dogtown and Z-Boys*, a 2001 documentary about skateboarding, was financed by the skate accessory company Vans, and it functions as a very cleverly cloaked commercial.

What at first glance looks like a historical documentary about the birth of anti-authoritarian skate culture turns out to be something else. After watching a number of carefully edited shots, you can't help but notice the relatively constant presence of Vans on the feet of the skaters. Because it's a documentary—a genre associated with "truth" and "transparency"—*Dogtown* successfully solidifies the association between skate culture and the company. When I grew up in the skate and surf town of Virginia Beach during the 1980s, I was well aware of the existence of Vans—heck, I even owned a checkerboard pair, just like Spicoli in *Fast Times at Ridgemont High*. But the way the brand is so often placed in the frame, *Dogtown and Z-Boys* creates a false or exaggerated kind of impression of their ubiquity.

"We really try to connect emotionally with the kids and find new ways of doing things," says Jay Wilson, vice president of marketing at Vans. Speaking about the film, Wilson notes, "We're getting more public relations on this thing than we ever imagined."[22] In the 1990s Vans dramatically raised its profile and expanded its market share by sponsoring The Vans Warped Tour, the punk-and-extreme-sports summer festival. It was a smart move, and financing *Dogtown* further solidified its reputation as the official outfitter of disenfranchised youth, one of the arbiters of over-the-counter culture cool.

Increasingly, our cultural activities are tied up with carefully researched and marketed products and services. There's an interesting kind of synergy happening when people can play a Tony Hawk video game, watch the *X Games* on ESPN, take in an extreme-sports-and-punk-rock concert at the local stop of the Warped Tour, drive to the mall and buy Quiksilver gear, eat an Extreme® Taco Bell meal at the food court, and check out *Dogtown* at the multiplex—all without ever having to skateboard once. When I was growing up not that long ago, the consumption options that now surround skateboarding simply didn't exist. It pretty much cost nothing (save for the board's price tag) to hang out and skate in a parking lot while a boom box played Black Flag. Now skateboarding is a cross-marketing dream or nightmare, depending on your point of view—or the contents of your stock portfolio.

PEOPLE AS BRANDS

In promoting her line of perfumes, Elizabeth Taylor flatly acknowl-edges that "I am my own commodity."[23] It's a telling statement, one that highlights the extent to which people are willing to think of themselves as commodified beings, or even intellectual properties. Tony Hawk, for instance, is far more valuable as an abstract brand than a corporeal being, which isn't to say that the brand's value won't decline as his skateboarding skills do. The legal doctrine that protects celebrity images, called "right of publicity," is a relatively recent invention, emerging in the mid-twentieth century (unlike copyright, which developed in the eighteenth century). It helped create a new kind of private property, adding to the growing list of things that have been fenced off and nailed down with a price tag.

Although right of publicity emerged with the rise of the twentieth-century celebrity industry, celebrity culture itself has been around for hundreds, if not thousands, of years. Following the invention of the printing press in the late fifteenth century, it was common for famous people to be plastered on mass-produced consumer goods. Historian Elizabeth Eisenstein documents that sixteenth-century mass-produced portraits of Erasmus and Martin Luther were frequently duplicated and quite popular. Artists and engravers had previously made their living from the aristocracy-funded patronage system, which by the eighteenth century was in decline. This meant that these professions increasingly had to please mass audiences, and the sale of celebrity likenesses became big business during and after the American Revolution.[24]

In 1774 businessman Josiah Wedgwood began a line of portrait medallions called "illustrious moderns," aimed at less-affluent audiences. Soon, the medallions outsold the tea services that had been Wedgwood's primary business, and his catalog included classical-music composers, popes, monarchs, poets, and artists, as well as America's Founding Fathers. The image of Ben Franklin—a hugely popular figure in America and Europe during and after the Revolution—appeared on fans, perfume bottles, and over a hundred other items of fashion. By the time Franklin was an old man, "his own face was displayed all over Europe in the shape of engravings, busts, statues, paintings, and even little statuettes and painted fans that looked like souvenir keepsakes."[25]

Mass-produced celebrity images flourished throughout the nineteenth century, but it wasn't until the twentieth century that famous people began to think of themselves as legally protected commodities. It would have been inconceivable for Martin Luther to seek to regulate the reproduction of his image in the same way that the estate of Martin Luther King Jr. does. Phillip Jones, president of the firm that manages the King estate, reminds us, "King may belong to the public spiritually, but King's family is entitled to control the use of his image and words." Elvis Presley's estate controls his image just as tightly. Almost every imaginable word and image associated with the other departed King has been privatized by Elvis Presley Enterprises (EPE).

Since it was founded in 1979, EPE has filed thousands of lawsuits over the unauthorized use of Elvis's image. For instance, in 1998 a U.S. Circuit Court of Appeals barred a tavern from calling itself The Velvet Elvis. The establishment's owner claimed that it parodied 1960s kitsch and the restaurant's overall content had little to do with Elvis, but the court disagreed. The judge stated that even though the idea of the velvet Elvis painting is a necessary component of a kitschy 1960s parody, it still created "a likelihood of confusion in relating to EPE's marks."[26] The estate so emphatically polices the King's image and performance rights that it attempted to exert its control in other ghostly dimensions. EPE seriously considered suing a company that distributed the book *Is Elvis Alive?*, which came with an audiocassette that allegedly contained a conversation with Elvis.

Stupid idea for a book, yes, but copyright infringement? EPE lawyers claimed that if this truly was a recording of Elvis, living or dead, this paranormal bootleg infringed on the estate's performance rights. The author is dead; long live the author! The lawsuit idea was dropped after the book didn't sell enough copies to justify the expense of legal action against it. In 2004 California governor Arnold Schwarzenegger sued Ohio Discount Merchandise Inc., a family-owned business in Canton that makes bobbleheads. The Governator's likeness appeared in a line of wobbly-headed caricatures of political figures, including John Kerry, Howard Dean, and others.

Schwarzenegger's lawyers claimed that the bobblehead makers infringed on his right of publicity. "No other politician has done this," company president Todd Bosley told the *New York Times.* "Jimmy Carter sent me a book. . . . Rudy Giuliani carried his around with him to several of his speeches. We've never had a problem like this." He decided to fight the suit with the help of a California law firm, which took on the case pro bono. "There's a lot at risk here for me and a lot at risk in the future for people like me," said Mr. Bosley. "Do we succumb to threats and heavy-handedness? Or do we stand up for what America really is?" We truly live in strange times when the frontlines in the fight to protect the First Amendment includes a bobblehead manufacturer.

"Over the years, right of publicity protection has expanded," legal scholar Rosemary Coombe writes. "It is no longer limited to the name or likeness of the individual, but now extends to a person's nickname, signature, physical pose, characterizations, singing style, vocal characteristics, body parts, frequently used phrases, car, performance style, and mannerisms and gestures, provided that these are distinctive and publicly identified with the person claiming the right."[27] Right-of-publicity law often overlaps with trademark law. For instance, Donald Trump's catchphrase and accompanying gesture, "You're fired," is trademarked, but right of publicity more generally protects his persona.

In the *Vanna White v. Samsung Electronics America, Inc.* case, the U.S. Court of Appeals for the Ninth Circuit enlarged publicity protection even further. In that problematic case, a Samsung commercial featured a robot wearing a blond wig, jewelry, and an evening gown that stood in front of a display board. It was meant to resemble the set of the game show, *Wheel of Fortune,* which featured Ms. White as a piece of eye candy who turned vowels and consonants on the board. The court ruled that the commercial infringed on White's right of publicity, even though no reasonable person would mistake the blond robot for the real Vanna White.

"Right of publicity" has also been stretched to protect a singer's voice from *imitation.* Courts had previously rejected the idea that a singer's vocal style could be protected under right of publicity, but two significant precedents have expanded that right. In 1988 pop star Bette Midler successfully sued the Ford Motor Company and its advertising agency for deliberately imitating one of her songs in a television commercial. They argued that it wasn't simply a case of imitation, but of trespassing on the property that is her famous voice (and, by extension, her valuable personality). In *Midler v. Ford Motor Co.*, the California court held that "Midler had a legitimate claim under the common law right of publicity."

After the Midler decision, the neo-beatnik singer-songwriter Tom Waits successfully sued Frito-Lay for using a singer who imitated his raspy style for a commercial. The Ninth Circuit drew upon the Midler decision, awarding Waits and his lawyers $2 million in punitive damages. Legal scholar Russell Stamets points out that this decision "represents a dramatic expansion of the publicity right defined in Midler. In the Midler case, Ford's advertising agency admitted trying to imitate Midler in a version of a song she made a hit." He continues, "Unlike Ford, however, Frito-Lay's sound-alike was given an original tune to sing, a tune never associated with the plaintiff."[28]

When civil-rights figurehead Rosa Parks objected to Outkast naming a song "Rosa Parks"—whose chorus playfully goes, "Ah-ha, hush that fuss / everybody move to the back of the bus"—she sued in 1999. Her lawyers invoked right-of-publicity law to try to squash the hip-hop song, and after six years the case is still winding its way through the courts. Also in 1999 children's television host Mister Rogers sued a T-shirt manufacturer that sold shirts that juxtaposed his image with the captions "Pervert" and "Serial Killer." Rogers also sued another company that sold a T-shirt of Rogers holding a gun. Invoking "right of publicity" and trademark infringement, his lawyers stated, "It is antithetical to Rogers' and FCI's philosophy, image and business practice to be associated with the corrupted depiction of Rogers shown in defendant's shirt."

Of course it goes against Fred Rogers's *intended* image; that's the point. Many of those who grew up on a steady diet of his programs believe that there was something a little *off* about the guy. His strangely calm demeanor left enough of an imprint on me that I made a collage piece about his weirdness as an adult. Using words and images from his television program, I excerpted pieces of his disturbing stories and songs, including a quite troubling up-tempo number: "Just for once I want you all to myself / Just for once let's *play alone* / I'll be the only one with you." Over the course of my collage, titled *Won't You Be My Neighbor?,* he chronicles the fears of a "four-year-old friend" who watched in horror after his toy dog's appendages fell off (it didn't survive a particularly perilous trip to the washing machine).

"But that's just with toys," he sloooowly assures his little friend, "It doesn't happen with people." With a dark sense of dread bubbling just below the surface, Rogers calmly adds, "Little boys' and girls' arms and legs don't fall off when you put them in water." Thanks for the reassurance, Fred—and for planting the idea in my head. This collage piece is available as a free download on my Web site and has played at film festivals, so I'm a bit worried about being sued by his estate, or by PBS, which broadcasts *Mister Rogers' Neighborhood.* However, I felt compelled to say something about a man who occupied my imagination when I was a kid, and damn the consequences. Judging from the reaction of many who have seen it—"I *knew* he was weird, I just couldn't put my finger on it"— I'm not alone. I also confidently believe that my creation is a fair use of these copyrighted broadcasts, because it's for the purpose of social commentary and satire.

MEDIA PIRATES

Ironically, Fred Rogers helped pave the way for me to create this collage. When the entertainment industry did its best to prevent the

VCR from entering the U.S. market, Rogers took a contrary position. A California court ruled at the time that the VCR could be banned because of its copyright-infringing capabilities, but Mister Rogers testified in the early 1980s that this was wrong. He believed that ordinary people should have the right to record his television show so that they could become "much more active in the programming of their family's television life." In classic Fred Rogers style, he argued, "My whole approach in broadcasting has always been 'You are an important person just the way you are. You can make healthy decisions.' " He concluded, "I just feel that anything that allows a person to be more active in the control of his or her life, in a healthy way, is important." He had a point.

The kind of borrowing I speak of isn't the same thing as "piracy," though film scholar Patti Zimmermann reappropriates the meaning of the term and puts a new spin on it. If the commercial pirate makes *counterfeits,* she argues, the media pirate produces counter-*discourses* by poaching from pop culture in a witty and subversive way. For instance, in *Día de la Independencia,* video artist Alex Rivera takes on the 1996 Hollywood blockbuster *Independence Day,* mocking the nationalistic themes that run through it. He plays with the idea that alien films have as much to do with our anxieties about immigration and ethnicity as they are simply sci-fi entertainment. Pirating the most well-known sequence from the film—a spaceship hovering over the White House—Rivera slyly replaces the vessel with a digitized sombrero.

Flashily edited to mimic a trailer, it subverts the original material by assuming a Spanish-speaking audience, rather than English, as it warns of an impending Chicano invasion. At the end of the trailer, the sombrero blows up the White House, playing on racially charged fears about nonwhite people overrunning the United States, a feeling that has only intensified post-9/11. Appropriation and collages aren't just techniques used by lefty artists—it's been a useful tool for right-leaning folks, from the Futurists to contemporary conservative talk-radio jocks. For instance, Howard Dean was the frontrunner for the 2004 Democratic Presidential nomination, until the Iowa caucuses. Although he had already slipped in the polls, Dean's post-caucus "I Have a Scream" speech precipitated one of the quickest freefalls in recent political memory.

The next morning, and for the next couple of weeks, the Dean howl was replayed on radio and television, sometimes being incorporated into elaborate and humorous montages. There were other factors that contributed to Dean's spectacular downfall, but the endless loops and collages of his yowling "YIPPIE!" played a big role. On the other side of the political spectrum, the day after the Dean debacle, Bush gave his State of the Union address. Almost immediately, the Internet was filled with dozens of downloadable remixes of the broadcast that parodied and undermined the president's speech. That year, Negativland mined Mel Gibson's controversial *The Passion of the Christ* and other religious films to create a biting audiovisual remix, *The Mashin' of the Christ*. Gibson's movie, by the way, was one of the most downloaded films on the Internet, but that didn't stop the *Passion* from raking in nearly $1 billion in 2004. Nevertheless, I'm sure the MPAA has reserved a special place in hell for all those Jesus-loving thieves.

Another example of "media piracy" is Robert Greenwald's independently produced and distributed *Outfoxed*. This 2004 documentary focused on Fox News's Republican bias, and to demonstrate this the producer needed to include clips from its copyrighted broadcasts. Not surprisingly, the fair and balanced® network argued that it was an "illegal copyright infringement." Given the cable news channel's litigious history, Greenwald was quite nervous, and the production of the documentary was kept secret in order to avoid a costly legal battle that might have slowed or stopped its production. "I want to make a great film," Greenwald told the *New York Times*. "But I'd like to do so without losing my house and spending the rest of my life in court."

Much like some copyright owners refuse hip-hop artists permission to sample, CBS and PBS-affiliate WGBH, among others, refused to allow Greenwald to use relevant clips from their broadcasts. For them, *Outfoxed* was too controversial, and they didn't want to be associated with it. Fox News certainly didn't give permission for its broadcasts to be excerpted, but, as Stanford Law Professor Lawrence Lessig stated in an op-ed piece published by *Variety*, this appropriation was clearly protected by the fair-use statute. Lessig, who advised Greenwald on copyright matters, reasoned that a commitment to free speech "is a commitment to fighting wars of ideas with more speech, and fewer lawsuits." He rightly argued, "It is as shameful for Fox to sue Al Franken for using 'fair and balanced' as it is for Michael Moore to threaten to sue his critics for defamation. We need more debate in America, not less. And we will get more critical and insightful debate if filmmakers like Greenwald can do their work without the law requiring that lawyers look over his editor's shoulder."

Media piracy doesn't always have to express an overtly political or high-minded statement; it needs only to be a creative act, even of the most trivial kind. Such is the case with *The Phantom Re-Edit: Episode 1.1*, a version of George Lucas's *Star Wars: Episode I—The Phantom Menace* cut by a fan. The adaptation, which has been freely floating around since 2000, significantly alters the role of the much-loathed Jar Jar Binks by garbling his speech and adding subtitles. Rather than being an annoying, goofy presence, the phantom editor turned Jar Jar into a wizened Jedi knight who actively shapes the story. It's both an improvement on the original film *and* quite funny. The creator also made other changes, from plot tweaks to cutting down the film's running time to quicken its pace.[29] Although it wasn't 100 percent new and original, at the very least this person chose not to be a passive, catatonic consumer.

ALTERING BILLBOARDS ON THE INFORMATION STUPOR-HIGHWAY

Fortunately for our democracy, intellectual-property laws are less effective in protecting political figures from satirical attacks than other kinds of celebrities. Massachusetts computer consultant Zack Exley demonstrated this when he successfully registered gwbush .com, gwbush.org, and gbush.org in 1999. Exley created a Web site that closely mimicked the look of the Bush campaign's homepage, but highlighted what Exley viewed as hypocrisies in Bush's policies. The best part of the story is that in a fit of paranoia the Bush campaign bought 260 more domain names, including "bushsucks .com," "bushsux.com," and "bushblows.com." For at least a year after Bush 2.0 entered office, if you typed in the domain names bushblows.com or bushbites.com, it sent you directly to the official Bush-Cheney Web site.

In constructing the site, Exley was aided by an organization named ®™ark, pronounced "art-mark." It's less a real organization than the brainchild of two men, Mike Bonanno and Andy Bichlbaum. Collectively, they're known as the Yes Men, and they scroll through numerous pseudonyms that create the illusion that they're an army of pranksters engaged in widespread subterfuge. (Their anti-authoritarian antics are captured in *The Yes Men*, a hilarious documentary by Sarah Price and Chris Smith.) Without breaking character, ®™ark presents itself as a corporation whose Web site acts as a think tank that funds nonviolent "cultural sabotage"— such as Exley's Web page, and the Barbie Liberation Front. In 1993 the BLF purchased multiple Barbie and G. I. Joe dolls, switched their voice boxes, and "reverse shoplifted" these gender-bending toys back into stores. During Christmas that year, in select toy stores, Barbie grunted, "Dead men tell no lies," and G. I. Joe gushed, "I like to go shopping with you." After they sent out press kits to news organizations, the story broke nationally.

"Artmark" also helped promote *Deconstructing Beck,* a CD that compiles tracks constructed entirely from unauthorized samples of Beck's music. (Part of the joke, and the serious commentary, was that Beck's own music is often made out of samples.) Negativland's Seeland record label released this collection in conjunction with the label Illegal Art. Beck's attorney, Brian McPhereson, fired off an angry e-mail: "Bragging about copyright infringement is incredibly stupid. You will be hearing from me, Universal Music Group, BMG Music Publishing, and Geffen Records very shortly." Beck's publishing company, BMG, also sent a letter threatening a lawsuit, but the matter was quietly dropped. Although Beck never publicly responded to the deconstruction, it's likely the hipster musician did behind-the-scenes work to avoid a PR-damaging debacle akin to the Negativland-U2 blow-up.

Because the gwbush.com parody fit with its prankish nature, when Zack Exley sought help, ®™ark obliged. "In the beginning," said Exley, "I wanted to do a copy of the Bush site. Back then I had no reason to think anyone would ever hear about or visit the site. But I thought it would be funny if the Bush people finally stumbled upon the site and found an exact copy—maybe with a few minor and unsettling changes." Exley continued, "I had been to ®™ark's site, and seen their copies of corporate Web sites and figured they had a program that copied them automatically. I e-mailed them and that was indeed the case."[30] He duplicated the layout and photos on the Bush campaign site, but he filled it with slogans like "Hypocrisy with Bravado."

The parallel-universe political page also invited people to engage in ®™ark-sponsored acts of symbolic protest—such as inserting "slaughtered cow" plastic toys into Happy Meals or jumping the fence into Disneyland and demanding political asylum. Responding to his doppelgänger site, candidate Bush was frighteningly candid: "There ought to be limits to freedom."[31] Perhaps it's the most honest thing Bush said before he was elected, and one that anticipated many of his administration's policies. Although Bush's campaign used a cease-and-desist letter to scare Exley into removing copyrighted and trademarked images, they weren't able to further muzzle him. And when *USA Today* and *Newsweek* reported the story, the Web site racked up six million hits in May 1999. In comparison, the Bush campaign managed only thirty thousand that month.

For the time being, no politicians have successfully won back a domain name that bears their name. In 2002 the World Intellectual Property Organization issued rules stating, "Persons who have gained eminence and respect, but who have not profited from their reputation in commerce" cannot protect their names against "parasitic registrations." On the other hand, it has become increasingly easier for celebrities to secure control of an Internet address that mirrors their name. For instance, Madonna took control of Madonna.com after her lawyers persuaded WIPO's domain name–arbitration panel to allow her to do so; it did the same for Julia Roberts, even though her name is a quite common name in the United States.

THE FICTION OF "CORPORATE PERSONHOOD"

In 1993 the artist-formerly-and-now-currently-known-as-Prince changed his name to an unpronounceable symbol or glyph, which he trademarked. In doing so, he pushed the notion of the branded person to its furthest logical extreme. Then, in 1999, Prince's lawyers began suing fan Web sites that offered MP3 live recordings, archived his lyrics, and reprinted his trademarked logo. Says Alex Hahn, a lawyer who represented one of the defendants, "The notion that a person can change his name to a symbol, ask everyone to use that symbol, and then sue them for using it is legally absurd."[32] Through trademark law, Prince had the power to control the contexts in which his "name" appeared, in much the same way that corporations can restrict the use of their logos.

This case works as a kind of a secular parable. For much of the 1990s, Prince insisted that he should only be referred to as a trademarked symbol, transforming himself into a branded corporate product. Conversely, under a U.S. legal convention referred to as "corporate personhood," businesses are considered to be one of us, they are "individuals." In an unsettling example of (ill)logical jurisprudence, the U.S. Supreme Court reinterpreted the Fourteenth Amendment—written to safeguard freed slaves—by defining corporations as "individuals" in 1886. Since the *Santa Clara County v. Southern Pacific Railroad* case, corporations receive many legal protections individuals enjoy.

Responding to this line of reasoning, ®™ark (again, another Yes Men identity) offers two thousand dollars to the first U.S. court that imprisons a corporation under the "three strikes" law, or which sentences a corporation to death. "Artmark" also argues that "since U.S. corporations are by law U.S. citizens, it should be possible to marry one," and it offers a two-hundred-dollar grant for the first person to do so. Another target of the Yes Men was the World Trade Organization, which administers the General Agreement on Tariffs and Trade (GATT), a controversial treaty that governs world commerce. They successfully registered the domain name gatt.org, and soon before the 1999 WTO conference in Seattle it introduced the clone "WTO/GATT Home Page." The Web site enraged the actual

WTO director-general, whose name is, strangely enough, Michael Moore. He complained, "It's illegal and it's unfair," but the ensuing press coverage only boosted visits to gatt.org.

In their Web pages and press releases, the Yes Men reappropriate corporate-speak. They flip familiar phrases in a deconstructive attempt to show how language conceals power—how bland-sounding expressions can hide unsettling ideas. They demonstrated this when the organizers of the Textiles of the Future Conference unwittingly emailed gatt.org and invited a "WTO representative" to deliver a keynote address. The merry pranksters answered in the affirmative, and in August 2001 the Yes Men/®™ark flew to Tampere, Finland, to create a spectacle that would make their Situationist forebearers proud. Posing as "Dr. Hank Hardy Unruh of the WTO," Andy Bichlbaum delivered a speech—wrapped in such terms as "market liberalization"—that favorably compared sweatshops to slavery.

During a subsection of his speech, titled "British Empire: Its Lessons for Managers," Dr. Unruh dismissed Mohandas Gandhi as "a likeable, well-meaning fellow who wanted to help his fellow workers along, but did not understand the benefits of open markets and free trade." As was documented in the *Yes Men* movie, his assistant removed Unruh's tear-away business suit at the conclusion of his speech. Underneath was a gold body suit with a giant and shiny inflatable phallus that contained a video screen. This contraption was supposedly designed to monitor workers in the Third World, which they illustrated in Power Point. None of the international scientists, businesspeople, officials, and academics did much more than to blink; they just politely applauded.

"We use this language because it is so effective," says Frank Guerrero, another Yes Men pseudonym. "We think that by adopting the language, mannerisms, legal rights, and cultural customs of corporations, we are able to engage them in their own terms, and also perhaps to reveal something about how downright absurd it can get." Although they don't directly acknowledge their debt to the Situationists and other radical artists concerned with transforming everyday life, the connection is clear. "It is impossible to get rid of a world," wrote Situationist Mustapha Khayati in 1966, "without getting rid of the language that conceals and protects it."[33] To toss out the Old World Order we have to deconstruct its words, ideologies, and institutions—and continue to reconstruct them, creating a better place to live.

This tactic might include the *détournement* of copyrighted images. Or it can be a more general kind of appropriation, like the way gay and lesbian communities took back the word "queer," embracing it as their own. Today's culture jammers (a term coined by Negativland to describe those who skillfully alter the messages of billboard advertisements) do both. They "steal" the logos of private corporations, recontextualizing them; and they manipulate corporate-speak to reveal its hidden assumptions. During the May 1968 riots in Paris—when catchy graffiti slogans such as "live without dead time" adorned city walls—the newspaper *France-Soir* observed that students were "fighting advertising on its own terrain with its own weapons." It's a Situationist tactic employed in the battle against what Guy Debord called "the spectacle." The term describes our hyper-commercialized, privatized world where virtually everything that used to be directly experienced is turned into a representation. In other words, rather than experiencing "the real thing"—life—we substitute it for what Coca-Cola calls "the real thing."

An exaggerated example of this would include the time when I stayed at the Egyptian-themed Luxor Hotel in Las Vegas (near the city-in-a-casino, "New York, New York," with an indoor Central

Park). The Luxor's lobby looked familiar, and then I realized it was where they filmed Will Smith's "Gettin' Jiggy Wit It" video, where he traveled around the world. (Only, Smith was roaming in a simulacrum, going from exotic Vegas hotel to hotel.) To remind us this was a prestigious set location, the Luxor mounted a gigantic TV that endlessly looped that part of the video. Not only were we standing in a Vegas-ized forgery of Egypt, we were sucked into watching a plasma screen that contained a representation of that fake world. It was a mind-melting, money-drenched feedback loop of image-upon-reality-upon-image—in other words, the spectacle.

Culture jammers such as the Yes Men lead their armies in a symbolic war across a media-saturated terrain by messing with images that erupt from the spectacle. But, as I've argued, it's a terrain that intellectual-property owners have attempted to fence off. Even though we still have the ability to say what we want in the physical world (at least in designated "free-speech zones"), companies have an ever-growing power to police what is said in cyberspace. For instance, when the Yes Men targeted Dow Chemical, what they said was erased. Literally. They snagged the domain name DowChemical.com and hosted a clone of Dow's official Web site, which spotlighted the infamous Bhopal chemical spill. In 1984 a pesticide plant in Bhopal, India, owned by Union Carbide, now part of Dow, sprung a leak and killed five thousand residents. The plant was abandoned without a cleanup, claiming an additional fifteen thousand lives since.

On the clearly satirical Web site and press release, the Yes Men shoved words into Dow's mouth:

"We are being portrayed as a heartless giant which doesn't care about the 20,000 lives lost due to Bhopal over the years," said Dow President and CEO Michael D. Parker. "But this just isn't true. Many individuals within Dow feel tremendous sorrow about the Bhopal disaster, and many individuals within Dow would like the corporation to admit its responsibility, so that the public can then decide on the best course of action, as is appropriate in any democracy. Unfortunately, we have responsibilities to our shareholders and our industry colleagues that make action on Bhopal impossible. And being clear about this has been a very big step."

Soon after the Web site went online in 2002, lawyers for Dow sent the parody site's Internet service provider (ISP) a cease-and-desist letter, claiming that the site "displays numerous trademarks, images, texts and designs taken directly from Dow's website," and therefore violated the Digital Millennium Copyright Act—a law that is one of the biggest threats to free speech online. The DMCA, which was passed in 1998, stipulates that ISPs can be immune from prosecution only if they immediately comply to "take down" requests by copyright owners. Even if the copyrighted materials appear in a fair-use context, the DMCA still makes it harder for freedom of expression® to prosper online.

By threatening ISPs and search engines, intellectual-property owners can simply make you disappear if they do not like what you have to say, something that was much more difficult in a nondigital world. Dow went over the head of the Yes Men's ISP—Thing.net—and straight to Verio, the company that provided its hardwired connection to the Internet. Verio shut down the entire ISP for a day, blacking out artforum.com, rtmark.com, and many other activist and academic sites. "Verio's actions are nothing short of outrageous," said Wolfgang Staehle, Thing.net's executive director. "They could have resolved the matter with the Dow parodists directly; instead they chose to shut down our entire network. This self-appointed enforcement of the DMCA could have a serious, chilling effect on free speech and has already damaged our business."

Before the Yes Men could fight for their right to keep the parody site, Dow took over DowChemical.com after one of the Yes Men's pranks backfired on them. Before the controversy began, they thought it would be funny to register the domain in the name of Dow CEO Michael Parker's son, Jimmy Parker, even using his real street address. Jimmy Parker and Dow's lawyers sent the proper authorities a Xerox of his driver's license via FedEx, stating that the domain name was his, and that was that. "Very creative work there, Jimmy!" the Yes Men conceded on their Web site.

Under the DMCA, the decision about what is fair use is shifted to intellectual-property owners, and they aren't necessarily fair and balanced®. Although this law has dissuaded some activists from creating parody sites, many others don't seem to give a damn, for there is power in numbers. After the gatt.org flap two years earlier, the Yes Men released to the world a free "parodyware" package called Reamweaver (a play on Dreamweaver, the popular software program used to create Web pages). Their subversive software automatically downloads all the files from a satirist's target, such as Dow.com, so that the parody site can exactly mirror the original site, though with key changes.

One of its features is to automate the changing of key words in the original Web site's text—from "investment opportunity," for instance, to "enslave and pillage." "Using this software, it takes five minutes to set up a convincing, personalized, evolving parody of the wto.org Web site, or any other Web site of your choice," the Yes Men's Web site states. "All you need is a place to put it, say, wtoo.org, worldtradeorg.com, whatever." The Yes Men add, "The idea is to insure that even if they shut down our Web site, hundreds of others will continue our work of translation. The more they try to fight it, the funnier they're going to look." One flaw in this strategy is the fact that domain names are increasingly being treated like trademarks, making it easier for companies such as Mattel to take back addresses such as "badbarbies.com."

FREEDOM OF EXPRESSION® ON(THE)LINE

"A guy in Libya, in just five minutes, can register for $70 a site called CokeSucks that is filled with offensive material," Porsche intellectual-property lawyer Gregory Phillips complained to the *San Francisco Chronicle*. "It is the functional equivalent of constructing misleading road signs on a highway to divert people. You'll see a Chevron sign but when you turn off the exit, you pull into a Podunk gas station." A guy in Libya? Why not Baghdad? Even ignoring Phillips's inflammatory example, his logic doesn't hold water because cokesucks.com is less like a billboard and more like a spray-painted sign made by an activist. It's free speech, though some lawyers and judges don't agree. "Courts as a whole are bending over backward to respect trademark rights," says Sally M. Abel, a member of the International Trademark Association board of directors.[34]

Search engines are potentially liable under the law for simply linking users to Web sites, though they, too, can avoid lawsuits if they cave in to the demands of overzealous copyright bozos. For instance, the Church of Scientology invoked the DMCA when it threatened Google with a costly suit. In doing so, it forced the Internet search engine to block links to Web sites that criticized the church, sites that reprinted fragments of the church's copyrighted materials. "Had we not removed these URLs," stated Google, "we would be subject to a claim for copyright infringement, regardless of its merits."[35] The search engine bowed to the church's demands because it would have simply been too costly to go to court, and Google is not in business to protect our freedom of expression®.

Scientology is an interesting example of a religion that emerged in the age of intellectual property. The equivalent of their bible is copyrighted and their religious icons are trademarked, which means that any theological criticism of the church that reproduces their religious materials, no matter how fragmentary, can result in an expensive lawsuit. The Church of Scientology is extremely litigious, and it won some of the very first copyright cases that undermined the First Amendment on the Internet. One of the most effective weapons Scientology has in its arsenal is the DMCA, which allows them to exterminate offending Web sites that reprint its copyrighted materials to criticize the church. Another DMCA victim was Marina Chong, an Australian resident who hosted an anti-Scientology Web site on an American ISP. Soon after the DMCA was signed into law, the ISP notified Chong that it had removed her site after Bridge Publications, a subsidiary of the Church of Scientology, claimed she had violated its copyrights.

"Because I am not a resident of the U.S.A. and because I have no inclination to fight the case in court, I agreed to remove the page," Chong explained in 1999. She added, "This legislation is a new weapon in the Church of Scientology arsenal, and I am sure the Church of Scientology will use it to close down as many sites as possible." The same kind of copyright censorship happened to Susan Mullaney, another activist whose Web site was erased when the church complained.[36] Because of the DMCA, the Scientology critics at xenu.net had to move their Web site to a hosting company in Amsterdam. Unfortunately, these critics couldn't find an ISP that would host it in America, the home of the brave and the land of the free.*

Carrie McLaren's illegal-art.org Web site was briefly removed from the Internet because the DMCA was invoked by Sony Enter-

---

*Certain restrictions apply. Void where prohibited.

tainment, which co-owns with Michael Jackson the Beatles catalog. Sony took exception to the fact that the Illegal Art site was making Danger Mouse's *Grey Album* available, even after EMI/Capitol stopped harassing McLaren. The Online Policy Group, an advocacy organization that owns its own server, volunteered to host illegal-art.org and, fortunately for McLaren, Sony never filed a lawsuit. Unlike the Online Policy Group, most ISPs and Web hosting companies are very squeamish about hosting content that could get them sued. For instance, after the ISP Interport received a threatening letter from Mattel, which objected to a Web site it hosted that satirized Barbie, it forwarded Mattel's letter to the Web-site creator, along with its own statement that justified its need to remove the offending images.

"Interport is not qualified to verify Mattel's claim and has absolutely no opinion on whether Mattel's claim is true or not," the ISP stated. "Regardless, Interport is in a position of potential liability [and] is compelled to act accordingly in a manner which limits our liability." In 1999, a year after the DMCA was passed, trademark-owning corporations won a major lobbying victory when Congress passed the Anti–Cyber Squatting Consumer Protection Act. Since then, companies have aggressively pursued legal action against those who incorporate their trademarks into domain names. The Anti–Cyber Squatting Act imposes stiff criminal penalties against offenders, though companies can also use an arbitration process to get control of a domain name they don't like. When so much of our culture and language is privately owned, it becomes all the more difficult to play with language, even in nonconfrontational ways.

Mike Rowe, a seventeen-year-old Canadian high-school student, discovered this problem when he registered the domain name mikerowesoft.com. Of course, Microsoft went after him. Using a now-common tactic, the software company offered ten dollars for the name. "I had spent a lot of time building up my site, and I had only been offered ten dollars for my work," Rowe said. "I responded by asking for ten thousand dollars, which I regret doing now, for my work and domain name." This allowed Microsoft to claim it was a "bad faith" registration and it started proceedings that would strip him of the domain name. After a slew of negative news stories, Microsoft backed off, slightly, with a company representative doing some damage control: "We appreciate that Mike Rowe is a young entrepreneur who came up with a creative domain name. We take our trademark seriously, but maybe a little too seriously in this case."[37] Microsoft still insisted on controlling the domain name, but it gave the young Rowe a better deal (and even threw in a free Xbox video-game console—woohoo!).

It's not surprising that domain-name disputes are unfairly balanced in favor of corporate trademark owners, something demonstrated in two studies conducted by Professor Michael Geist of the University of Ottawa. Two organizations that are sympathetic to corporate interests—the World Intellectual Property Organization and the National Arbitration Forum (NAF)—control the lion's share of domain disputes—93.7 percent, to be exact. Why do they dominate the process? Trademark owners (the complainants) can choose where a case is heard, and of course they want the best odds of winning. Professor Geist's studies suggest that WIPO and NAF actively pick judges who favor complainants because doing so ensures the two organizations more revenue. On numerous occasions, WIPO's arbitration panel has removed custody of domain names and turned them over to corporate trademark owners, who then return as satisfied customers.

WIPO hasn't just ruled against people who squat on nike.com, mcdonalds.com, or vivendiuniversal.com (Vivendi Universal is—or was—one of the major media powerhouses that dominate the multibillion-dollar entertainment industries). It has also stripped domain names from those who have had the audacity to register a *variation* of that trademark. In 2001 WIPO ruled against vivendi universalsucks.com, stating that this domain name might cause public confusion. In one of WIPO's more surreal and silly decisions, the panel argued that "certain members of the public in general and 'Internauts' in particular,"—Internauts?—"not being English speakers and/or aware of the meaning of the word 'sucks' in the Internet world, would be likely to understand 'sucks' as a banal and obscure addition to the reasonably well-known mark VIVENDI UNIVERSAL."

Granted, WIPO *might* be engaging in subtle cultural criticism—acknowledging that this media mega-giant *does* suck. But somehow I don't think that was their intention. Straying from the humorless norms of intellectual-property rulings, panelist David E. Sorkin dissented from the vivendiuniversalsucks.com case. His comments give me hope that there are voices of reason out there.

> [It] may be unwise to adopt a *per se* rule holding that "sucks" domain names can never be found confusingly similar to the trademarks they contain. But the Complainant in this proceeding does not claim to be known as a manufacturer of vacuum cleaners or suction pumps, or as a self-deprecating alternative rock band, or a test laboratory for beverage straws, or a porn star, a black hole, or any other sort of entity that people are likely to associate with sucking.[38]

As we look back twenty years from now, Mattel and other businesses like Fox News may ironically be remembered as some of the greatest promoters of fair use. After all, their brand of copyright bozo zealotry has helped breed an army of activists, young and old.

Virtually every time these companies try to step on freedom of expression® in court they end up expanding the parameters of fair use in case law, and they also intensify the backlash against this kind of behavior. One example of this is the formation in 2004 of FreeCulture.org, a student movement devoted to promoting and defending a free and open cultural space. A couple weeks after the Tom Forsythe ruling discussed in the last chapter, FreeCulture.org announced plans for "Barbie in a Blender Day." On July 27, 2004, the organization displayed on its online gallery guerrilla works of art that remixed Barbie in various devious and hilarious ways.

"This campaign is a celebration of our free speech rights, rights that we must defend by exercising them," said Rebekah Baglini, one of the cofounders of FreeCulture.org. Nelson Pavlosky, another cofounder, told me, "I think the main purpose of projects like 'Barbie in a Blender' is to make the copyright wars less abstract, to anchor the issues in concrete examples." The event was planned without Forsythe's knowledge, and when I told the artist about it, he responded enthusiastically. "I always pursued this case to make the point that corporations can't silence free speech if people are willing to stand up for their constitutional rights," he told me. "It's inspiring to see a student movement use the case to encourage creative expression. Who knows, if this catches on maybe every brand will become like Kleenex—simply a generic word for a product we use to dispose of our snot."

TOWARD A "FAIR" WORLD (OR AT LEAST A FAIRER COUNTRY)

The internal policies that regulate the behavior and output of universities, movie studios, book-publishing houses, and other culture-producing entities have grown more conservative and cautious in recent years. At the same time, ironically, some American judges have increasingly been reaffirming the value of free speech when commenting on privately owned images, logos, or phrases. Although no tidal wave has swept across the judicial system, washing away all overzealous trademark bozos, a few key recent cases have established important precedents. One is *MasterCard v. Nader.* When Ralph Nader's 2000 presidential campaign parodied Master-Card's ubiquitous "Priceless" ad campaign, the financial institution sued, and lost. Nader's campaign produced a political ad that read: "Grilled tenderloin for fund-raiser: $1,000 a plate . . . campaign ads filled with half-truths: $10 million . . . promises to special interest groups: over $100 billion . . . finding out the truth: priceless. There are some things that money can't buy."

In 2004 the U.S. District Court stated that the derivative ad created little likelihood of consumer confusion, ruling against Master-Card's trademark-infringement claim. It also ruled against MasterCard's assertion that Nader infringed on the ad campaign's copyrights, stating that it was a fair use of the company's intellectual property. Quoting the influential 2 Live Crew Supreme Court decision, the majority asserted that in literature, science, and art there are "few, if any, things which, in an abstract sense, are strictly new and original throughout. Every book in literature, science and art, borrows, and must necessarily borrow, and use much which was well known and used before." The court went on to cite another important decision that upheld fair use even in the most commercial of contexts.

Photographer Annie Leibovitz lost a case against Paramount Pictures when it exactly mimicked her photograph of a nude, pregnant Demi Moore, but with a twist. The focus of *Leibovitz v. Paramount* was the studio's *Naked Gun 33⅓* movie poster, which depicted a digitally manipulated picture of a nude, pregnant Leslie Nielson striking a familiar pose. Additionally, in 2003 the Supreme

Court unanimously ruled that Victor's Little Secret—the name of a relatively seedy adult-toy store located in a Kentucky strip mall—did not violate the Federal Trademark Dilution Act. Writing for the majority, Justice John Paul Stevens stated that the federal statute requires proof of *actual* harm, not merely the likelihood of dilution.

Even when it works against their particular interests, intellectual-property activists acknowledge the importance of cultivating open flows of information. There is, for instance, a competing illegal art.*com* that criticizes illegal-art.org for associating itself with a "corporate-backed" venue such as San Francisco MOMA. It exactly imitates the graphic design of Carrie McLaren's site and is obviously a parody. McLaren theoretically could have taken action, but it never crossed her mind. Similarly, Naomi Klein, author of the influential anti–consumer culture book *No Logo,* went against her publisher's wishes and didn't trademark the title of her book. Now there is a trademarked No Logo shoe company, food company, and cell-phone company. "It's frustrating for me because I actually get e-mail from people who say that they think I've produced products," Klein told WORT, a community radio station in Madison, Wisconsin.

"That does bother me," she said. "But the alternative would be doing exactly what I argue against in the book, which is trying to own ideas and keep them from spreading. Which is exactly the opposite of what most activists want. You want ideas to spread." In another important 2004 decision that cited the unanimous 2 Live Crew ruling, the U.S. Court of Appeals for the 2nd Circuit vigorously defended the fair-use statute as something that protects freedom of expression® in a commercialized world. In *NXIVM Corporation v. The Ross Institute,* the court argued that if the new work of criticism damages the market share of the original—because its critique is convincing—it still does not constitute copyright infringement. In this case, thankfully, free speech trumped property rights. Quoting the Supreme Court, the Court of Appeals stated that a "lethal parody, like a scathing theater review, kills demand for the original, [but] does not produce a harm cognizable under the Copyright Act."

The court went on to say that if criticisms "kill the demand for plaintiffs' service, that is the price that, under the First Amendment, must be paid in the open marketplace of ideas." In his concurring opinion, Judge Dennis Jacobs stated that "copyright is not about virtue; it is about the encouragement of creative output, including the output of transformative quotation." Arguing more generally for the importance of fair use in a democratic society, he stated, "Certainly, no critic should need an author's permission to make such a criticism . . . nor should publication be inhibited by a publisher's anxiety or uncertainty about an author's ethics if his secondary work is transformative."

Fair use isn't a blank check; courts have stated that there need to be good reasons why a use that causes economic harm should be considered fair—reasons such as cultural criticism, parody, and political commentary. When looking beyond the United States, whose strong fair-use legal tradition is unique, it is clear that its effectiveness as a weapon of free speech is quite limited by geography. Professor Rosemary Coombe, reminding us that America isn't the world, refers to fair use as "a local ordinance in a global information economy."

Nevertheless, it's comforting for Americans such as myself that we have these rulings that reaffirm fair-use rights. Comfort is nice, but it's even more important to not back down when the brand bullies try to shake us down. For instance, in 1992 the satirical, anti–consumer culture magazine *Adbusters* produced a parody of Absolut Vodka's long-running ad campaign. In the fake ad copy's fine print, it stated, "Any suggestion that our advertising campaigns have contributed to alcoholism, drunk driving, or wife and child beating is absolute nonsense. No one pays attention to advertising." Absolut quickly threatened a lawsuit, demanding a retraction and the destruction of all remaining issues containing the spoof ad— which the magazine refused to do. Instead, *Adbusters* sent out a press release, "Absolut Vodka Tries to Censor Magazine," and printed in its next issue another mock ad featuring a coffin shaped like an Absolut bottle.

Keith McIntyre, an executive at Absolut Vodka Canada, warned the magazine, "If you want Absolut to play hardball, then Absolut will play hardball." It never did, most likely because *Adbusters* made it clear it would fight Absolut in the court of public opinion.[39] The fact that a forceful criticism may economically hurt a copyright or trademark holder is a worst-case scenario, though it's necessary to ensure that freedom of expression® thrives in the corporate age. It's possible that *Adbusters*'s anti-ad dissuaded a few people from buying the company's vodka, and perhaps from driving drunk, but the latter is clearly a good thing, right? In most instances, though, derivative works don't harm the value of the original. For instance, 2 Live Crew's ugly reworking of "Pretty Woman" didn't supercede or make obsolescent Roy Orbison's original; it simply added diversity to the available pool of culture. That, in a nutshell, is the purpose of copyright.

CHAPTER FIVE

OUR PRIVATIZED WORLD

selling off the public square, culture, education, our democracy,

and everything else

One of my favorite modern day parables involves a Wisconsin performance-art troupe named, fittingly enough, Nu Parable. During the 1980s this group was notable for enacting what they called "Dances of Death," which dramatized the carnage of nuclear war by using dozens of writhing, choreographed bodies. Nu Parable could freely dance in areas that were designated as public spaces, such as downtowns. However, when they ventured into the private property of a shopping mall and other such spaces, they were arrested for trespassing. The funniest and saddest part of the story is that some Nu Parable members were successfully prosecuted for passing out copies of the First Amendment. The problem was that they distributed this founding document of American free speech against the mall management's wishes, sending them straight from the food court to state court.

The shopping mall works as an apt metaphor for what has happened to cultural and economic life in America, a symptom and a cause of the erosion of our freedom of expression®. We've all heard of these things called "downtowns." They still exist in more than a few cities and towns throughout the United States, but they have increasingly become anomalies in a landscape cluttered with suburban shopping and strip malls. Downtown was where people used to mix with other community members for economic and social reasons, and occasionally participate in societal change by exercising their First Amendment rights of free assembly and free speech.

The deterioration of the American downtown began after World War II, and its slow, choking death wasn't natural. It had more to do with certain local and federal government policies, including those that undermined public transportation in favor of the automobile and an elaborate interstate system. It also didn't help that General Motors bought up public-transportation companies in most American cities and systematically dismantled the streetcar system. In doing so, they replaced it with a fleet of GM buses, ripping up trolley tracks, and making way for the post–WWII flood of automobiles. The streetcars were the arteries that made downtowns accessible to large numbers of people, but by 1950 the number of streetcars in the United States fell to eighteen thousand, down from seventy-three thousand in 1936—despite an explosion in the nation's population.

In 1949 the federal government found GM (and its partners in crime, Firestone and Standard Oil) guilty of "conspiracy to monopolize the local transportation field," and seven high-ranking executives at those companies were individually found guilty. However, the companies were fined only five thousand dollars each and the execs were slapped on the wrist with a one-dollar fine. Investigative journalist Jonathan Kwitny argues that the case was "a fine example of what can happen when important matters of public policy are abandoned by government to the self-interest of corporations."

These are the first of many instances to come in this chapter that show how the privatization of public resources—whether cultural or physical—can be socially damaging when the controlling private interests are subject to little oversight.

FREEDOM OF EXPRESSION® GOES TO THE MALL

The displacement of the downtown as the center of social and economic life in America brought many significant changes. The downtown belonged to everyone—in theory, at least, and sometimes in practice; but most state courts and legislatures have claimed that the free-speech rights we are guaranteed in public places do not extend equally to private property. This makes it possible for someone in a mall to be arrested for wearing an "objectionable" T-shirt. During the buildup to Gulf War 2.0, on March 3, 2003, a lawyer named Steve Downs was arrested for trespassing at the Crossgates Mall in Albany, New York, because he refused to remove a T-shirt that declared "Peace on Earth" and "Give Peace a Chance." (The most absurd detail: the offending shirt had been purchased *at the mall*.)

Officials claimed that it violated a mall policy that banned clothing that is "disruptive," stating that the mall's management "is committed to maintaining the mall as a family-friendly facility that provides a secure and enjoyable experience." The press release reminded us, "While Crossgates Mall is perceived by some to be a public place, it is privately owned." After it had made its chilling point, the mall quietly dropped the charges. This outrageous incident induced in me a bout of self-righteous indignation. I sped to the Coral Ridge Mall in Coralville, Iowa—a strip-mauled town that doesn't seem to believe in zoning laws—armed with a stack of First Amendment fliers, and nothing else. It took less than five minutes before a mall-security officer informed me of the establishment's solicitation policy. With a friendly Iowan smile I explained that I wasn't selling anything. I deadpanned that I was passing out copies of the First Amendment because I worried that these shoppers weren't aware that it existed.

Regardless, the security man told me, I was not allowed to distribute unauthorized literature on the mall's property—not just inside, but outside in the parking lot as well. I handed him a copy of the First Amendment, which he refused to accept. "Our Constitution guarantees me the right to do exactly what I'm doing," I argued earnestly. With a matching Midwestern smile, he informed me that he would call the police if I didn't obey his instructions. I called his bluff, only it wasn't a bluff, because I soon found myself talking to two of Coralville's finest, who sized me up and checked my ID (this is post-9/11, after all). They politely, though condescendingly, told me that if I did not leave I would be arrested for trespassing. (Also, the Coralville cops confiscated my copies of the First Amendment. Where are the irony police when you need them?) Realizing that I should choose my battles carefully, I vacated the premises as directed.

In the urban downtowns, retail superstores such as the Virgin Megastore, Barnes & Noble, and Borders have replaced public squares much like suburban shopping malls have. Even the things that traditionally have been regarded as public squares are being branded and privatized, Naomi Klein points out. In 1997 anti-tobacco protesters were forcibly removed from Nathan Phillips Square in front of Toronto's city hall during a jazz festival. The festival was sponsored by a tobacco company, and during the week of the festival this public space essentially became the private property of the company, which exercised its policing power by kicking dissenters out. That same year, anti-tobacco protesters were removed from their own campus in Toronto during the du Maurier Tennis

Open because the students objected to the fact that it was sponsored by a tobacco giant. Throughout North America, business districts are being turned into little more than outdoor malls with real cops, rather than rent-a-cops, policing the area.

When it hosted the 2002 Winter Olympics, Salt Lake City set up "free-speech zones" (George Orwell, please phone home) placed away from the heavy pedestrian traffic flow. This procedure severely limited the impact of so-called free speech. In Seattle, during the 1999 World Trade Organization meetings, protest was approved for certain regions, but police fiercely protected other areas, provoking riots. Similarly, the Secret Service, charged with protecting the U.S. president, has also set up free-speech zones to keep protesters away from Bush 2.0. For instance, on Labor Day of 2002, sixty-five-year-old retired steelworker Bill Neel was arrested for holding a sign critical of Bush. When he refused to move to a distant baseball field surrounded by a chain-link fence, Neel was charged with "disorderly conduct" and his sign was confiscated.

"As far as I'm concerned," said Neel, "the whole country is a free-speech zone." He was later acquitted, as was Brett Bursey, who was charged with trespassing when he held a No War for Oil sign. Bursey refused to move to a designated area roughly a half mile from the location where Bush was to speak. He got off because South Carolina law prohibits trespassing arrests on public property—another example of how public land, a kind of commons, helps enable freedom of expression®. However, John Ashcroft's Justice Department took over the case and charged Bursey with violating an obscure federal law regarding "entering a restricted area around the president of the United States."[1] If citizens can only legally express themselves in certain free-speech zones it begs the question, what is the rest of the city called? I'm reminded of an old Guerrilla Girls' poster, the one that asks:

Q: If February is Black History Month and March is Women's History Month, what happens the rest of the year?

A: Discrimination.

Intellectual property and physical property also intersect when a number of companies go to extreme lengths to control visual reproductions of their buildings. The director of publishing at FPG International, one of the largest stock-photo agencies, claims this kind of representation has increasingly affected the firm's business. If someone wants to use an existing photograph of a building in FPG's stock-photo library, FPG often informs the customer that certain property owners require special releases or, in some cases, "licensing fees" (imagine having to pay to "sample" a building). "What's happened," says Rebecca Taylor, "is we've had to establish certain business practices based on the harassment factor. It's become part of doing business—it's just one more thing we have to worry about." Because of this harassment factor, FPG tells photographers who are currently shooting images that certain buildings aren't worth the trouble.

"Whether these property owners really have these trademark rights is questionable," says Taylor, "but we've decided it's an issue that's not worth fighting over." Among the Manhattan property owners who aggressively protect their trademarks are the New York Stock Exchange, the Chrysler Building, Rockefeller Center, and even the New York Public Library. "It's sort of a pain for us," says Taylor, speaking of the impact of these licensing arrangements on freedom of expression®. "But," she explains, "it's far riskier for small companies that don't have the legal resources we have." Nancy Wolff, an intellectual property–law attorney in New York City, agrees. "Photographers and designers don't have the budgets to get releases for everything," she says. "And even though there is very little legal basis for preventing artists from using these images, they are often too small to fight because the cost of litigation is so great."[2]

Not everyone in the United States and abroad is allowing our public and cultural space to be colonized without a fight. Citizens were up in arms when, in 2003 Vienna's Karlsplatz—a public square of historical importance—displayed the "Nike Infobox." It was a slick walk-in container with two floors that sported a sign that declared to passersby: "This square will soon be called Nikeplatz. Come inside to find out more." During its monthlong residency, which ended on October 28, 2003, thousands of brochures were also distributed throughout the city that laid out plans for the "Nike Ground" campaign. "Nike is introducing its legendary brand into squares, streets, parks and boulevards," declared the propaganda found inside the Nike Infobox. "Nikesquare, Nike Street, Piazzanike, Plazanike or Nikestrasse will appear in major world capitals over the coming years!"

If that wasn't enough to rile up the average Viennese resident, the Infobox went on to promise that a 36 × 18 meter monument in the shape of Nike's "Swoosh" logo would be placed in the center of "Nikeplatz." People freaked out, and soon thousands of e-mails and handwritten letters descended on Austrian newspapers and city governments. The incident turned out to be a clever prank engineered by a band of media artists collectively known as 0100101110101101.ORG. Its intent was to create a mass hallucination in which Vienna itself was the theater; as Shakespeare famously observed, all the world is a stage.

In a press release, the collective stated, "It is our duty to directly intervene into urban and media space, to bring up the issues of symbolic domination in public space by private interests. We see Nike Ground as a statement for the artistic freedom to manipulate the symbols of everyday life." Their intent was to provoke conversation and debate, and judging by the intense negative feedback generated, they succeeded. The artists also provoked a lawsuit from Nike, which objected to their satirical use of its trademarked name and logo. "These actions have gone beyond a joke," Nike stated. "This is not just a prank, it's a breach of our copyright and therefore Nike will take legal action against the instigators of this phony campaign."

Nike lost the first round on a technicality (it filed in the wrong jurisdiction), which meant that the Nike Ground display was allowed to remain for the planned monthlong period—before Nike could file for another injunction. After a torrent of bad publicity, first brought on by the activists and then by its own lawsuit, Nike declined to pursue the matter. The nikeground.com Web site, hosted by the Austrian media activists at Public Netbase, stayed online, and freedom of expression® remained untrammeled. "We won!" declared 0100101110101101.ORG spokesman Franco Birkut. "Our victory is proof of at least one thing: the famous 'Swoosh' logo belongs to the people who actually wear it every day. These commercial giants think they can beat anyone who annoys them, and they're unable to distinguish an artistic or critical project from unfair competition or commercial fraud."

Public Netbase director Konrad Becker said, "It was worth the risk in order to insist on the right to free artistic expression in urban spaces." Like other antiglobalization and anti-sweatshop activists, 0100101110101101.ORG uses the lumbering cultural weight of the Swoosh against Nike like a Derridaian judo master who trips up her philosophical opponent. They tacitly acknowledged this tactic when the group's spokesperson Ted Pikul stated, "Nike is a perfect subject for a work of art. The Swoosh is probably the most viewable brand on earth, more than any political or religious symbol. Now these giants are losing control over their own brands, which in the hands of pop culture are turning into boomerangs."[3]

PRIVATIZING NATURE

At the inauguration of Everglades National Park in 1948, President Harry S Truman said, "We have to remain constantly vigilant to prevent raids by those who would selfishly exploit our common heritage for their private gain. Such raids on our natural resources are not examples of enterprise and initiative. They are attempts to take from all the people for the benefit of a few." These words of wisdom—a strong argument for maintaining the commons—are being drowned out by the loud, well-funded voices who cheer on the cause of privatization. "We in Western society are going through a period of intensifying belief in private ownership, to the detriment of the public good," lamented John Sulston, who won the Nobel Prize for spearheading the British effort to map the human genome.[4]

Private corporations argue that *they* can better manage the common wealth—national parks, the radio spectrum, and water supplies, for instance—that is supposed to belong to all. They say "corporate management is obviously more ideal because market norms are the grease that lubricate the wheels of efficiency and innovation." Put that way, it's hard to imagine another system ever working, but one did, for decades. Some things were purchased, some things were freely traded, and not everything was nailed down with a price tag and managed by private interests. The existence of a commons is an essential part of what some economists and social scientists refer to as the gift economy. Today's successful open-source software movement, and the rise of the Internet itself, is proof that a gift economy still exists and thrives.

The collection and free distribution of weather data, untethered to any intellectual-property rights, is a kind of U.S. government–sponsored gift economy. It's an informational commons that both directly and indirectly benefits Americans by bolstering public safety and protecting the nation's economic assets. Also, because the U.S. government freely distributes this data, it produces raw material for a booming meteorology and risk-management industry valued in the billions. Conversely, some E.U. governments actually enforce restrictive data policies regarding national meteorological services, which has stunted the growth of these sectors in Europe.[5] "There's no such thing as a free lunch," the old adage goes, but there are many cases where gift-giving can generate many rich returns—both economically *and* socially.

"Gift economies are potent systems for eliciting and developing behaviors that the market cannot—sharing, collaboration, honor, trust, sociability, loyalty," writes David Bollier, the cofounder of Public Knowledge, an advocacy group dedicated to defending the commons of the Internet, science, and culture. "In this capacity," Bollier continues, "gift economies are an important force in creating wealth—both the material kind prized by the market as well as the social and spiritual kind needed by any happy, integrated human being."[6] We should remember that market norms, which are often taken to their extreme by private industry, run counter to social norms such as *ethics*.

A notorious example of this conflict of values is Ford Motor Company's decision to not replace potentially explosive gas tanks in Pinto cars in the 1970s. The company's cost-benefit analysis demonstrated that it was cheaper to pay settlements on the 180 or so annual burn-related deaths than to spend eleven dollars more per vehicle for a safer gas tank. This is a decision guided by market norms, not the kind of social norms that benefit humanity. In Philip Morris's attempt to squash proposed cigarette taxes in the

Czech Republic, the tobacco company sponsored a study that claimed that the government would actually *save* $147.1 million from the premature deaths of smokers. "The truth is," argues John Sulston, "that companies don't have to behave ethically: they can if they want to, but there's no social constraint on their pushing acquisitiveness to the legal limit; or indeed beyond."[7]

It is true that privatization sometimes succeeds in improving service and efficiency, but the privatizations that go badly can be catastrophic. We see this time and time again with the privatization schemes insisted upon by the World Bank and International Monetary Fund (IMF). These organizations require developing countries to agree to unfavorable terms if money is to be loaned. An unsettling case is Bolivia, which felt the impact of these policies when it borrowed heavily from the World Bank and the IMF in the 1980s. In return, it agreed to open its borders to trade and privatize its industries. Seventeen years later, Bolivia remains the poorest country in South America, with its labor unions smashed and hundreds of thousands of workers tossed into the "informal sector" of sweatshops and street peddling.

The country's railroad, which was turned over to a consortium led by the private Chilean multinational Cruz Blanca, cut service on routes it considered unprofitable. This meant that numerous freight and passenger lines were closed, including one that connected Bolivia's capital with its third largest city—a move that helped cripple the country's infrastructure. This decision was guided by market norms that didn't take into consideration the economic and *social* impact of shutting down those "inefficient" routes. Nobel Prize–winning economist Joseph E. Stiglitz said that during his time at the World Bank, "I saw decisions were often made because of ideology and politics. As a result many wrongheaded actions were taken, ones that did not solve the problem at hand but that fit with the interests or beliefs of people in power."

The issue of water-resource management is one of the many areas that undermine the arguments about the benefits of privatization. Developing countries are pressured to liberalize and open up their markets to outside investors, which buy up existing water infrastructures and control the cost of water. Once this public resource becomes private property, its distribution is overseen by "the market." That's a fancy way of saying that water is redirected to those who can pay for it. Coca-Cola, for instance, owns a bottling plant in Planchimara, India, that consumes six hundred thousand liters of fresh water daily; the residents of the village, on the other hand, suffer from water shortages.[8]

Some say that in times of scarcity, unregulated markets work more efficiently. But who do you think can decide how to better handle resources more efficiently: the foreign company that uses thousands of cubic tons of water to irrigate crops to feed cattle that will be slaughtered and shipped off to the First World—or the local community that would use only one percent of that water for crops to feed itself? Applying the ideology of the free market, the first choice is economically profitable, albeit socially destructive, and the second choice is not.

Warfare is another unfortunate area of modern life that has been transformed by privatization. For instance, during the first Gulf War in 1991, the government employed one private contractor for every hundred soldiers, but by the second Gulf War, that ratio had changed to roughly one in ten. As much as one-third of the steadily growing cost of occupying Iraq fills the coffers of private U.S. firms that profit handsomely from the carnage of war.[9] Not only did American taxpayers pay Halliburton to import oil *into* Iraq, the company charged us nearly three times the going rate until this fact was made public.[10] This is what I mean by "inefficient and costly" privatization schemes. And by "irrational and destructive," I mean war itself, especially preemptive wars that are waged at a high cost to human life, the environment, and domestic social programs at home.

INTELLECTUAL PROPERTY V. FREE SPEECH AND DEMOCRACY

INTELLECTUAL PROPERTY V. FREE SPEECH AND DEMOCRACY

If you saw the headline "File-Trading Students Out to Save Democracy," you'd think it might be a spoof. But it's literally true. These students weren't trading MP3 files on peer-to-peer networks and on the Web. Rather, in late 2003 college students received cease-and-desist letters from a company named Diebold, which makes voting machines. This unlikely scenario unfolded when a handful of student voting activists posted fifteen thousand copyrighted documents on their Web sites, which prompted a familiar sequence of events: the company sent colleges threatening letters, which in turn removed the content from their networks, which made the students really, really mad.

What were the documents? They were thousands of internal memos, e-mails, and discussion-list postings that were leaked and then posted on an electronic-voting activist's Web site. After that, they multiplied like bionic bunnies. The contents painted a behind-the-scenes picture of Diebold that wasn't flattering, to say the least. In these documents are a myriad of statements that suggest the company's electronic voting machines contain many security problems and bugs in the software, as well as last-minute changes that are illegal after election authorities certify software for an election. Among the most disturbing was the following frantic missive concerning the reliability of the company's machines during the 2000 presidential election:

> I need some answers! Our department is being audited by the County. I have been waiting for someone to give me an explanation as to why Precinct 216 gave Al Gore a minus 16022 when it

was uploaded. Will someone please explain this so that I have the information to give the auditor instead of standing here "looking dumb." I would appreciate an explanation on why the memory cards start giving check sum messages. We had this happen in several precincts and one of these precincts managed to get her memory card out of election mode and then back in it, continued to read ballots, not realizing that the 300+ ballots she had read earlier were no longer stored in her memory card. Needless to say when we did our hand count this was discovered.

Any explantations [sic] you all can give me will be greatly appreciated.

Thanks bunches,

Lana [Hires]

Diebold claimed that it owned the copyright to these memos, which was true. But these vote- and boat-rocking students argued that their postings were a fair use of the company's materials because it was in the context of news reporting and criticism. What was most obvious was that Diebold used copyright law as a tool to attempt to censor embarrassing revelations, and nothing more. This is yet another disturbing way that the Digital Millennium Copyright Act gives copyright owners more power to erase dissent, merely by sending a "take down" notice to ISPs or Web hosting companies. "The DMCA issues do muddy the water," said John Palfrey, executive director of the Berkman Center for Internet and Society at Harvard Law School. "I don't think this is a slam dunk on either side." Although some students continued to keep the documents on their own servers, others felt the chilling effect of cease-and-desist letters. "I'm starting to worry about the ramifications for my entire family if I end up in some sort of legal action," said Zac Elliott, a student at Indiana University.[11]

However, Diebold's attempt to put out this digital fire only fanned the flames. The documents exponentially multiplied as computer-savvy voting activists linked to other Web sites and distributed them across peer-to-peer file-sharing networks. Within weeks the memos spread to dozens of colleges, including Duke University, Harvard University, Massachusetts Institute of Technology, and Grinnell College, down the road from me in a neighboring Iowa town. If Dr. Dre, Metallica, and the entire music industry couldn't stop music downloading, what made this company think it could stop these committed students? In the midst of the controversy, a Diebold spokesman said with a straight face, "We reserve the right to protect that which we feel is proprietary." A Swarthmore College sophomore astutely countered, "If I were Diebold I wouldn't claim copyright protection; I'd claim I hadn't written the memos."[12]

Another Swarthmore student, Nelson Pavlosky, one of the co-organizers of FreeCulture.org's "Barbie in a Blender Day," was on the front line of the anti-Diebold resistance. Still only a teenager when Diebold aimed its copyright guns at him, the tall, thin, and unassuming Pavlosky seemed an unlikely activist when I first met him in 2004. What was a nineteen-year-old undergrad doing fighting to preserve the fundamental mechanics of the democratic voting process? "Well, I grew up Quaker and was taught to witness for the truth," Pavlosky tells me. "I guess my family is nonconformist, and I was brought up to do what's right, and this seemed like the right thing to do—and something I could make a difference in." And he did; Pavlosky sued Diebold.

The student voting activists' electronic civil disobedience is but a fragment of a larger, more important controversy. It's a story about handing over the nuts and bolts of the democratic voting process to private interests. Unfortunately, states have signed contracts that make it not only difficult, but often illegal, to have the machines examined by a third party because the company's software is heavily fortified by copyright, patent, and trade-secrecy law. This means that there are few legal ways for citizens to look for security flaws and other errors in electronic-voting software and machines. For instance, a Georgia woman claimed she could crack Diebold's system in minutes, and Secretary of State Cathy Cox accepted that challenge. But the woman had to back down after being informed it was a criminal offense to be given the programming code that operated the e-voting machine.

After the Georgia election, a Diebold technician admitted that at first the machines performed erratically when they were shipped to Georgia and they had to be fixed with a last-minute software "patch." Because the programmer was in Canada, the patch—and the entire software package—was transmitted via Internet, through an unsecured FTP, or file transfer protocol, server. (One of Diebold's competitors, Sequoia, also suffered embarrassment in 2003 when its software was left unprotected on an open FTP server.) Any computer expert will tell you that this is a fundamental breach of security, and the only good thing to come out of this leak was that it allowed analysts to peer into Diebold's tightly protected software, because it was copied from the server by e-voting activists and openly posted on the Internet.

Numerous people did the same thing, including Roxanne Jekot, a computer programmer with over twenty years' experience. She found enough shoddy programming in her line-by-line review to, as she said, "stand your hair on end." Littered throughout the code were programmers' comments such as "This doesn't really work." Diebold issued several press releases denying the conclusions of various negative studies, but the bad reviews kept coming in. The state of Maryland, which purchased Diebold machines, commissioned a study that found 328 software flaws, 26 of them critical, something that put the system "at high risk of compromise."[13] A later report presented to Maryland state legislators found that Diebold's voting machines "have such poor computer security and physical security that an election could be disrupted or even stolen by corrupt insiders or determined outsiders."

One reason the privatized election business should be more transparent is that these companies can and do contribute to political parties. Diebold, for instance, is a heavy Republican supporter. In the two years after 2000, the company gave $195,000 to the Republican Party, and its CEO, Walden W. O'Dell, wrote to campaign contributors in 2003 that he was "committed to helping Ohio deliver its electoral votes to the president next year." I'm sure he did not literally mean that he would use his company to tamper with voting machines to illegally swing the Ohio elections Bush's way; nevertheless, this statement makes me uneasy, and I feel no better now that the company announced that O'Dell would take a lower political profile. (I *want* to know what he's up to.)

In another eyebrow-raising situation, in 1996 Chuck Hagel became the first Republican in twenty-four years to be elected to the Senate by Nebraskans, thanks in part to the efforts of campaign director Michael McCarthy. Interestingly, the McCarthy Group owns Election Systems and Software (ES&S), the voting-machine company that counted—under the usual terms of confidentiality—the election results that sent Hagel to Congress. If you suspect the McCarthy who served as Hagel's campaign director in 1996 and 2002 has any affiliation with the McCarthy Group, you're right. Michael McCarthy founded the company. Also, according to Mr. McCarthy, "Hagel still owns up to $5 million in the ES&S parent company, the McCarthy Group."[14] The state's largest newspaper, the *Omaha World-Herald,* declined to report on this conflict of interest, most likely because—get this—the paper also owns a stake in ES&S.

What is sorely missing in this picture is a public policy that regu-

lates, and prevents, these kinds of conflicts of interest from occurring. Government regulation is hugely important in matters like
these because the free market just *does not care* about the democratic process. In fact, the principles of the free-market economy
work against the egalitarianism of democratic theory. It doesn't
ease concerns to know that the government agency that sets standards for e-voting, the U.S. Election Assistance Commission, is ter-
ribly underfunded. The commission released a report in 2004 that
stated that the lack of funding made it impossible to develop a national system for testing voting machines before that year's presidential elections. This, despite the fact there are a lot of profits to be
made in e-voting—billions, in fact. In 2001 President Bush signed
the Help America Vote Act (HAVA), which allocated $3.9 billion to
states that adopt electronic polling machines. Cash registers rang,
and so did alarm bells.

During the 2002 Georgia state elections, run by Diebold, there
were numerous unsettling incidents that cut to the heart of the
e-voting controversies. In downtown Atlanta, sixty-seven memory
cards from the voting machines disappeared, which delayed election certification for ten days. In nearby DeKalb County, ten memory cards went missing and were later found in the terminals that
had broken down. In these cases, and others, it is unclear how the
results from the missing cards were tabulated (or if they were
counted at all) because the election results are the company's private property, protected by copyright and trade-secrecy laws. One
of HAVA's major flaws is that it doesn't require paper documentation of votes; it only calls for electronically stored results, forcing us
to trust companies such as Diebold to do the right thing—or at
least be competent.[15]

In Fairfax, Virginia, voters reported malfunctions during the
2003 elections that may have swung another close race. County of-

ficials tested one machine and discovered that it seemed to subtract a vote for Republican Rita S. Thompson in "one out of a hundred tries."[16] After the 2004 presidential primaries, Alameda County, California, the oldest West Coast customer of Diebold, cited "disappointment and dissatisfaction" with the company's voting machines after it used poorly tested, uncertified voter-card encoders that broke down in two hundred polling stations. In Oakland, poorly tested and faulty Diebold software and hardware caused voters to be turned away during the 2004 primaries.

One senior California elections official observed, "Diebold may suffer from gross incompetence, or gross negligence. I don't know whether there's any malevolence involved." The head of California's elections office, Kevin Shelley, called for a criminal investigation, claiming that Diebold's actions amounted to "reprehensible" fraud. After its primaries in Indiana, Marion County officials discovered ES&S had unlawfully installed software used to compile and tabulate votes and failed to notify the county clerk. The Marion county clerk Doris Anne Sadler, a Republican, blasted ES&S, stating that this was "criminal activity of the worst level: an absolute, total attempt to deceive."[17] None of these early field tests bolstered confidence in the way the 2004 presidential elections were counted.

These anecdotes all illustrate compelling reasons why the workings of electronic-voting systems should be more transparent, and why the software code should be "open source," rather than proprietary. With open source, anyone can examine the code, and the stellar security track record for open-source software such as Linux and Apache demonstrates the benefits of this approach. These open-source programs tend to be far more secure than their Microsoft counterparts, which are cloaked in secrecy. "Our society and our democracy is better served by open voting systems," said Cindy Cohn, an attorney at the Electronic Frontier Foundation (EFF). She told *Wired News,* "The way to create a more secure system is to open the source code and to have as many people as possible try to break into the system and figure out all the holes. The clearest way to have an insecure system is to lock it up and show it to only a few people." E-voting companies really don't have much to fear, because this kind of product would be extremely difficult to pirate (it's highly unlikely states are going to buy bootleg voting machines from shady characters).

At the end of 2003 Diebold gave up trying to protect the fifteen thousand "copyrighted" documents after weathering a torrential public-relations storm. More important, it gave up after the Electronic Frontier Foundation and the Stanford Cyberlaw Clinic filed a lawsuit to protect these e-voting activists' First Amendment rights. Only through these efforts did things begin to change. The negative publicity surrounding the Diebold memos, and what they revealed, helped gain momentum for a campaign to make e-voting safer. Kevin Shelley, California's top elections official, mandated that e-voting machines must have a "voter verified paper audit trail," and a handful of states such as Ohio did the same thing. However, the vast majority of states instituted no such policy.

In so many instances of overzealous copyright bozoism, the law is not on the side of those who try to apply it improperly. Many times, all it takes is an individual to call a company's bluff or an organization such as the Electronic Frontier Foundation to counter attacks on free speech. In fact, many of these censorious uses of copyright law have had a boomerang effect. In making frivolous claims on its copyrights, Diebold succeeded only in setting a precedent that opened up *more* possibilities for freedom of expression® online. This event demonstrated to activists and ordinary people that they need not be afraid of threats that are based on unfounded assertions of intellectual-property rights. Or, at least, they should be less fearful.

PRIVATIZING PUBLIC INFORMATION

Not only is e-voting information proprietary, even facts about *us* are being privatized. Companies that sell information to marketers collect and sort the data trails we leave behind with our ATM withdrawals, credit-card purchases, plane flights, and the vast data drawn from public records. The government's Total Information Awareness (TIA) database, which was designed to collect and cross-reference data about private citizens drawn from these commercial databases, was axed by Congress because of privacy concerns. But what has arisen in its place is something worse: similar databases run by private companies. The scariest is called the MATRIX. The poorly chosen acronym stands for Multistate Anti-TeRrorism Information eXchange (I guess they thought they'd beat *The Onion* and other satirists to the punch).

"The power of this technology—to take seemingly isolated bits of data and tie them together to get a clear picture in seconds—is vital to strengthening our domestic security," said James "Tim" Moore, commissioner of the Florida Department of Law Enforcement when the state entered the MATRIX. Phil Ramer, Florida's intelligence chief, had another opinion. "It's scary," he said candidly. "It could be abused. I mean, I can call up everything about you, your pictures and pictures of your neighbors." Seisint, Inc., owns and operates the database, which is funded by individual states, though it was developed with a federal grant. The MATRIX was also earmarked for funds from the Justice Department and the Department of Homeland Security.

This information is proprietary, which means we citizens don't have the same rights under the Freedom of Information Act to peer into our files, another hidden cost of privatization. "I won't lie to you," admitted Lt. Col. Ralph Periandi, deputy commissioner for operations with the Pennsylvania state police. "This system is not just being used to investigate terrorism." Asked whether or not the MATRIX could lead to a world where authorities can monitor everything, much as the machines do in *The Matrix,* the motion picture, Periandi said with a laugh, and I imagine it to be a sinister laugh, "I guess it comes down to whether you trust the police or not."[18]

Late in 2002 a confidential source gave CNet reporter Declan McCullagh a password that could have aided his research. This opened up encrypted documents on the Transportation Security Administration (TSA) Web site—documents that contained details of the working relationships of federal and local police and airport security. The DMCA states that "no person shall circumvent a technological measure" that protects copyrighted information, nor can one publish information that circumvents "a technological measure that effectively controls access" to a copyrighted document. The reporter thought twice about entering the password, so he called the Justice Department, though his phone call further muddied the waters.

"There are always determinations that must be made in any allegation of criminal wrongdoing," stated Brian Sierra, a department spokesman, cryptically. "Our policy is to enforce the law. If the law is being violated we will investigate, and we may prosecute." Materials prepared by government employees cannot be copyrighted. And because the DMCA only makes it a criminal act to break the encryption on *copyrighted* goods, McCullagh should've had nothing to worry about. However, the government has privatized many of its operations by outsourcing information collection and processing. Sure enough, these documents were copyrighted by Deloitte Consulting, making it a tougher call for the reporter because he could very well be charged with DMCA violations. "It's not every day," McCullagh wrote in 2002, "that I fret about committing a string of federal felonies that could land me in prison until some-time in 2008."

Although it's possible that a court would consider this type of DMCA breach to be fair use, because it was for the purpose of news reporting, McCullagh chose not to find out the hard way. Under the current DMCA regime—and in the way its authority has been overreached several times—it's more difficult to publish something akin to the Pentagon Papers. In 1971 former Pentagon official Daniel Ellsberg leaked the military's internal history of the Vietnam War, which proved the government had lied to its citizens in several important ways. Ellsberg's leak to the *New York Times* and the *Washington Post* contributed to a chain of events that helped end the war, an example of how free information flow is important for democracy.

Under the DMCA, however, the federal government would have grounds to prosecute an informant who leaked the protected infor-mation or password, or a journalist who picked the digital lock on a federal document prepared by a private company. As the U.S. gov-ernment continues to increase secrecy and roll back civil liberties, it's quite possible that the DMCA might be used by the Department of Justice for repressive purposes. This possibility highlights one of the main problems with this law: It contains very narrow "fair use" exemptions, and the few exemptions that do exist are vague enough to scare away potential do-gooders and whistle-blowers.

In an example of DMCA prosecution gone awry, on July 16, 2001, a foreign computer programmer was arrested and detained for months when he gave a conference presentation in Nevada. No, he wasn't an al-Qaeda operative. Dmitry Sklyarov was a software programmer representing his company, ElcomSoft, based in Russia. Federal agents arrested Mr. Sklyarov for violating the DMCA and charged him with trafficking in and offering to the public a software program that allowed a consumer to copy e-books onto one's laptop computer or PDA. The interesting thing is that Sklyarov and company weren't accused of infringing any copyrights, and their Advanced eBook Processor was designed so that it could be used only by people who had already lawfully purchased an e-book from a retailer. However, merely *designing* a software program that breaks copy protection is a criminal act.

Sklyarov was held in jail for nearly a month, then released on fifty thousand dollars bail, though his movements were restricted to northern California. On December 13, 2001, Sklyarov was released from U.S. custody and allowed to return to his home in Russia, but only after he agreed to testify against his employer. During the two-week trial, government prosecutors claimed ElcomSoft created "a tool for burglars." It also characterized the company as "an affiliate of hacker networks that was determined to sell the Advanced eBook Processor despite its questionable legality," something that just wasn't true. ElcomSoft was eventually acquitted by a jury; it decided that the software was illegal but the company didn't know it was violating the law. In other words, this decision upheld the legality of the DMCA, and the defendants were merely lucky because— this time, at least—the jury felt that the company was ignorant of American law.

Even old-school copyright-infringement claims can scare away people who are legitimately using the "unauthorized" material for educational, historical, or other similar purposes. Such was the case with Simon Waldman, the director of digital publishing for Guardian Newspapers who published on his personal Web site a 1938 *Homes & Gardens* puff piece on Adolf Hitler. "There is nothing pretentious about the Führer's little estate," the fawning *Homes & Gardens* article observed. "It is one that any merchant of Munich

or Nuremberg might possess in these lovely hills." When Waldman e-mailed the magazine's current editorial director, Isobel
McKenzie-Price, to inform her about his interesting find, she responded by demanding that he remove the copyrighted article
from his Web site. It was, she said, an "unauthorized reproduction
of IPC's material"; IPC Media is a subsidiary of TimeWarner.

The article referred to Hitler as a "droll raconteur" whose "bright,
airy chalet" had "the fairest view in all of Europe." The magazine
and its parent company obviously didn't want to remind people of
this prose, but as the Bozo-battling Tim Quirk reminded us, "Copyright isn't a right to not look like an idiot." As was the case with the
equally scary Diebold memos, copies of the article replicated themselves throughout the Internet, multiplying much faster after word
leaked that *Homes & Gardens* tried to suppress it. More people
found out about the article because of IPC's protests (and the ensuing articles in the *New York Times* and other papers), making this
attempt at copyright censorship backfire.

EDUCATION IN A PRIVATIZED WORLD

When it comes to education in particular, you'd think that copyright wouldn't trump freedom of expression®, but it does, quite often. There's a professor out there, who I'll refer to as Dr. Nancy X,
who doesn't want me to share the particulars of a copyright horror
story she lived through. Therefore, I've changed some superficial
details to throw the copyright police dogs off her scent. Because of
the nature of her analysis, Dr. X needed to reprint in her book a certain amount of lyrics quoted from the performances of the cover
bands she studied. Going the legitimate route, she sought the permission of song publishers whenever more than two lines of a song
were quoted, which meant she had to pay hundreds of dollars to

several companies. The labyrinthine formula publishing companies used to determine the licensing fee was extremely arbitrary, says the professor, with some representatives from Company Y arriving at a figure by asking her what Company Z charged.

But the real problem occurred when she tried to quote five lines of a song by a popular recording artist. She sent the manuscript pages, just as the song publisher asked, but the context wasn't flattering (the cover performer she wrote about injected sarcastic comments into the lyrics). In response, the company denied her permission to reprint those lyrics or any other lyrics controlled by the publisher—just to be vindictive. "Along with the letter denying permission," Dr. X told me, "they sent me a form to sign promising that I wouldn't use the songs. They've since sent me the same form again. My response has been to ignore these missives, though I'm always afraid this will come back to bite me in the ass."

Dr. X was especially nervous because she went ahead and used the two forbidden songs, though she pared the quotes down to a couple lines each in the published book. It was a seemingly inconsequential amount, but she still didn't want to take any chances, which is why I altered the surface details of the story. After I gave her the chance to preview this manuscript, she even asked me to change how I came to know about the story, because it contained traces of evidence that could identify her book, and her transgression. "Probably, it was idiotic of me to call attention to this at all," she sighed, knowing I was going to write about it—though she doesn't blame me for wanting to tell her tale. "I, too, collected horror stories of this sort for a while," she said, "if only to put my own experience in context, mostly having to do with the exorbitant fees requested of academic authors to reprint a few lines of lyrics in books that barely sell a few hundred copies."

It's a sad day when a scholar has to feel as paranoid as a drug dealer just for doing her job. This isn't an isolated story, either. It happens with shocking regularity to scholars who choose to write about popular culture, something Professor Sheila Whitely commented on in her article " 'The Sound of Silence': Academic Freedom and Copyright." Responding to Whitely's piece, Professor Timothy Taylor concurred in his essay "Fair Use Isn't Fair," giving examples of the way his publisher's copyright policies constrained the contents of his book *Global Pop*. Taylor stated,

> My editor at Routledge tended to be extremely cautious about such matters; if we had a refusal from anyone, no matter how unconsidered, he wouldn't allow anything to be reprinted save the usual four or five lines of lyrics. I don't think this is an unusual practice on his part, but simply cautious; no editor wants to be the person of whom an example is made in a lawsuit. And this, of course, is the way the "industry" operates: they can't go after everyone, but they can go after someone in enforcing their extremely narrow (and, to them, profitable) notion of what "fair use" means.

The fifteenth edition of the *Chicago Manual of Style,* a venerable resource for writers and editors, points out that "many publishers tend to seek permission if they have the slightest doubt whether a particular use is fair. This is unfortunate. The right of fair use is valuable to scholarship, and it should not be allowed to decay because scholars fail to employ it boldly." The chilling atmosphere that blankets copyright won't lift until the Routledges and Random Houses of the world begin loosening their restrictive internal policies—policies that don't reflect the possibilities that the fair-use statute grants. These kinds of policies for permissions were set in stone at most big publishing houses before the fair-use statute was codified in the 1976 Copyright Act, a federal law. At the time, fair use was an amalgamation of state and common law, so it's understandable that some presses were cautious.

Today, however, there's no reason why they should remain so conservative, especially after numerous Supreme Court decisions have expanded what is allowable under fair use. I don't mean to just pick on corporations, because there are countless instances when universities have not stood up for practices that are clearly fair use. If any institution can confidently invoke the fair-use statute, it is universities, but their lawyers often tend to apply the same kind of overly cautious "risk assessments" that for-profit corporations do. Quite simply, many schools don't want to risk a costly lawsuit, even if it's clear the university will prevail—especially in times of budget cuts.

It's the reason why Indiana University Press withdrew from circulation a book about an obscure composer, the deceased Rebecca Clarke, after the copyright owner of her unpublished writings and music cried foul. Liane Curtis, the editor of *A Rebecca Clarke Reader,* told the *Chronicle of Higher Education* that the alleged infringements added up to 94 lines in a 241-page book. For Curtis, the quoting of this unpublished work in a scholarly context was a fair use, but the university press chose not to find out in court. This kind of overcautious behavior even trickles down to graduate student research. When my Ph.D. advisee Hugo Burgos attempted to reproduce five images that he analyzed in his dissertation, an examiner at the University of Iowa's graduate college told him he would likely have to get permission from the copyright holders. For a freakin' dissertation! Hugo insisted it was fair use, but he still had to meet with a university attorney to do a "risk assessment" before he could keep the images. "They reacted as if I asked to reproduce kiddie porn," observed Hugo, shaking his head.

The Supreme Court ruled that the commercial nature of a work doesn't disqualify it from being "fair," which is the case with my book. No reasonable person could accuse me of excerpting in this tome the lyrics of 2 Live Crew, Woody Guthrie, Ghostface Killah, and the Carter Family as a strategy to boost sales. Nor am I taking away anything from those artists. By quoting them, I'm not undermining their access to the market, because it's very unlikely someone will purchase *Freedom of Expression*® as a substitute for a hip-hop album by Ghostface Killah. The freedom to borrow parts of these songs without having to ask permission is a right the fair-use statute gives me. Unfortunately, I'm not *guaranteed* that right when I work with a big publishing house, a university, or any of the other institutions that I typically deal with in my daily work. However, there are possibilities for individual resistance.

When James Twitchell, a University of Florida professor who studies advertising, received a legal threat after he published his book *Living It Up*, he fought back. Melinda Davis, a representative from the marketing firm the Next Group, discovered he had used in his book an advertising-related term she "coined" in her own public presentations and her book *The New Culture of Desire*. Davis explained in her cease-and-desist letter, "I am sure that you, as an author and speaker yourself, understand all too well that our words and ideas are our product—it is how we live. My business is built on the proprietary communication of concept, and I must protect it." Davis cordially added, "I am copying this letter, not for drama but for administrative thoroughness, to our lawyer, who handles our intellectual property issues."

Twitchell responded to Davis and her attorney—copying me, as well—stating that if the paperback should go to a second edition, he proposed the following changes to his manuscript:

We understand each other not by sharing religion, politics or ideas. We share branded things. We speak the Esperanto© of advertising, *luxe populi©*. (A Melinda Davis has written me, with copies dutifully sent to her legal staff, wishing it be known that she holds the copyright to the second term. She believes she owns the play-on-words and, to some degree, the underlying concept. Ms. Davis is in the brand-consulting business and must, she tells me, be ever vigilant about "the proprietary communication of concept." Hmmmm. Whatever.)

"I want you to understand I have no problem whatsoever with legal protection for a process or an invention," Twitchell told Davis in his biting letter. "But common language—even at its cleverest—is too important to tie up for a spot of porridge. That's where the rubber hits the road. You may have a legal right, but if you ever try to assert it, you should be mocked and derided and shamed." Sut Jhally is another professor who studies advertising and who has been at the receiving end of a cease-and-desist letter. Jhally is also the founder and executive director of the Media Education Foundation (MEF), a nonprofit video-production house based in Northampton, Massachusetts. MEF has been referred to as "the house that *Dreamworlds* built," a reference to a widely viewed educational video about sexist images in music videos, titled *Dreamworlds: Desire/Sex/Power in Rock Video.*

After Jhally began selling *Dreamworlds* to other university professors for classroom use, MTV's lawyers threatened to sue him (and the University of Massachusetts) for copyright and trademark infringement. It's clear that this educational video, which featured a sober British voice lecturing over the video images—without music—did not threaten MTV's market share. MTV simply didn't like what the video said and tried to shut down Jhally's dissenting opinion. Although the University of Massachusetts lawyers acknowledged that the video fit the definition of fair use, they advised Jhally to back down. This kind of self-censorship is extremely insidious and damaging to freedom of expression® in the corporate age, and it's quite common. How in the world are commentators supposed to critique the ubiquitous, privately owned things that help shape our consciousness if we can't reproduce them? ("Okay kids, close your eyes and imagine an MTV video, now . . .")

Sut Jhally is a stubborn, intimidating man, and he can be very persuasive. But when he insisted on distributing *Dreamworlds,* the spineless university lawyers told him he'd get no institutional support. On his own, he played a game of legal chicken with MTV, and the cable channel blinked. Soon after, Jhally founded the Media Education Foundation to shield him from personal legal and financial liability. Thanks in part to the overzealous copyright bozoism of MTV, since 1991 the nationally visible MEF has fairly used *thousands* of fragments of copyrighted materials in the dozens of educational videos it sells—all without being sued for copyright infringement, something that sets an important precedent that others have followed.

I know Sut Jhally because he was my dissertation adviser, and when I finished my Ph.D. he tapped me to produce a critical examination of the music industry. The resulting documentary—*Money for Nothing: Behind the Business of Pop Music*—was narrated by Sonic Youth's Thurston Moore, a favorite musician from my teenage riot years. It featured interviews with independent musicians Ani Difranco, Chuck D, Michael Franti, and Kathleen Hanna, as well as media critic Robert McChesney, Dave Marsh, and others. There are *many* video and audio clips used throughout *Money for Nothing* that are needed to illustrate the things the talking heads discuss, but these images and sounds are owned by a handful of media conglomerates.

The administrative costs of requesting copyright clearance (not including the expensive licensing fees) would make such an endeavor impossible for a small nonprofit such as MEF. Anyway, these corporations would probably say no. That's why a liberal interpretation of fair use is so important. As the distribution channels for educational materials increasingly become controlled by corporations that are not willing to take risks, it becomes crucial for independent nonprofits such as the Media Education Foundation to survive and prosper. This necessity also makes the university setting all the more important in carving out a space where fair use can actively be practiced. Without the free exchange of ideas and images, we can't foster a functioning democracy comprising active, informed citizens.

When books are subjected to copyright censorship and companies that ensnare schools in exclusive contracts brand our educational environments, it's much harder for these democratic ideals to manifest themselves. Some academic presses have resisted the erosion of fair use, but they are in the minority. "Duke University Press has been a strong supporter of fair use," editor-in-chief Ken Wissoker tells me. "We are lucky to have intellectual-property legal advisers through our University Counsel's office who are strong supporters themselves."

Susan Olive is Duke University's external legal council on intellectual-property issues, and she has well over a quarter century of legal experience. "I think it's important for academic publishers to *inform the nation* and not hide behind a cover of fear," she tells me.

"People who think academic publishers should be scared first and publish second are flatly wrong," though she's careful to note that scholarly books published by big commercial houses are also protected by fair use. Susan Olive has very strong views on the subject—strong, but not radical. After all, they are backed up by the law itself and many legal decisions. When I tell her about how U. Mass's lawyers caved to threats from MTV, Olive says, "I think that that kind of behavior is atrocious. They should be ashamed of themselves."

Fair use doesn't give people a free ride to do *anything* with copyrighted materials in the name of "criticism," for there are limits. Duke's editor-in-chief gives the example of using stills from a motion picture. "If the material is being used for the purpose of criticism—to make the criticism clear—that's likely to be fair use. If it is serving only as an illustration or an embellishment, it's not," Wissoker states. "If the author is discussing a scene in *On the Waterfront* and uses a frame enlargement of that scene, it's fair use." But if the author only uses a still of Marlon Brando to more generally illustrate 1950s masculinity, Duke University Press probably wouldn't consider it a fair use.

The Supreme Court has in many cases set reasonable limits on what is fair and what is not. For instance, in *Robinson v. Random House*, the court rejected a fair-use defense in a court battle involving two books, one of which quoted and very closely paraphrased over 25 percent from a competing book. The high court ruled that the book published by Random House amounted to an unfair market substitution, rather than legitimate criticism. The only lawsuit the Media Education Foundation has been slapped with is *Cambridge Documentary Films, Inc. v. Jean Kilbourne and Media Education Foundation*. It's an ugly case. Jean Kilbourne, a well-known media critic, had produced a series of documentaries based on her college campus lectures about the representation of women in advertising. The series was called *Killing Us Softly* and had been distributed by Cambridge Documentary Films, a feminist documentary collective.

Kilbourne was dissatisfied with Cambridge for a number of reasons, so she decided to do *Killing Us Softly 3* with MEF when I was working there. Cambridge quietly registered the trademark Killing Us Softly, then sued Kilbourne and MEF for trademark infringement. Feminists gone wild with litigation. At the same time, Cambridge rush-produced *Beyond Killing Us Softly,* interviewing activists such as Gloria Steinem, but neglecting to tell some interviewees what they were up to. Kilbourne's lawyers eventually won back the Killing Us Softly trademark, which allowed Kilbourne and MEF to legally distribute *Killing Us Softly 3* without fear of litigation.

Another risk that has emerged for organizations such as the Media Education Foundation is that damned DMCA. The law makes it a criminal offense to bypass copy protection on digitally stored works, such as when you make an unauthorized copy of a DVD or e-book. Even if it's for completely legal, fair-use purposes—with few exceptions—the *act* of circumvention is a criminal act. For example, I recall one instance while making *Money for Nothing* where one of the coproducers (may or may not have) bypassed the copy protection on a DVD so that we could include a very brief clip in the documentary. Although our *intent* clearly falls under the domain of fair use, the *act* of circumventing the copy protection on a DVD is quite illegal under the DMCA, especially because the documentary is for sale. It's an awful catch-22.

Additionally, I teach undergrad classes on the media, and I often compile clips from movies and TV shows to use as examples and provoke discussions. (It's far more efficient to do this than to bring a stack of videos and DVDs to class, especially when I'm using a lot of examples.) This kind of educational practice is absolutely a fair use and doesn't require me to ask permission of the copyright owner to duplicate or show clips. But if I wanted to draw from a DVD—a director's commentary track, bonus feature, or simply a scene from a movie—I would have to break the encryption on the disc. Even though this use is for educational purposes, and is fair, to do so I would have to acquire a banned software program, which is against the law. As the media we consume increasingly moves into the digital sphere, these kinds of situations will become all the more common, unless Congress lifts these stifling DMCA restrictions.

RESEARCH IN A PRIVATIZED WORLD

It was 2000, and the music industry was just coming to terms with the reality of digital downloading. The Recording Industry Association of America (RIAA) halfheartedly founded the Secure Digital Music Initiative (SDMI) to explore "safe" ways of distributing music online. Issuing a challenge to the professional cryptography community, the SDMI encouraged researchers to defeat its copy-protection technology to test its security. Dr. Edward Felten, a professor of computer science at Princeton University, led a team of researchers from Xerox, Princeton, and Rice University who successfully met this challenge. Felten's team detailed their findings in a paper and prepared to present them at an academic conference.

Then the SDMI and the RIAA got nervous and asked Felten to remove the parts of the paper that reveal the technology's weaknesses, but the researcher refused. These music-industry organizations asserted that "any presentation of the paper at a conference or subsequent publication of the paper in the conference proceedings would subject these persons and their institutions to liability under the DMCA." The SDMI and RIAA made clear their intention to take legal action, and after meeting with lawyers, Felten and his team pulled out of the conference because of the potentially high costs of litigation. Felten read the following statement at the Pittsburgh conference:

On behalf of the authors of the paper "Reading Between the Lines: Lessons from the SDMI Challenge," I am disappointed to tell you that we will not be presenting today. Our paper was submitted via the normal academic peer-review process. The reviewers, who were chosen for their scientific reputations and credentials, enthusiastically recommended the paper for publication, due to their judgment of the paper's scientific merit. . . . Litigation is costly, time-consuming, and uncertain, regardless of the merits of the other side's case. Ultimately we, the authors, reached a collective decision not to expose ourselves, our employers, and the conference organizers to litigation at this time.

The RIAA eventually said it would not sue Felten, but the activist lawyers at the Electronic Frontier Foundation wanted a court order that would prevent this from happening again. However, District Judge Garrett E. Brown ruled against Felten and EFF, dismissively stating, "Plaintiffs liken themselves to modern Galileos persecuted by the authorities. I fear that a more apt analogy would be to modern day Don Quixotes feeling threatened by windmills which they perceive as giants."[19] Later, in 2003, a lone Princeton grad student was threatened by SunnComm after he published on his Web site an academic paper titled "Analysis of the MediaMax CD3 Copy-Prevention System." In the paper, Alex Halderman gave detailed instructions about how to disable the technology encoded on a music CD that prevented consumers from digitally copying music files.

The paper gained attention, and after SunnComm's stock price dropped the company went on the offensive. The funny thing is that Halderman's "circumvention" entailed holding down the Shift key when loading the CD in the computer, which prevented Windows from launching SunnComm's technology. For that, an enraged SunnComm CEO Peter Jacobs told reporters the company was considering both criminal and civil suits; it would also refer this DMCA violation to federal authorities. "SunnComm is taking a stand here because we believe that those who own property, whether physical or digital, have the ultimate authority over how their property is used." A few days later, Jacobs came to his senses and decided not to pursue a case against the grad student.[20] But it was only because of the good graces of SunnComm that the student didn't face the kind of exorbitant legal bills that come from defending oneself against an intellectual-property lawsuit.

These threats and arrests have engendered a climate of fear among computer scientists and security experts throughout the world. After Professor Felten's team was prevented from presenting their findings at the International Information Hiding Workshop in Pittsburgh, it made sure its next conference would be outside the United States. (The DMCA is an American law, though the U.S. government is pushing other countries to adopt versions of it.) The organization—populated by professionals who test the security of data-protection systems—didn't want a repeat of what happened at the U.S. conference (or worse). Fred Cohen, a well-known security consultant removed his evidence-gathering tool from his Web site, stating, "When they started to arrest people and threaten researchers, I decided the legal risk was not worth it." Another security expert, Dug Song, pulled his own site down in protest, replacing the text with "Censored by the Digital Millennium Copyright Act."[21]

Even the former head of Bush's White House Office of Cyberspace Security, the now-famous (or infamous) Richard Clarke, called for an amendment to the DMCA—with no success—because of what he called its "chilling effect on vulnerability research."[22] The more eyes that can peer into a tool or program, the more likely it is for flaws to be discovered. This presupposes a freedom to examine without asking permission, something that the DMCA prevents. In response, researchers have withheld the publishing of their papers, such as Dutch encryption expert Niels Ferguson. "I travel to the U.S. regularly, for both professional and for personal reasons," he wrote in an online statement. "I simply cannot afford to be sued or prosecuted in the U.S." He pulled his research that discovered fatal flaws in a system named High-Bandwidth Digital Content Protection (HDCP).

"What do you do when you find a result like this? First, you have to write it down and explain it," Ferguson wrote.

> Then you publish a paper so that the mistakes can be fixed, and others can learn from it. That is how all science works. I wrote a paper on HDCP, but I cannot publish it. . . . Instead of fixing HDCP *now* before it is deployed on a large scale, the industry will be confronted with all the expense of building HDCP into every device, only to have it rendered useless. The DMCA ends up costing the industry money. No points guessing who ends up paying for it in the end.[23]

The negative effects of the DMCA are merely exaggerated symptoms of the growing desire among information elites for even greater control of every imaginable combination of 1's and 0's. This quest for more proprietary power, in turn, has undermined the basic mechanics of Western science's gift economy, where the norms of openness fueled the explosion of scientific discoveries over the past two centuries.[24] Today, private companies are buying up the rights to academic journals in the sciences, arts, and humanities, something that undermines the free sharing of knowledge that has characterized academia. We academic authors are in a precarious position, because our tenure and promotion hinges on publishing in peer-reviewed journals. In most cases, we must give up our copyrights to what we write because it's a long-standing practice within the scholarly community. In the past, we scholars gave away our work—which was often referred to as a "contribution to the field"—in an act that resembles a gift exchange.

By giving our words (and even our copyrights) to journals, it was understood that we were increasing the intellectual richness of our area of study. If the knowledge we contributed for free is well received by our peers, we are rewarded with enhanced reputations and merit pay raises. It's a classic example of the circuitous rewards of the gift economy. Today, however, this kind of academic gift economy is being threatened by the privatization of scholarly information, which significantly raises the price of access.[25] On a related note, you wouldn't believe the number of professors and grad students I've talked to who have had to remove a journal article (or book chapter) from a course pack because the copyright holder wanted a staggering licensing fee. Some publishers will ask for up to one dollar per page, which means the cost of photocopying a forty-page chapter can exceed the retail cost of an entire book. When material is dropped from a course packet, no one gets paid and fewer people read it, which undermines one of the most basic missions of education: the dissemination of knowledge.

The free flow of information is becoming less and less free in many areas, especially within the field of genetics. This is due in part to the blossoming university-industrial complex, where partnerships such as the one between the Swiss biotech giant Novartis and Berkeley's Department of Plant and Microbial Biology are becoming more common. In this case, Novartis shelled out $5 million a year for five years in exchange for first rights to license a discovery. Former Harvard University president Derek Bok argued that the contracts university scientists sign under these partnerships with private companies can undermine the norm of openness. "Accordingly," says Bok, "company officials regularly insist that information concerning the work they support be kept in confidence while the research is going on and for a long enough time thereafter to allow them to decide whether to file for a patent."[26]

University of Iowa president David Skorton, a prominent scientist (and part-time jazz musician), explained to me why these events are troubling for certain folks. "At the more basic end of scientific research, any serious impediments to the free flow of ideas is to be avoided and resisted," he says as I sit in his office. "The number-one reason is that it will eventually inhibit the march of science. It sounds so corny, but I really believe it's true." Skorton breaks it down for me, an outsider from the arts and humanities: "If you take a scientific discovery that's really important in the medical field, and you try to walk backwards in time and see what F led to G, what E led to F, what D led to E, it's not a linear path often. It's not the sort of thing where you could predict today, 'Doctor X is doing this research and that's definitely going to lead to something down the line'; it's often a circuitous path. So, in order to allow those circuits to occur, you have to allow the openness of exchange. . . . In generalities, very broad generalities, I think it's important to protect the freedom of exchange, and, by the way, not just in the scientific areas that you're asking about."

However, David Skorton isn't just a scientist working disinterestedly for a higher good; he's the president of a public university in a cash-strapped state. "Having said that, at the nadir of a tough recession, it's clear that society—whether society means rank-and-file people on the street or legislators—expects us to do the best we can to commercialize technologies developed in the universities for the state's good." But he quickly adds, "My own point of view has been, and will remain, that I am more concerned with the freedom of ex-

pression® than with the commercial imperative." When we change our conversational course and start talking about his other life as a jazz musician, he grows more animated. "I think that the jazz solo could be viewed in some crackpot way as an exercise in improvisation similar to a scientific experiment," he muses. "In a scientific experiment, you have a set of knowledge—observations, wisdom—based on past observations.

"You have some concept of a leap that might be taken, an educated guess, a postulate. Then you test it out by gathering information and seeing if it works or not." He now seems a little taller in his leather chair, perhaps less weighed down by professional talk and the crushing state-funding cuts that face him every day. As he riffs on this subject, it's obvious why he never put the saxophone down. "I've thought about this often, as I'm nervously awaiting my chance for a solo—you know, the chord structure of the song, what other people perhaps have done with a similar harmonic progression. And then you step up and try something that may work, may not work. . . ." Then there's a pause, because we've veered completely off course. He smiles, cuts himself off, and tells me, "Of course, that has nothing to do with science or intellectual-property law."

But in his response I found something that does. I point out to him that the existence of jazz music is predicated on the ability to borrow, experiment, and freely play with musical information, which is true of Skorton's explanations of science. Jazz musicians are enabled by a kind of "open source" culture, where pre-existing melodic fragments and larger musical frameworks are freely processed and reworked, creating something new and beautiful. Unfortunately, the freedom of many university researchers to "play" with genetic information has been significantly constrained over the past two decades. A recent survey of nearly two thousand university-based geneticists in the United States showed that one-

third agreed that withholding data was becoming more common in their field. Over half reported that, in the previous three years, they were denied access to scientific information relating to *already published research* because of financial concerns.[27]

Unfortunately, many universities don't have guidelines that can prevent the overzealous guarding of scientific information. According to a study, only 12 percent of these institutions have clear policies that limit secrecy to the minimum necessary to protect commercial interests. Some have no written policy at all. Unsurprisingly, given the direction the money flows, company research directors report few problems getting as much silence as they want. Not everyone from private industry thinks this is a good thing. A report cited by Bok from the National Institutes of Health found that virtually every firm polled stated that access to research tools—patented genes, for instance—are being overly restricted. Not only do they think this is impeding the rapid advance of research, these companies believe the problem is getting worse, especially in their dealings with universities.

"Over and over again," the report states, "firms complained to us that universities 'wear the mortarboard' when they seek access to [research] tools developed by others, yet they impose the same sorts of restrictions when they enter into agreements to give firms access to their own tools." They claim universities—in order to obtain a higher portion of revenues—regularly hold up requests for materials, though MediGene's Helena Chaye isn't as cynical. She simply feels that many university technology-transfer employees are overworked and backlogged. Because of high turnover, low pay, and tight resources, it's a system that Chaye says "becomes really inefficient." On the flip side of the coin, private companies worry that their information might get into the hands of university researchers under contract with rival firms, which means they also insist on

many muzzling restrictions. Over 90 percent of life-science companies have some kind of formal relationship with academic scientists. The *Journal of the American Medical Association* reports that
universities' share in gene patents rose from 55 percent to 73 percent in the 1990s.

The financial windfall that patents provide has become so important for universities that it has resulted in some bizarre scenarios. In the early 1990s, an undergrad researcher at the University of
South Florida was accused of stealing the university's intellectual
property when he registered a patent on a biological product that
he invented. The problem was that Petr Taborsky used the university's facilities when he concocted an ammonia-absorbing sub-
stance that could be used for kitty litter, and the university asserted
its contractual rights of ownership. When Taborsky refused to reas-
sign the patent in the university's name, he was convicted of a
felony, received a three-and-a-half-year sentence, and was initially
assigned to a chain gang.

Florida's governor, Lawton Chiles, finally stepped in and moved
him from the chain gang to a minimum-security prison. "There are
a lot of things in this case that raise your eyebrows," said Dexter
Douglass, legal counsel to the governor's office. "We are concerned
that the government overreached in this young man's case."[28] With
time off for good behavior—the budding scientist was no tough
guy—he was released in 1997 to face eleven years' probation. Free at
last. Why did the university spend so much money prosecuting one
of its students, ensuring bad publicity for itself in the process? It
was afraid that by *not* doing so, this would undermine confidence
in future corporate partnerships.

If this sounds like the paranoid speculation of an activist professor, listen to what the in-house attorney for the University of South
Florida has to say. "We are concerned that potential sponsors will

view it as a black eye for the institution if we allow student researchers to steal information," argued Henry Lavendera. The case
is no different for him than a student who steals books from the library or a VCR from a classroom. "The university has taken heat in
the media that Taborsky wound up in prison," said Lavendera, "but
the fact is he stole property that didn't belong to him."[29]

Other dark scenarios have emerged when drug companies use
heavy-handed techniques to suppress the unfavorable findings of
university researchers. Such was the case with Betty Dong and
Nancy Olivieri, of the University of California, San Francisco, and
University of Toronto, respectively. A pharmaceutical firm gave
Dong a grant to find out if its drug Synthroid was superior to the
generic versions of the drugs. When Dong's research suggested
there was no significant difference, things turned sour. After being
informed of these unfavorable results, the company accused her of
methodological errors and unspecified ethical lapses. It even hired a
private investigator to try to uncover any conflicts of interest, which
proved fruitless.

Dong tried to submit the results to a professional journal,
prompting the company to threaten a lawsuit based on a secrecy
clause in their agreement, and the university refused to assist her
in her fight. It took seven years for the paper to be published.
Nancy Olivieri experienced a very similar fate at the University of
Toronto's Hospital for Sick Children. In her capacity as a university
professor and researcher, she insisted on publishing the results of
her experiments that shed a negative light on a drug produced by
Apotex. She claimed that the drug she tested not only was less effective at treating thalassemia—a genetic blood disorder—it was potentially hazardous to patients.

The company threatened legal actions and canceled her research
contract, which led her to be falsely accused by her hospital of dis-

regarding regulations. The hospital also directed her not to discuss the incident publicly. "Olivieri and Dong are by no means the only investigators who have been pressured by companies," writes Bok. "There are plenty of anecdotes involving researchers threatened by lawsuits or attacks on their reputation in an effort to suppress unfavorable results." The former Harvard president continues, "No one knows how extensive this problem is, since no one can be sure how many scientists have quietly succumbed to pressure and suppressed their findings rather than undergo the harassment and delay endured by Dong and Olivieri."[30]

The varied—and sometimes mind-blowing—stories collected in this chapter vividly illustrate the perils of embracing an unregulated system that is solely managed by private interests. This is what happens when an increasing amount of our physical and cultural resources are turned over to private hands. It is true that not all privatization schemes are necessarily bad, and in some cases they can improve efficiency while also working for the public good—sometimes, but not always. Without a guiding public policy that balances the profit motive of a few with the interests of most citizens, we run the risk of more fenced-off public squares, secretive elections, DMCA arrests, cease-and-desist letters, slowed research, and a shrinking public domain.

CHAPTER SIX

THE DIGITAL FUTURE

and the analog past

Talk about the law being blind and dumb. Not until late 2003 did it become legal for blind people to listen to certain e-books without a copyright owner's permission. For whatever overprotective reasons, it wasn't unusual for publishers to disable the "read aloud" voice synthesis function on the computers that stored e-books. Software companies were too scared to pick this digital lock—no matter how easy it was, or how much common sense it made—because it was a violation of the Digital Millennium Copyright Act. Among other things, they were chilled by the 2001 arrest of Dmitry Sklyarov, the Russian computer programmer mentioned in the last chapter who was jailed on DMCA charges. His employer developed software that broke a publisher's restrictive rules, such as the following ones that appeared on the copyright page of Adobe's e-book edition of *Alice in Wonderland*:

COPY No text selections can be copied from the book to the clipboard.

PRINT No printing is permitted of this book.

LEND This book cannot be lent or given to someone else.

GIVE This book cannot be given to someone else.

READ ALOUD This book cannot be read aloud.

Only after intense lobbying from the American Foundation for the Blind did the Librarian of Congress grant a DMCA exemption that legalized the unsavory crime of reading e-books aloud. Copyright was originally conceived as a way of dispersing knowledge and culture. But for nearly five years the DMCA was pretty much responsible for keeping blind people from accessing e-books such as *Alice in Wonderland*. Even though *Alice* and many other e-books are in the public domain, by converting them into digital form, companies can recapture works whose copyrights have lapsed. In doing so, they create newer, more innovative ways of eroding our cultural commons that go beyond the mere extension of copyright-protection terms. Also, they can create protections that are virtually infinite, rather than respecting the balanced bargain that has been at the core of copyright for over two centuries. It's a sign of the times when overzealous copyright bozos move to make *everything* a billable event, tightly controlling all access to their property.

In the old days, for instance, we could purchase a book and take it home, read it, mark it up, store it for years on our bookshelves, photocopy a chapter, loan it to a friend, or whatever. Such uses are protected by what lawyers call the "first sale doctrine," which essentially states that when you purchase a copyrighted good, you can re-sell it, give it to a friend, or make personal copies, among other things. Unfortunately, this doctrine is quickly evaporating in the digital world. Under the DMCA, content providers can now regulate who can see its product, how long it can be viewed, whether or not it can be copied, and what can be done with it. This significantly rewrites rules that had been in place for years and struck a balance between copyright holders and the public.

EMBRACING A RENTED FUTURE
(WHILE FORGETTING THE PAST)

Soon after Apple introduced its iTunes store—which legally sells digital music files with "locks" that prevent free copying—a Web developer stirred up a digital hornet's nest with his online performance-art piece. George Hotelling placed a song he purchased from the iTunes store on the Web auction site eBay, promising to donate any surplus proceeds to the Electronic Frontier Foundation. "I'd just like to know that if I buy something, whether it's physical or intellectual property, that I'll have my right of 'First Sale,' " stated Hotelling. "It underscores the fact," added Fred von Lohmann, a senior staff attorney at the EFF, "that when you purchase digital music online today, you may be getting quite a bit less for your money than when you purchase a CD in a store."[1] Eventually eBay yanked Hotelling's song for violating a ban on goods purchased and distributed electronically. Because Apple never had a chance to weigh in on the debate, the status of the first-sale doctrine for legally downloaded music remained murky.

Justifying their actions, copyright owners argue that without strong protections against digital leaks, they'll no longer be able to make money. They constantly remind us that the Internet and digital distribution are different from that which came before. Although this is partially true, they are still dehistoricizing the current situation. Virtually every time a new technology has been introduced, copyright industries have hysterically and hyperbolically responded the same way. After all, even the *phonograph* was supposed to destroy the music industry at the beginning of the twentieth century. Of course, there was a reorganization of the music industry, but music itself didn't suffer—instead, the industry got much, much bigger.

"What we find, historically, is that the folks who do best are those who embrace the new technologies," says Brian Zisk, co-founder of the Future of Music Coalition. "The King Olivers and those folks who are early and got their stuff on records built this following." But the early twentieth-century musicians who wouldn't let their music be recorded have been forgotten. "They may have thought they had a legitimate reason to say, 'We don't want people to copy our licks,' " Zisk continues, "but it's really about how to get as many people to hear your music as possible." Then radio was supposed to ruin the newly emerging recording industry because, well, if people don't have to pay for the music they hear, why would they go out and purchase records? The answer soon became obvious: The more people heard certain songs for free, the more likely they would buy a familiar record. Radio turned out to be a fantastic promotional tool.

"Radio was also supposed to end live music because people were going to stay home," says Steve Albini, someone who knows more than a thing or two about the music industry. Over the past quarter century, Albini has produced or engineered over one thousand albums for more than one thousand artists—ranging from relatively obscure critical darlings (Nina Nastasia, Man or Astro-man?, Low), midlevel acts (the Pixies, P. J. Harvey, Weezer), and multiplatinum stars (Nirvana, Bush, Cheap Trick). "What actually happens is that every single one of these [innovations] increased the general public's participation in music," the recording engineer tells me. Albini said this before literally suiting up—in a specially designed jumpsuit all his engineers wear—and getting to work in his Electrical Audio studios in Chicago. They look like a team of über-cool crime fighters.

"This stuff came about *because* of these technological advances," he says, "not in spite of them. The radio made people excited about hearing live bands because they'd hear live bands in a ballroom with this excitement going on, and the ballrooms exploded in popularity after radio." With hindsight, it's perhaps too easy to sit back and make fun of the shortsightedness of those who believed that radio would spell the end of the music business. But one can imagine why people thought that; this was a new technology, after all, a wireless medium of communication that would supposedly reorganize society—sort of like what we've heard about the Internet.

Stanford law professor Lawrence Lessig argues that controversies over cable television foreshadowed the first Napster controversy. As a newly adopted commercial technology, cable television raised the hackles of the three television networks because cable companies were "stealing" their content. (Cable companies were pulling broadcasts from the airwaves and copying it onto their wires.) Under pressure, the Federal Communications Commission (FCC) halted cable's expansion in the 1960s, yet another example of how copyright conflicts can slow the development of significant new media technologies. When the FCC began reversing itself in the early 1970s, television program–copyright owners took the cable companies to court twice.

Judges sided with cable and left it up to Congress to strike a compromise, which legislated a compulsory "blanket license," similar to what radio and live-music venues purchase from royalty-collection agencies such as ASCAP. This license allows radio and television to broadcast copyrighted materials by paying a statutory fee set by Congress, not by copyright owners. It limits the monopoly rights of copyright owners by ensuring that they can't stifle competition by setting artificially high prices. Under the compulsory blanket-licensing system, copyright owners don't have the right to arbitrarily refuse permission to rebroadcast their programs or to favor one company in its pricing schemes. This way, the cable industry was allowed to thrive, consumers had new entertainment options, and copyright owners were fairly compensated.

These blanket licenses are curious constructs. In chapter four I wrote about the legal fiction of the "corporate individual," and the way this plays out in broadcast and cable television raises important questions. First of all, who is the "author" of a television show or a movie? The multiple writers, the director, the actors, the producers who put up the money, the editors, other technicians necessary in such a production, or the channel that broadcasts it? Practically speaking, it's a puzzling problem, one that displays the cracks in the smooth veneer of the culture industry's conception of "the author." In his essay, "What Is an Author?," Michel Foucault argued that "we should reexamine the empty space left by the author's disappearance; we should attentively observe, along its gaps and fault lines, its new demarcations."[2]

In Hollywood, the death of the author leaves behind a chalky police outline of a homicide victim, a merely cartoonlike representation of a person. It's an imitation author, a corporate individual. The television or movie studio that funds and produces entertainment becomes a virtual author, which takes ownership of property created by a multitude of people. When a show is broadcast on cable television, cable companies pay statutory fees to an independent collection agency that then redistributes payments to individual copyright owners. Under the compulsory blanket-licensing system, the product has been turned into a *simulation* of property; a statistical formula based in part on Nielsen ratings is used to dole out slices of the royalty pie. As media scholar Thomas Streeter points out, with the blanket licenses there is no actual exchange of copyrighted products for money—it's more like paying and collecting taxes.

Although cable television was similar to Napster in important ways, some say that the decentralized nature of the Internet could make it harder for a similar licensing system to work. Comparatively, there are a much smaller number of cable companies than individual peer-to-peer network users, which makes it easier to regulate the cable broadcasters. In dealing with a rogue company, copyright owners can literally follow the hardwired cables back to the source and demand payment. The same isn't true of the Internet, where physical addresses are harder to track down—but it's not impossible, for there are technologies that can monitor file-sharing activities. After the dust settles on all the RIAA lawsuits, and after much legislative wrangling, the most likely and reasonable compromise on the file-sharing issue will be a relatively small fee tacked on to the Internet-service bills of individual consumers. The money could then be redistributed in a manner similar to what has worked for decades with broadcasters, something I'll return to later.

Also predictive of the Napster controversy was the introduction of the VCR. Hollywood viewed the VCR as nothing less than a mass murderer that would pick off movie studios like frightened teens in a slasher film such as *Halloween*. I'm not exaggerating in the least. Jack Valenti, CEO of the Motion Picture Association of America for years, tactfully told Congress the following in 1982: "I say to you that the VCR is to the American film producer and the American public as the Boston Strangler is to the woman home alone." In the introduction, I quoted Valenti arguing that the VCR would lead to a "lessened supply of high quality, expensive high budget material where its investment recoupment is now in serious doubt."

Earlier, in the 1970s, RCA was developing a version of the VCR, but when they approached Hollywood studios, they were rebuked. Companies such as Disney balked at the idea of losing control of their copyrighted works, even when RCA suggested a mechanical version of today's digital rights management technologies. The scheme: When a videotape played all the way through, it would lock up and could only be unlocked when the consumer returned it to the video store and paid a fee. But this was still troubling. "How could they know," asked a disturbed Disney executive, "how many people are going to be sitting there watching? . . . What's to stop someone else coming in and watching for free?"[3]

The idea that audiences could freely record and watch entertainment was a novel one, just as the Internet just recently felt wholly new, and it's understandable why executives felt threatened. But Hollywood was nevertheless very shortsighted and completely off base. The movie studios were forced to relent after they lost the Betamax Supreme Court case in 1984. The high court thankfully decided that the public had a right to record and watch movies as many times as they want—with as many people in the living room as they'd like—to the chagrin of Disney execs. Little did Disney know that letting millions of kids watch its movies over and over and over would boost the sales of its T-shirts, toys, and other related products.

As the market penetration of VCRs exploded, box-office receipts steadily increased, and VHS and DVD revenue became a major moneymaker for previously unnerved entertainment companies. Box-office numbers have continued to rise since the 1980s, and, in 2002, home-video revenue totaled $11.9 billion, surpassing the $4.2 billion in theater ticket sales. Also in 2002, Jack Valenti said about movie downloads, "It's getting clear—alarmingly clear, I might add—that we are in the midst of the possibility of Armageddon."[4] He wasn't talking about the Ben Affleck film, but he was beginning to sound more and more like Chicken Little freaking out about the sky falling.

At the beginning of the 1990s the RIAA lined up digital audiotape (DAT) recorders in front of the firing squad. Using lawsuits, legislation and, regulatory tactics, the RIAA severely stalled the introduction of DATs into the U.S. market and eventually killed potential mass market demand for this new technology. At the end of the decade, it sued to keep portable MP3 players from being sold in the United States (the RIAA lost this time). After that, Hollywood attacked personal video recorders (PVRs). PVRs such as Tivo allow people to digitally record television programming by using keywords and menus, something TV networks and studios have tried to ban. Although MGM's 2002 lawsuit targeted SonicBlue, which produces the most sophisticated batch of PVRs, it was also aimed at all PVR companies. MGM lawyers argued that their searchable keyword functions would "cause substantial harm to the market for prerecorded DVD, videocassette, and other copies of those episodes and films."[5]

I don't doubt that many entertainment executives are genuinely scared. Artists have worried no less than corporations that the new recording, reproduction, and distribution technologies would strip them of their livelihoods as their work becomes infinitely reproducible for free. This fear has proven to be unfounded so far—and is likely to be so in the future. In fact, these recent changes have the potential to disseminate a more diverse and democratic array of art than what was allowed to bubble up through the culture industries of old. It's for this reason that we shouldn't kill the creative potential of these new technologies before they have a chance to positively enhance the ways we produce, distribute, and consume culture.

FILE-SHARING AND CD BURNING ARE KILLING HOME TAPING

In the early 1980s, when the music industry slumped after its disco- and-cocaine-fueled high—during a recession, by the way—record companies blamed tape recorders, and the people who used them, for lackluster sales. They even came up with a bumper sticker–ready slogan, "Home Taping Is Killing Music." Record-company execs feared that the convenience of cassette tapes would raise an entire generation of people who believed they didn't have to pay for music. "Never before"—a phrase that pops up frequently in these debates—did so many music fans have the ability to copy music themselves. So, at the urging of the RIAA, Congress initiated a study of home taping, but the Office of Technology Assessment (OTA) issued a report that contradicted many of the industry's claims. The OTA report stated that, among other things, home tapers bought more records than nontapers and, conversely, the majority of nontapers didn't listen to or purchase prerecorded music.[6]

The only study of home taping initiated by a record company, Warner Brothers Records, also concluded that there is a direct correlation between how much you tape and how much you buy. "These findings imply that, although related, taping may best be seen as independent ways of expressing a more general, underlying commitment to music," the Warner report stated. "In fact, the data clearly indicate that the stronger this commitment, the more likely one is to both tape and buy prerecorded music and engage in a variety of behaviors that also express this commitment to and interest in music."[7] Congress's report also found that home taping has a "stimulative" effect that fuels record sales, though it claimed that record companies need to find ways to get consumers to spend *all* their money on records, and *none* on blank cassettes.

Trading music is very much a social act. The sharing of songs with like-minded people exposes them to new music, increasing the chances of someone buying a new record. This is corroborated by my own experiences, the experiences of others, and the reports issued by Congress and Warner. I've been notorious for making lots of music compilations for friends, which I know has generated album sales. For instance, I gave my friend Megan Levad a mix-CD that included a song, "Iowa City," about our little college town. Eleni Mandell sings this pretty ditty as a country waltz with a chorus that goes, "Iowa, Iowa, skies are blue / Not so Chicago, Never New York . . ." Upon hearing it, Megan bought Mandell's CD for someone who had recently moved away from our beloved Midwestern town as a kind of musical postcard. When Mandell stopped in "the I.C." during a 2004 tour, I nervously told her this story, not knowing if she'd be offended by my piracy. The Los Angeles–based musician responded simply: "Cool."

Iowa City's best-known musical export is folkster Greg Brown, who is one of the crusty crown jewels of the town's roots rock scene. Another in the upper echelon of the local music hierarchy is David Zollo, a thirty-five-year-old piano player, singer, bandleader, record-label owner and, more recently, father of baby boy, Rocco (yes, his name is Rocco Zollo). A few weeks after the birth of his son, I dropped by Dave's house to talk about life, kids, music, and, as the conversation wore on, copyright law. I admitted to him that I obviously have no problem making mix-CDs of other people's music, but when it came to Dave's records, I've felt uncomfortable doing so. He laughed, and said he appreciated my sensitivity. But, Dave said, "I've *always* made mix-tapes. It's the idea that you actually become involved with the art and become an artist, in a way. And any time someone is actually involved, it makes them a part of the experience." One of the ways he courted his wife, Beth, was to make her tapes. Putting together music mixes has been a key part of mating rituals since music-possessed geeks learned how to press the record button on the cassette recorder.

"The act of making a mix-tape is an act of creative engagement," Dave Zollo insists. "I might listen to a Chuck Berry record and then write a song, so I am engaged in this music that has influenced me.

I've reinterpreted the music, released a record, and someone takes that song that I made and puts it on a mix-tape. And someone will tell me about it." Dave doesn't really make a hard distinction between the creative acts that music fans engage in and the music-making that he does—in part, because he's doing both. "Once my music has been put on someone's mix-tape, the work lives. It's been placed in another context, and been given importance because of what it's alongside. Like, first Tom Waits, then David Zollo. Holy shit, how did I get there? Then all of a sudden, that validates the work."

Sonic Youth guitarist Lee Ranaldo told me about how he and his wife, Leah, started a tradition of making mix-CDs of "classic oldies" for their kids' summer birthdays. "All the kids who come to the parties get one, and (hopefully) get turned on to all this music that is outside the realm of 'kids' music,'" he said in an e-mail. "Last year it was themed about colors, so yellow submarine, white wedding, 99 red balloons, good-bye yellow brick road, Michael Jackson's black or white, purple rain, green river, etc." These musical juxtapositions, however, will be harder to create if the recording industry fully embraces protected, proprietary digital files, either online or on CDs. If they get their way, we'll no longer own the music in the same way people did when they bought records and tapes—when they stored them in their homes and built libraries of music.

The introduction into the marketplace of CDs that can't be copied is one example of how intellectual-property owners are willing to protect their products at all costs, even if it means alienating consumers. One of those companies is EMI, part of the major label system that controls the distribution of 80 percent of the music sold in the world (it's down to only four companies now). EMI's response to Holger Turck—a consumer who in 2002 wrote a letter of complaint after he bought a CD with copy protection that was not clearly labeled as such—demonstrates the arrogance (mixed with fear) of a corporation that feels threatened.

> Even without formal study in economics, it should be clear to anyone reading this that the music industry cannot continue to exist if the trend holds. The widespread copying of prerecorded audio material via the burning of CD-Rs can only be countered one way: namely, copy protection. We fear, however, that all these facts will not interest you in the slightest, as these measures will herald the end of free music, which surely won't please you at all.... In the event that you plan to protest future releases of copy-protected CDs, we can assure you that it is only a matter of months until more or less every CD released worldwide will include copy protection. To that end, we will do everything in our power, whether you like it or not.
>
> Sincerely,
>
> Your EMI Team

True to EMI's condescending threat, which ignored the fact that this customer *bought* the album, in 2003 major labels began releasing copy-protected CDs into the marketplace. Although a few hundred million of these CDs had already been released in Europe, it was the first time the technology was deployed in the United States, though on a limited scale. By 2004, the number of CDs embedded with copy protections (the industry term is "digital rights management") had significantly increased in America—making it difficult or impossible to, for instance, place certain CDs on our iPods.

Companies such as EMI are increasingly treating their own customers like criminals. In 2003 the RIAA hired the former director of the Bureau of Alcohol, Tobacco and Firearms to head up its antipiracy efforts. The next year, the RIAA won the FBI's approval to begin using the law-enforcement agency's logo in its packaging. This has ruffled the feathers of quite a few artists on major labels, who have no choice but to deal with the fact that an "FBI Anti-Piracy Warning" dominates the lower fifth of their CD art. "Yeah, the FBI thing totally creeps me out," Lee Ranaldo says. "It's stupid in the extreme." Sonic Youth's 2004 record *Sonic Nurse* sported the mandatory layout the first week it was rolled out. "We happened to have our release right on the schedule for this new design invasion," Thurston Moore tells me. "Everyone was PISSED—I can see why—but, in a way, it was so absurd I kinda liked it."

As I've argued throughout this book, copyright was conceived of as a bargain, one that is supposed to balance the interests of both the creator and the public. Copy-protection technologies, however, only respect one side of this balance. "Hollywood and the recording industry," writes Robin Gross, an intellectual-property lawyer at the Electronic Frontier Foundation, "take all the privileges from the government-created monopoly but none of the responsibilities like ensuring fair use and contributing to the public domain."[8] When the RIAA and MPAA argue that theft is on the rise, and that it has steadily increased since the introduction of copying technologies, they are conceiving of copyright in relatively new terms.

Up until the 1970s, most legal briefs, judicial decisions, law articles, and books understood copyright as something that strikes a balance between the public and the creator. It didn't hand over *complete* control to the author, for the law was designed to provide a more porous kind of protection—not an airtight barrier.[9] Today, however, any activity that goes beyond adhering to the rules set by a copyright owner is considered theft, a quite significant change in the way we understand the role of intellectual property.

SHARING MUSIC AND SELLING MUSIC

"When I was young," musician and record producer Thom Monahan tells me, "the way that I got into bands was by people making
me tapes. You know, file-sharing, just in a different way. I had tons
of tapes, and I bought records of bands because people gave me a
song." Much like Dave Zollo, he has spent most of his adult life as a
working musician, and he's played more shows than he has gray
hairs. We first got to know each other while coproducing, along
with Jeremy Smith, the Media Education Foundation documentary
Money for Nothing, and have stayed in touch since. As a member of
the Pernice Brothers (and formerly the bassist in another indie-
rock band, the Lilys), Thom has toured the United States and Europe several times. Whenever his band comes through town, we'll
grab a post–sound check drink and fill each other in on what's
worth reading, watching, and listening to—chitchat common among
music-loving nerds.

The last time I saw him, the subject turned to the current state of
the music industry, and how bands such as the Pernice Brothers are
doing in these uncertain times. I wasn't surprised to find that, when
it comes to his music, Thom had no problem with file-sharing. It's a
term he uses interchangeably with tape trading; for him, it's the
same thing. "I've watched the tape-trading thing going on with Pernice Brothers," he tells me. "As soon as it was posted on our Web site
that Joe Pernice was okay with people taping shows," Thom says,
"there's been a lot of activity with people posting shows and posting links to shows because they know it's okay with the band."

By allowing their music to be freely traded, the band receives no
direct compensation. For some, it would make no sense to give
something away when you could charge a fee, but that's the beauty

of the gift economy. Although there is no quid pro quo transaction, the goodwill and community it builds rewards the band in less-direct ways. "It actually works to really generate traffic and interest and activity at the Web site, and in the band," says Thom. During the same time when major-label CD sales declined, according to Nielsen/Soundscan each Pernice Brothers album since their 1998 debut sold more than its predecessor, something that's true of similar artists. In his fictionalized memoir, *Meat Is Murder*, songwriter Joe Pernice described how his older friend Ray helped him discover new bands as a kid.

"I got a lot of my music back then from Ray. I never had much money to spend on records, or anything else for that matter," he wrote. "So Ray would give me tapes of albums he thought were important. Tapes, but no cases, and rarely any writing on them. A band name and an album title at best, and always abbreviated. It was his trademark. 'Clash: Rope,' 'U2: Oct,' 'Costello: Aim.' I'd break his balls and say it was his way of making me earn it, meaning I'd have to do the legwork to learn more about an album or band. Maybe it was." A lot of budding music fans had a musical mentor like Ray in their lives.

During the mid-1980s—in the same town where Joe Pernice grew up, Boston—an important American indie rock band emerged: Galaxie 500. Damon Krukowski, the group's drummer, talked to me in 2004 about his nearly twenty-year career in the music industry. He pointed out that before the Internet, college radio and mixtapes were great ways of promoting bands ignored by the mainstream. "When we started in the 1980s, college radio was our principle means of getting the name out and getting the music heard." After the demise of Galaxie 500, Krukowski cofounded Damon & Naomi, and the duo discovered that file-sharing was a lot like college radio. "When Napster was up and working well,"

Krukowski tells me, "the only thing we had heard about it was from people who hadn't heard of us before, but were coming to our shows and saying, 'I heard about your band through Napster.' That was no different to us than hearing, 'I heard about you on college radio or a friend gave me a tape of your record.' "

Even the Dave Matthews Band developed its initial fan base by encouraging people to record their shows and give them to friends. This built a word-of-mouth following in the early 1990s that expanded the group's reach from Charlottesville, Virginia, to the southeastern tour circuit and beyond. They followed a road paved by the Grateful Dead, which was one of the first to encourage tape trading. "The Grateful Dead sort of got it together," film archivist Rick Prelinger tells me. "They got the whole intellectual-property thing together while a million lawyers and activists were still spitting in their soup [like babies]. They figured out that there are going to be some things that are sold and some things that are traded. And the cohesiveness of that fan base kept it free. There's a real strong ethic that we can learn from; they had a trading policy that really worked. It meant that the fans get all their music, and they'd still buy."

The Dave Matthews Band have been hailed as the multimillion-selling successors to the Grateful Dead. In the beginning, though, Matthews was just another local musician when I worked at Plan 9 Records during the first half of the 1990s. We sold Matthews's independently released debut, *Remember Two Things,* as well as concert tickets, posters, and other merchandise. My record-store job gave me a vacation from my academic life because, at the time, I was an unhappy grad student in sociology at the University of Virginia with an interest in copyright law. Despite my best intentions, my music and scholarly lives intertwined. One day, Dave Matthews came into Plan 9, and from behind the raised checkout counter I questioned him about why he allowed his music to be copied and traded. "You work at a record store," he said in his easygoing tone, "and I'm sure you make mix-tapes for friends.

"You're probably choosing songs that you think are good, or songs you think a friend would like. I mean, how else are they going to hear about a band and possibly buy the whole record unless they're exposed to the music?" He had a point. I hadn't quite thought of it in that way, I'm embarrassed to admit, until Dave Matthews said this to me. "So, no," Matthews said, "I don't think it's the same thing as stealing. The whole tape scene has served us well. We can't get on mainstream radio, and who knows if we ever will"—little did he know!—"so, it's a way of getting word out about the band, and with each year there are more tapes and bigger audiences." The popularity of the Dave Matthews Band rose through the late 1990s, and so did the Internet, which made this kind of music swapping easier and more efficient. In many ways, the band still benefits from the culture of trading—online and off—because it's part of what maintains connections among fans.

The spread of cassette-tape technology also created new outlets for disseminating music and ideas that had been silenced by governments and corporations around the world. For example, it created a seismic shift in India's musical landscape, which had previously been dominated by one record company until the 1980s. This monopoly created an extremely narrow selection of music that didn't reflect the diversity of tastes of the country's population. Before the spread of cassette technology, only large companies could afford to manufacture and distribute LPs; then, suddenly, a plethora of choices emerged from the ground up. Egypt, Thailand, Indonesia, and Sri Lanka also experienced similar transformations, some of which carried over into politics.[10]

Hip-hop thrived in the 1970s long before the record industry paid attention; this also had a lot to do with the recent affordability of cassette recorders. During this time, the only way to hear hip-hop music was at live performances in South Bronx parks, public-school gyms, small nightclubs, or on boom boxes. DJs and crews sold dubbed copies of their live performances, and their fans copied these cassettes—passing them on from friend to friend, acquaintance to acquaintance. "Around 1977," said DJ Disco Wiz, "we used to record all our battles. Every party we had we always had a boom box on the side, and we used to record what we did and who we did it to. And those things used to sell—we used to sell them in high school." Jazzy Jay, an MC in Afrika Bambaataa's Soulsonic Force, boasted, "I mean, we had tapes that went platinum before we was even involved with the music industry." An exaggerating Grand-master Flash said that tapes of his performances sold at "a buck a minute."[11]

Hip-hop prospered because of the wide diffusion of bootlegged tapes. This is true for hip-hop even today, because record companies frequently leak exclusive tracks to popular DJs who make and sell illegal mix-tapes. Giving away tracks that float around the underground mix-tape circuit is a way of promoting up-and-coming artists and building buzz for an established act's new record. "At first," said Rob Love, an executive at the seminal hip-hop label Def Jam, "I was anti–mix-tape, because I thought it was stealing and I thought that the resale of [the recordings] did not benefit the artist." But Love changed his mind when he realized mix-tapes were extremely effective promotional tools; the success of mix-tape favorite 50 Cent (and others) demonstrates this.[12] Even Metallica, in the early 1980s, directly benefited from the unauthorized trading of their tapes, an irony that would rear its ugly head years later.

WORLD WAR MP3

In the spring of 2000, Metallica's Lars Ulrich carted into the Napster offices boxes of printouts naming the downloaders who violated his group's copyrights. It's the kind of grunt work typically done by an intern, but the heavy-metal drummer's sacrifice was for a higher purpose: a stage-managed media event, complete with press conference. An outraged Lars Ulrich had earlier explained that his band goes through a "grueling creative process" when writing and recording each of their songs. "It is therefore sickening to know that our art is being treated like a commodity," the multiplatinum rocker said. "From a business standpoint, this is about piracy—aka taking something that doesn't belong to you, and that is morally and legally wrong."

"Fuck you, Lars," screamed a member of the teenage peanut gallery that spontaneously formed at the scene. "It's our music, too!"[13] Indeed, in recent concerts the group had changed the lyrics of "Whiplash" from "We're Metallica" to "We'll never stop, we'll never quit, 'cause *you're* Metallica." In doing so, they emphasized a supposed communal connection between the band and its fans. As recently as 1996, Metallica allowed fans to tape shows and trade their music for free, setting up special recording sections in arenas. It was a nod to their early fan base, because in the early 1980s Metallica was just one of many unknown hard-core metal groups slogging it out. They got their first big break from the world of bootleg-tape trading, and the group has gratefully acknowledged this debt on a number of occasions.

"The brutal irony of the Metallica beef," Steve Albini tells me, shaking his head, "is that Metallica's early fan base was all kids that traded cassette copies of the Metallica demo. That's how I first heard Metallica—on a fucking cassette dub of a demo. They owe their career to the exact same practice, in a different form, and for them to get bent out of shape about it now is fucking retarded." Along with long-forgotten groups (Jaguar, Blitzkrieg, and Anvil Chorus), Metallica's demo *No Life 'Til Leather* tape was a favorite among fans who scoured the pages of British metal magazines such as *Kerrang!* and *Sounds.* "Back in the Stone Age," remembers early Metallica fan Brian Lew, "tape trades took weeks to complete as letters and packages were sent and received."[14] His description highlights an important difference between tape trading and file-sharing—a difference in volume, scale, and speed of delivery. But to say tape trading is *nothing* like file-sharing is just as disingenuous as saying the opposite, for there are significant similarities.

"The difference between tape trading and file trading that the major labels hype up is the idea that people can go and get whole records, so they never bother to buy the music," says Thom Monahan. "I actually don't buy into that at all." For Thom and others like him, both file-sharing and tape trading are a kind of underground radio, spreading the word about bands that aren't pumped out through more mainstream outlets. "I see the file-trading thing as a different kind of listening booth, that's all it is," says Albini. "It's like a special radio that you can program yourself, but it's not the real thing. Nobody listening to a downloaded file is actually getting the record, they're not actually getting the same sound quality. . . . You're getting a cheapened simulacrum, which might excite you about the real thing."

For a rock star whose band made rebellion their stock-in-trade, Lars Ulrich showing up at the Napster offices with a lawyer wasn't exactly the best image enhancer. In doing so, Ulrich volunteered to be the File-Sharing Nation's first whipping boy—even though Dr. Dre and other non-Lars superstars also sued Napster. He was eviscerated on many Web sites and booed by the kids in the balcony when presenting an MTV Video Award later in 2000. It's quite possible that on the day he entered the Napster offices, Ulrich may very well have realized just what he got himself into. Joseph Menn reported that the drummer grew increasingly uneasy when he realized that Napster was housed in a decrepit building over a bank, and he looked miserable on the elevator ride up. Upon entering the Napster offices, Lars was swamped by employees who told him they were fans, some of whom had gone to Metallica concerts since junior high. Upon hearing this, "Ulrich seemed to slump," wrote Menn.

In 2003, three years after Lars Ulrich entered the Napster offices, the RIAA began its lawsuit campaign against hundreds of file-trading consumers, which sought $150,000 in damages per song. Among the evildoers were a working mom, a seventy-one-year-old grandfather, and a twelve-year-old honors student named Briana Lahara, who lived in New York City public housing. "I am very sorry for what I have done," said the little girl in an RIAA press release, after her mom shelled out a two-thousand-dollar settlement. The girl continued, under duress from the RIAA, "I love music and I don't want to hurt the artists I love."[15] By 2004, the RIAA had racked up over three thousand lawsuits against downloaders in the United States, and the international music industry began suing individuals in Italy, Germany, Denmark, and Canada. Perhaps realizing it's a bad idea to sue military personnel during the wartime occupation of another country, the music industry chose not to go after troops who shared music in Iraq (suing twelve-year-olds in public housing, I guess, isn't crossing the line).

During and after the second Gulf War, troops would upload songs on a central server for others to download. "Anytime anybody on the team gets a new CD," said Sgt. Thomas R. Mena, "they load it in, so we stay pretty current." Sgt. Daniel Kartchien added, "Everybody has their own MP3 player to pass the time."[16] Back in the homeland, a retired Massachusetts schoolteacher was served with papers—for downloading tracks such as Trick Daddy's "I'm a Thug" from KaZaA, even though this file-sharing software doesn't work on her Mac computer. While it's unlikely that a retiree was downloading hard-core rap, she still had to hire a lawyer to clear her name, and the RIAA only let her off with a warning, generously stating, "We decided to give her the benefit of the doubt."

A Colorado dad received a reprimand from his ISP when he downloaded "Happy Birthday to You" for his child, not knowing it was a copyrighted song. The list went on. It was a sign of desperation from an industry that had been for years hopelessly unwilling to adapt to changing times and shifting technologies. The recording industry spent the first couple of years before and after Napster's debut holding its breath, closing its eyes, and wishing file-sharing would go away—instead of developing a coherent, standardized business model for digital distribution. The major labels could have done just that when they launched the Secure Digital Music Initiative, but they dropped the ball, coming up with next to nothing.

Exactly one hundred years before the music industry began suing consumers, believe it or not, the same thing happened in the auto industry. In 1903 Henry Ford launched the Ford Motor Company and locked horns with the Association of Licensed Automobile Manufacturers. ALAM, much like the RIAA, represented the major auto companies of the time, and it guaranteed its market dominance through the Selden Patent. Through this patent, ALAM could collect royalties on "self-propelled vehicles powered by internal combustion engines." You know, cars. At the time, automobiles were expensive and out of the reach for most consumers, and ALAM wanted to keep it that way, so they refused to grant a patent license to Ford.

He made his cars anyway, and ALAM sued hundreds of Ford customers for purchasing these intellectual property–violating "unlicensed vehicles," quickly turning public sentiment against it. Reminiscent of RIAA's lawsuits and ads about downloading, ALAM placed the following notice in newspapers, stating that "any person making, selling, or using such machines made or sold by any unlicensed manufacturers or importers will be liable to prosecution for infringement."[17] Litigation lasted from 1903 to 1911, until an appeals court ruled in Ford's favor, and most of the ALAM-licensed companies failed after being left in the dust by technological advances. Moral of this hundred-year-old story: Don't sue your customers, or they'll move on. Also, embrace change.

In its relentless drive to stamp out any and all music trading on the Internet, the RIAA sent Penn State's Department of Astronomy and Astrophysics a threatening cease-and-desist letter. Apparently, the department was unlawfully distributing MP3s of R&B artist Usher. Just why was a department of astronomy illegally giving away Usher songs? Well, it wasn't, it's just that the RIAA's automated Web-crawling copyright bots found that the department's Web page contained a mention of emeritus professor Peter Usher and an MP3 file that contained an a capella song about the Swift gamma ray satellite. Sample lyric: "With a superbright explosion, never to repeat again, how are we supposed to know? / How 'bout a telescope rotation swiftly on to the location of its panchromatic afterglow . . ." That would be one weird slow jam. It's like a scene from Terry Gilliam's *Brazil*, the black comedy about authoritarian bureaucracy gone painfully awry. The RIAA later apologized after a slew of bad publicity.

Even more troubling was the RIAA's plan to plant "bombs" in the computers of those who download MP3s by posting fake viruslike files on peer-to-peer networks. The *New York Times* reported that record companies were preparing a program called Freeze, which "locks up a computer system for a certain duration—minutes or possibly even hours—risking the loss of data that was unsaved if the computer is restarted." To make things worse, the RIAA has many allies in Congress, from the barely contained lunacy of Republican senator Orrin Hatch to the relative moderation of Howard Berman, a California Democrat. "I'm all for destroying their machines," said Hatch in 2003 during a Congressional Committee hearing, referring to those who trade music files. "If you have a few hundred thousand of those [bombs], I think people would realize the seriousness of their actions."[18]

Interestingly, Hatch—a musician who distributes his gospel records independently—had previously been somewhat sympathetic toward file-sharing, and an outspoken critic of the RIAA. Now the Utah senator wanted new legislation that exempts copyright owners from being prosecuted for the crimes of property destruction and invasion of privacy. Although Hatch apparently believes there's an excuse for willful destruction of property, he says, "There's no excuse for anyone violating copyright laws." The next day, he cryptically clarified himself: "I do not favor extreme remedies—unless no moderate remedies can be found."[19] (He almost sounds like a by-any-means-necessary-espousing Black Panther.) Similarly, Representative Berman has advocated for the legal right of intellectual-property owners and their agents to hack computer systems that may be facilitating copyright infringement. In 2004 a couple of key bills were introduced in Congress that would significantly criminalize individual file-sharing activities, and similar laws began popping up around the world.

There was a far more troubling irony that emerged during the file-trading wars. It turned out major labels were using the same method of identifying and suing potential copyright infringers—tracking down one's IP address, kind of an online street address—

as a way of gathering marketing data. The firm BigChampagne monitors downloads on file-trading networks and collects the data, creating a sort of alternative *Billboard* charts for the digital era. BigChampagne has worked with most major labels, selling subscriptions to its database, though these record companies are loath to admit it. (By doing so, the companies would undermine the RIAA's position that file-sharing has no promotional value.) Jeremy Welt, head of new media at Maverick Records, Madonna's label, is more forthcoming. He calls it "fantastic," adding, "It actually shows us what people are doing of their own accord," because it allows labels to peer into the private preferences of downloading listeners.

IP addresses contain information akin to a zip code, allowing downloads to be sorted and ranked according to geographical location. (For instance, one month in 2003 38.35 percent of file-sharers in Omaha, Nebraska, had a song from 50 Cent's debut album.) Joe Fleischer, VP of Sales at BigChampagne, explained how a label executive uses their data. "He'll give this to promotions," he said. "They call these stations and say, 'You need to bang this shit. You're barely playing it, and it's already in the top fifteen among alt-rock downloaders in your market. You need to step on this at least twenty more times a week, and not while people are sleeping."

To use a concrete example, the Maverick Records–signed band Story of the Year's music was being downloaded as much as other popular artists, but the group wasn't getting much radio play. Armed with this data, their record company successfully lobbied radio to spin their music more, and soon after, Story of the Year's *Page Avenue* went gold. "In the world of what we do," says Gary Oseary, Madonna's business partner, "it's always good to have real information from real fans." BigChampagne chief executive Eric Garland marveled, "It's the most vast and scaleable sample audience that the world has ever seen."[20] File traders unknowingly are working—for free, and at risk of being sued—in an ongoing focus group. Something about this seems horribly wrong.

IS FILE-SHARING REALLY THAT BAD FOR BUSINESS?

Critics argued that file-sharing was directly responsible for the widely reported CD-sales slump from 2000 to 2003. The worst year was 2002, which saw total album sales drop 10.7 percent compared to 2001. However, blaming file-sharing for the decline ignores the fact that the economy was in a recession after 9/11 and many other industries suffered greater declines at that time. More important, the two primary markets that directly compete for young music buyers' dollars—video games and DVDs, media that are also heavily traded on the Internet—did quite well during the recession period. In 2003 DVD sales enjoyed a staggering growth rate of 46 percent, and video-game sales also rose over the previous year. If we accept the industry's rhetoric that each download equals a lost sale—an estimated 2.6 billion music files are downloaded a month—we would have seen sales decline to zero, something that obviously never happened.

Still, it's perfectly reasonable to assume that downloading, rather than the economy, was the cause of the post-2000 drop in CD sales—a certain number of those downloads surely accounted for lost sales, after all. However, some strange things began happening that complicated this simple narrative. The United Kingdom saw a 7.6 percent increase in CD sales in 2003, and that year turned out to be the Australian music industry's best year ever. In the first quarter of 2004, U.S. CD sales rose 10.6 percent over the previous year—and sales continued to rise in the following months—an upturn that the RIAA confidently attributed to the more than three thousand lawsuits it filed against downloaders. However, the Pew Internet & American Life Project released an April 2004 report that stated that the number of people who say they download music files "increased from an estimated 18 million to 23 million since the Project's November–December 2003 survey." Other nonsurvey-based estimates put that number at 60 million—more people than who voted for Bush in 2000—and the technology firm CacheLogic reported that file-sharing activity had doubled between mid-2003 and mid-2004.[21]

At the exact moment file-sharing activity rose, so did CD sales, numbers that confirmed the findings of an important two-year economic study on file-sharing. The paper Felix Oberholzer-Gee and Koleman S. Strumpf published contradicted the RIAA's position. Their findings indicated that file-sharing had no measurable effect on music sales and couldn't be attributed to their overall decline. "At most, file sharing can explain a tiny fraction of this decline," concluded the report. "This result is plausible given that movies, software, and video games are actively downloaded, and yet these industries have continued to grow since the advent of file sharing."

These men are not anti-copyright activists by any measure—Oberholzer-Gee is a professor at the prestigious Harvard Business School, and Strumpf is a Visiting Fellow at the conservative-leaning Cato Institute. In fact, they began the study with the assumption that file-sharing had a negative impact, but their analysis demonstrated otherwise. "No matter how we use our statistical models, we cannot find a connection between decreased sales and downloads," says Oberholzer-Gee. "The Internet is more like radio than we thought. People listen to two or three songs, and if they like it, they go out and buy the CD."[22] Sonic Youth's Lee Ranaldo agrees: "I view file-sharing in a manner similar to the way AM radio worked when I was young—it was a source of information about a lot of new music, a place where you could hear new sounds. If you liked it you went out and bought it."

For instance, Norah Jones's second album, released in 2004, had one of the biggest selling first weeks in history, selling over one million copies. "She is one of the most downloaded artists of all time," says BigChampagne's CEO, Eric Garland, "which disproves this idea that illegal downloads cannibalize CD sales." The director of marketing at Jones's label, Blue Note, cautiously agrees. "People who download [Jones] truly might be previewing it," he says. "If they like what they hear, they'll probably go out and buy the record, too."[23] This behavior doesn't just extend to acts that appeal to older consumers who are less likely to use file-sharing networks. *The Eminem Show,* Mathers's third album, was the biggest selling CD of 2002 despite heavy downloading. And Oberholzer-Gee and Strumpf's report notes that CD sales for Eminem's *8 Mile* soundtrack didn't decrease during or after several downloading spikes.

Too Much Joy's Tim Quirk explains this apparent contradiction by drawing from personal experience. Although Quirk isn't an old man, he's been in the music business long enough to watch LPs give birth to CDs, which then begat MP3s. Real Networks, his current employer, was one of the first music services to get in on the legal downloading game, so Tim can speak firsthand about the subject from the perspective of a businessman, musician, and fan. "I can listen to things for free all the time at my job," Tim tells me. "But I buy even more records than I did five years ago due to my access to more." He adds, "My personal take on file trading is the practical musician's take. To me, it's really not that much different from when I used to walk into a used-record store, and if I saw a used Too Much Joy CD in the used bin, I was happy," Tim explains. Someone would be more likely to buy his CD at a reduced price than for eighteen dollars, and it didn't matter to him either way because he never saw a penny of royalties from Warner Records. "As a musician, you want your music out there; you want it out in as many places as it can possibly be."

This increases the chances more people will pay to see your band when it comes through town (and perhaps buy merchandise), or that a newfound fan will purchase one of your other albums. While there are always going to be freeloaders who will never pay for music, that doesn't characterize the majority of fans who share music. A study of file-sharers conducted in 2000 by the Norman Lear Center at the University of Southern California backs up these anecdotes with numbers. It stated, "MP3 usage does not reduce students' CD consumption patterns. Fully 73 percent of students who download MP3s reported that they still bought either the same number of CDs or more." Those who are most likely to trade with friends are the very people who buy the most CDs, echoing the earlier Warner report, which noted that home taping demonstrates a commitment to music. Additionally, the Pew Internet & American Life Project conducted random digit-dial phone surveys during Napster's 2000 to mid-2001 heyday, and it concluded:

It is clear from the passion the Napster controversy has generated among music fans and musicians that a "commitment to music" is very much in play throughout the debate, as it was during the home taping controversy. That so many music downloaders in the surveys are not concerned with matters of copyright does not mean that they are criminals, or even scofflaws, or that they do not understand copyright law. Instead, as seems to have been the case with home taping, music downloaders believe music occupies a special place in their lives and in the world, a place that they believe is not subject to the same rules and regulations found in the world of commerce. In general, the Internet appears to have given them an opportunity to experience music in ways not as connected to income and commerce as music buying.[24]

A 2003 study by Jupiter Research found something similar among European downloaders. "There are strong music fans within the file-sharing community," Mark Mulligan, an analyst at Jupiter Research, told Reuters. "They are more likely to listen to digital radio and visit artists' Web sites. There is compelling evidence that this group is the bedrock community for those willing to pay for legitimate (online) music services in the future." All this isn't to say that consumers aren't disgruntled with the recording industry.

When consumers figured out that CDs cost as little as one dollar to manufacture but retail for upward of $19.99—while artists receive about one dollar in royalties per CD, or nothing—it's no wonder many have moved on to other more value-packed forms of entertainment such as DVDs. For instance, the list price of the DVD *High Fidelity* is $9.99, but the soundtrack CD is $18.99. It also didn't help that, during the 1990s, the major labels defrauded consumers out of millions upon millions of dollars by fixing CD prices. The week before I finished this book, I received a $13.86 settlement check—split many ways with other CD buyers—after participating in a class-action suit brought against the majors.

Even many in the porn industry have embraced the free trading of its pictures online. "It's direct marketing at its finest," says Randy Nicolau, president of playboy.com. The porn industry has always been among the first to exploit new technologies—the VCR, the Internet, and online payment systems, for instance—and it has grown savvy during the copyright wars. Nicolau doesn't worry about steering a different course than the RIAA, telling the *New York Times*, "I haven't spent much time thinking about it. It's like asking Henry Ford, 'What were the buggy-whip guys doing wrong?' " Although some porn companies are concerned about the issue, most don't go after their customers, opting to sue for-profit Web sites that reprint their photos. "We haven't gone after Joe Citizen who's sharing something he printed off something from the *Hustler* Web site with another guy," says Paul Cambria, a lawyer who represents *Hustler* and others.

Different musicians—from rock stars to obscure indie artists—have varying opinions about downloading. For instance, Missy Elliot hates it when people download her songs: "Copy-written, so don't copy me," she rapped in "Get UR Freak On." During the 2004 Consumer Electronics Show, actor Ben Affleck, singer Sheryl Crow, and U2 guitarist the Edge—remember him from the Negativland controversy?—took the stage to make a pitch against unauthorized digital downloading. "All the downloading of music, and all the sharing of music, I can't stand it," says indie hip-hop maestro Prefuse 73. "That person gets paid, they make a living, rather than just these kids downloading music." On the other hand, at the height of the RIAA lawsuits, Neil Young told *Rolling Stone,* "I'm not greedy to the point that I need to get paid for every little thing I do. I'm an artist. I should be fucking doing art, not standing up for artists' rights." He adds sarcastically, "We got Sheryl Crow and Don Henley—it's covered. I don't have to do it. When the copyright law is all over and I'm dead and gone, I'll have more songs."

"I personally don't know a single artist that takes any offense at file-sharing," says Steve Albini. "I think that it's a genuine expression of an appreciation of music, and most bands don't feel threatened by it all. They don't think that someone is downloading a song in order to *not* give them money. The big record labels look at downloading as a means for someone to not pay, and these bands look at it as yet another means for somebody to hear their music." Claudia Gonson—manager of the Magnetic Fields, and also a musician in the band—primarily makes her living administrating the band's finances. As someone who isn't very tech-savvy, she admits that the spread of file-sharing makes her nervous. "The learning curve is so steep, it's hard to acclimate to the changes the Internet has brought," she tells me. "So this makes it scary to a lot of people—it's a fear of the unknown." However, Gonson says she's reluctant to see downloading as a bad thing because of the many positive accounts she has heard from her musician peers.

When entering these debates, especially if you aren't a musician yourself, it might seem unethical to ignore the wishes of artists. A standard line I've heard, which sounds rather convincing, is that it should be up to the artists to decide whether or not their music can be freely distributed. Some artists such as the Beatles have even resisted allowing their music to be legitimately sold in downloadable form. Reasons for this are manifold, including the fact that artists spend a considerable amount of energy sequencing the tracks and designing album packaging. With iTunes, they say, anyone can ignore these intentions and simply pick, choose, and rearrange. However, the desire these artists have for full control ignores multiple historical precedents.

As I discussed earlier, radio doesn't give musicians the right to choose how their music will be presented. Radio stations purchase annual blanket compulsory licenses from organizations that collect songwriting royalties—ASCAP, BMI, and SESAC—something that gives these broadcast outlets the freedom to order songs in whatever ways they see fit. Once the song has been publicly released, copyright holders are given only *limited* control over their creative goods. The difference between current file-sharing and radio, at the moment, is that radio pays for what it plays. *Sort of.* The fee for these blanket licenses compensates the songwriter, not the performing artist. In other words, every time a commercial radio station played Frank Sinatra's signature song, "My Way," the crooner didn't see a dime, because late-1950s teen idol Paul Anka wrote it. Radio stations are essentially getting a free ride on the value Sinatra added to Anka's song.[25]

At first glance this payment practice seems unfair, but it really points to how the enforcement of copyright law has always involved compromise. The example of radio also shows how "free" can translate into cash. Radio broadcasts act as commercials that advertise the existence of a record, and it is in this indirect way that performing artists are remunerated for their efforts. If all copyright owners had their way—if they could manifest their own vision of a "perfect" world—our media culture would be quite different, and much more constrained. For instance, if early-twentieth-century song publishers had their way, we'd still be diligently buying their sheet music, just as if modern record companies had prevailed in court in 1999, there would be no MP3 players.

THE GIFT ECONOMY IN ACTION

When the Dave Matthews Band shelved an entire album recorded with longtime producer Steve Lilywhite, the songs leaked onto the Internet and fans devoured them. The band initially believed the album wasn't worth putting out, but the extensive downloads demonstrated otherwise. And when they released an official version of the album, *Busted Stuff*, it debuted at number one. Even though the audience for the CD overlapped with those who had already downloaded versions of those tracks, it sold about two million copies, according to Nielsen/Soundscan. The same scenario played out with the Chicago-based rock band Wilco, which was dropped by Warner after the major label deemed their album "uncommercial." As the group searched for a new label, the tracks leaked onto file-sharing networks—so they put the album on their Web site so that fans could listen to it for free.

By applying the major labels' logic, the band's gift should have cut into sales, but the exact opposite happened. Wilco's *Yankee Hotel Foxtrot* ended up debuting in the *Billboard* top twenty and went on to be the band's biggest album, selling a half million copies, double that of its last album. The publicity surrounding the plight of the record combined with the free distribution of their music on the Internet undoubtedly generated more sales for the little band that could. Wilco's next album, *A Ghost Is Born,* also spread on file-sharing networks long before its official release. "How do I feel about the record leaking on the Internet?" says Wilco business manager Tony Margherita. "Well, that's a little bit like asking me how I felt about the sun coming up today. It's an inevitable thing and not something we ever perceive as a problem."[26] The Magnetic Fields are signed to Nonesuch, Wilco's label. "When we went to Nonesuch," says Claudia Gonson, "they told us not to worry about downloading—because look at what happened with Wilco, and how their sales increased."

Responding to concerns about downloading, film archivist Rick Prelinger argues that the answer isn't the nearly impossible task of preventing unauthorized duplication. The solution is to sell more copies by creating incentives and positive reinforcements to purchase. Many people still collect CDs and DVDs because of the value that the packaging and supplementary materials add—and they download. "The biggest reason to make material available for free is that it feeds demand," Prelinger tells filmmakers and other creative types. "Think of a free download as a trailer, a preview, an ad, as a way of stimulating DVD sales."

In 1982 he founded the Prelinger Archives as a storehouse for ephemeral films about American history and culture that nobody else was collecting at that time: educational filmstrips, industrial films, and the like. It became a rather large collection that went to the Library of Congress, and since 2000 he's been working in a partnership with Brewster Kahle's Internet Archive to digitally distribute these materials. What's fascinating about the Prelinger Archives is that they've taken all the key films from the collection and put them online, for free. People who download the material can then reuse the footage in their own work without restriction; all that is asked for is a simple credit. "So if somebody wants to make a movie and they don't have money to get footage," Prelinger tells me, "they can access really a kind of wonderful library of historical footage for free."

"Why not free?" Prelinger says, turning my inevitable question around. "As long as it's possible for me to make a living out of that collection—it turns out that we actually make more money because we give things away." He put his money where his mouth is, demonstrating in practice the fact that the gift economy isn't just a nifty theoretical idea, that you can give things away and still have a viable product. "We have a two-tier model. If you want a very, very high-quality copy—a physical copy on tape—you can pay to license it from us," he says. "But if you want something for free, you go online and you download it. It's been exciting. I think archives are validated by what kind of use is made of them. There's been this profusion of work that wouldn't have happened if people hadn't had access to that material. So it's kind of an exercise in democracy."

Prelinger points out that in 2003 his company's sales were up roughly 20 percent from the previous year—this during a recession, something that wasn't true of his competitors. He attributes the increased profits to the easy availability of the archive's films online and the publicity that has generated, allowing Prelinger's outfit to compete with other archive companies with bigger marketing budgets. He says there are a lot of people out there whose jobs require them to find interesting imagery and recycle it into the culture—trend spotters, fashion people, MTV producers, ad people, and others. "It's kind of like the rising tide. I make more money," Prelinger says, "and all the other people that are involved with selling stock footage do better. I think it's kind of an amazing example."

At the exact moment when Hollywood successfully lobbied the FCC to mandate that television signals carry a "broadcast flag"— which prevents programs from being downloaded—the British Broadcasting Corporation took another course. After visits from Lawrence Lessig and Brewster Kahle, in 2003 the BBC announced it would make much of its archive available for download. BBC director-general Greg Dyke will make available free, digitized versions of the network's productions from the earliest radio broadcasts to its most current documentaries. It also allowed media-makers to reuse the BBC's material in their own work. Contemplating a question about whether or not file-sharing harms the BBC, Dyke pauses, then asks, "Wait a minute. Why do we care about them sharing our programs?" It's part of the BBC's charter: to make its material available to as wide an audience as possible. File-sharing only helps this cause.

The project is called the BBC Creative Archive and is inspired in part by the U.S.–based Creative Commons project, which Lessig helped found with involvement from Kahle, Prelinger, and others. The Creative Commons Web site offers simple boilerplate contracts that allow artists' works to be easily shared, and Brewster Kahle's Internet Archive offers free hosting of digitized works that carry a Creative Commons license. Sound-collage artists such as Negativland and Vicki Bennett have applied Creative Commons sampling licenses to their work, which encourages others to sample and transform it. The famous Brazilian artist Gilberto Gil, today Brazil's minister of culture, released his 2003 album with a Creative Commons license.

"You are free," the license stated, in part, "to make derivative works." Rather than all rights reserved, *some* rights are reserved. Gil retained his copyright on the album, but the license gives others more freedom to do something new and unexpected with fragments of his music, without dealing with lawyers. "I'm doing it as an artist," says Gil, though he acknowledges his leading role as a Brazilian government official. He says his ministry has been "getting interested in supporting projects concerning free use," not only for music but creative content in general.[27]

The gift economy also works in its own curious way for artists whose songs have been sampled, something that has frequently rekindled the commercial life of the original artist or song. Liquid Liquid was dealt a major legal headache when Grandmaster Flash appropriated their song "Cavern" for Flash's "White Lines," but it turned out to be a good thing over the years. "I don't have any bad feelings about the 'Cavern' thing," bassist Richard McGuire tells me, sitting in his immaculate Manhattan studio. "I think it helped keep our band alive. The band still has this following because of that, and it's given us so much more attention. The song will live on because of it."

OPEN-SOURCE AND FREE CULTURE

The same technological advances that made digital sampling possible also helped dramatically lower the price of home recording equipment. Garage bands and platinum-selling artists alike now use computer-based software and hardware systems that cost a fraction of a traditional professional studio. At a hugely reduced price, musicians can make a high-quality recording and put it directly onto the hard drive of a computer (though it still can't recreate the sonic richness and nuance of many traditional studios). With these programs, rather than patching your guitar through a physical reverb or distortion pedal, you can download "plug-ins" that generate those effects. Since the late 1990s, there's been an explosion in the number of free, freaky effects available for musicians and producers to download and do with what they want.

"There's all sorts of synthesis techniques that can be applied," says über-gearhead Thom Monahan. "Stuff that emulates analog circuitry, like stuff you might find in an old studio. You can do lots of things with plug-ins." Reason is a popular audio-production program, one that is designed to emulate a rackful of audio gear—drum machines, samplers, synthesizers, pianos, etc. The program allows you to use "sound sets" called Refills, which might contain, for instance, the full range of notes made by an organ. Propellerhead, the software company that makes Reason, opened the architecture of the software so that people could create their own Refills. For instance, the 808 drum machine, whose booming bass sound was the foundation of a lot of 1980s hip-hop and House records, has been fetishized by collectors to the point that it now sells for thousands.

"There's a guy in Italy who thought it was ridiculous," Monahan says, "so he took his 808 and he sampled the hell out of it, and put together this amazing Refill of his 808 drum machine and put it online so that people could do stuff with it." Similarly, Thomas O'Neill loved an eight-foot Baldwin grand piano that his parents had to get rid of, so he spent hours recording it. He then turned the digitally preserved piano into a Refill packet and posted it on the Web for anyone to download. "I hope you like this little gift to the Reason user community," O'Neill wrote on his Web site, "and that it finds its way into your music making." This is yet another example of the gift economy, which goes to the very communal heart of the open-source and free-software movements.

The "openness" of open source and the "freedom" of free software allows many people to collaborate and build upon each other's ideas, which are then transformed into something new and unexpected. This kind of creativity is possible because open-source code can be copied and freely built upon by an army of volunteers, then given back to the community, often in improved or expanded form. The surprising thing about the open-source and free-software movement is that its products often outcompete the products of their closed, proprietary competitors. For instance, the open source Sendmail routes over 80 percent of all e-mail on the Internet, and Linux commands 27 percent of the server market, much to Microsoft's chagrin. Bill Gates has a right to be concerned. In 2002 Britain, Russia, China, South Korea, and other countries began to seriously consider replacing their Microsoft servers with Linux-based PCs.

Other governments worldwide are expected to require state agencies to use free, open-source software, and Brazil, Thailand, India, and Germany have already begun to use open-source software on public computers. During these times of education budget cuts, many information technology (IT) workers in the United States are turning to open-source software. For instance, a University of Missouri IT employee told me that his department uses open source whenever possible, something that is increasingly common for his colleagues at other institutions. In 2003 Massachusetts adopted a broad-based strategy for the state government to use open-source software. State Administration and Finance Secretary Eric Kriss said that the state was motivated by reducing licensing fees, but also "by a philosophy that what the state has is a public good and should be open to all."[28]

It's not just governments shifting to open source; Amazon, eBay,

Google, and many others run on Linux. Even Motorola released a cell phone that runs on the open-source Linux and Java in order to speed the development of innovative features and applications, something that other companies followed. "We've been open, using Java, which is the key to applications," says Motorola senior VP Scott Durchslag. "But putting Linux under Java as our operating system is openness cubed."[29] By 2003 IBM was running television ads worldwide, proclaiming, "The Future Is Open."

Richard Stallman, the founder of the Free Software Foundation, explains that his use of the word "free" isn't economic. It's "free," as in "free speech," Stallman says, not "free," as in "free beer." Lawrence Lessig explains, "A resource is 'free' when (1) one can use it without the permission of anyone else or (2) the permission one needs is granted neutrally." Still, you might be wondering, *why* does the gift economy work? Is it some sort of magic increase machine? Intellectual-property scholar James Boyle says that it's fun to debate and imagine all the different explanations, but they're ultimately irrelevant. With open-source software, he writes, you have a global network of people, and it costs almost nothing to transmit, copy, and share digital materials.

With these assumptions, it just does not matter why they do it. In lots of cases, they *will* do it. One person works for love of the species, another in the hope of a better job, a third for the joy of solving puzzles, and so on. Each person has his own reserve price, the point at which he says, "Now I will turn off *Survivor* and go and create something." But on a global network, there are a *lot* of people, and with numbers that big and information overhead that small, even relatively hard projects will attract motivated and skilled people whose particular reserve price has been crossed.[30]

Robert Greenwald's *Outfoxed,* discussed in chapter four, used a kind of open-source methodology to produce this documentary. Although the medium was film, rather than computer software, it was similar to the way individual open-source programmers write certain sections of code, which are then compiled to create something larger than the sum of its parts, like Linux. In the case of *Outfoxed,* the *New York Times* reported that a group of volunteers was recruited to watch Fox News's broadcasts twenty-four hours a day, with each volunteer assigned to monitor a particular time slot. Greenwald created a list of categories—the sort of techniques used by Fox News to slant its coverage—and when a volunteer noticed an example on the producer's list they e-mailed the producer the exact date and time it aired.

This information was entered into a spreadsheet, and before long Greenwald's assistants had logged enough examples to begin constructing a general outline of the film. Soon after, a small army of highly skilled film editors (who worked for next to nothing because they sympathized with the film's politics) organized the clips into subsections that eventually created coherent narrative. Each worked as a separate node, often in different cities, and at the end of each day they posted their work on a secure Web site for Greenwald to review. *Outfoxed* was conceived and completed in just four and a half months, an astoundingly short amount of time to create a professional-looking documentary.

Interestingly, the ability of free or open-source software to remain unrestricted relies on the existence of copyright; it's another reason why copyright itself isn't inherently flawed. "Copyleft" is the term Richard Stallman uses to describe the method he and others apply to prevent their free-software code from being turned into proprietary software, that is, full of restrictions. "Copyleft uses copyright law," Stallman says, "but flips it over to serve the opposite of its usual purpose: Instead of a means of privatizing software, it becomes a means of keeping software free." The basic premise of copyleft is that it uses the legal-contractual force of copyright law to permit anyone to do anything with the code. You just can't add your own restrictions to it (all modifications must be free—again, as in freedom).

There are many companies that profit from open-source software, such as Red Hat, a company that packages and bundles Linux software and sells it for a price. But Red Hat also supports the development of new code and returns it to the open-source community, setting the information free. It's by honoring the very basic social contract that we learned when we were kids—to share, and share alike—that companies such as Red Hat can contribute to openness *and* make money. (Red Hat is profitable, has $328 million in the bank, and provides support for Amazon, DreamWorks, Reuters, British Petroleum, and others.) Red Hat claims that the open-source model "often builds better, more secure, more easily integrated software. And it does it at a vastly accelerated pace compared to proprietary models." Also, it's cheaper for consumers.

The fact that much of the (sometimes giddily over-the-top) discussion of cyberspace's "innovation commons" originates in the United States comes as no surprise to Eva Hemmungs Wirtén, a Swedish scholar. The way America's Wild West has been romanticized—freedom from constraints, rugged individualism, and ingenuity—overlaps closely with the tech talk of certain open-source and free software advocates. Those who lament the expansion of intellectual property and the enclosure of the Internet's public domain can occasionally sound like Libertarian cowboys who are repulsed by how the beautiful wide-open spaces have been fenced in by government (or corporate) regulation. At their worst, they come off like free-market yahoos whose primary mission is to protect the personal liberties of the programmer.

"Innovation is a poor excuse for democracy," Wirtén points out, "and the ultimate test of whether or not the Internet truly offers the possibility of a global public domain lies perhaps not in its capacity to stimulate further technological breakthroughs on the part of a privileged elite but in its capacity to ensure increased public and hence democratic participation."[31] I believe that for a "free culture" movement to grow into a broad-based coalition—rather than remain in an affluent technological ghetto—its raison d'être, its obsession should center around fostering genuinely democratic freedom of expression® and social justice, rather than merely developing cool gadgets and nifty software tools.

Given that, I'm encouraged by some in the next generation of open- and free-software converts. For instance, Nelson Pavlosky, the nineteen-year-old Swarthmore College student who sued Diebold over its copyright censorship, sees open and free software as something more than just an engine of innovation and individualistic creativity. "My friend installed Linux on my computer the summer before my freshman year," he tells me, "and I was instantly hooked. It was just so cool; it embodied everything I believe in." At the heart of the free-software ethos, Pavlosky sees an ideal of participatory democracy, one that comes from the bottom up—rather than a top-down privatized model. "This is at the core of my philosophy: that people should be active, not passive," the undergrad says, avoiding the cold, geeky technobanter some programmers can lapse into—instead, exuding a kind of earnest, humanistic warmth.

"The greatest barrier to positive change on our planet is apathy, and what better way to promote apathy than to prevent people from participating? What better way is there to prevent people from caring than to remove all sense of community, of involvement in the world around them, to make action and activity the domain of other people far away?" Reminding me of his religious background, he explains, "There is actually a lot of overlap with my Quakerism.

A Quaker meeting is very democratic. Anyone can speak in a meeting—that right is not reserved for a priest or preacher—and Quakers have a long tradition of direct action that opposes injustice."

"The importance of open-source software is not that it introduces us to a wholly new idea," writes Professor Boyle. "It makes us see clearly a very old idea."[32] He's talking about the long-standing ethic of resource sharing, and the Internet has opened up new opportunities for the gift economies to flourish. For instance, the prestigious Berklee College of Music has put a large amount of content online. With a Creative Commons license, Berklee encourages people to freely download more than one hundred music lessons that come with video, audio, and text files. These range from tips on Afro-Cuban conga rhythms to turntable tricks for DJs. There are a number of reasons why Berklee is wading knee-deep into the gift economy. "(One) it's free and easy—the best proven way to get your stuff widely disseminated right now," says Glenn Otis Brown, executive director of Creative Commons. "(Two) it's their audience. A lot of people using these networks are music lovers, so they know they're getting the attention of groups inclined to listen. This project really demonstrates that file-sharing is basically just a great communication tool, and there are very legitimate uses of this kind of technology."

The college is doing this to cheaply spread the Berklee name around the world, to educate students about careers in the music industry, and to cultivate a multisided conversation about file-sharing. After quietly introducing these lessons in late 2003, within a month the files spread to more than ten thousand Web sites, generating over one hundred thousand downloads during that brief period. While Dave Kusek, associate vice president of the school, and other faculty members were surprised at this overwhelming positive response, they were even more amazed to discover that these users were also uploading their music to file-sharing networks. "When you look at the big picture, most musicians, if they're not songwriters, make most of their money performing," says Kusek. "It's a great way for new artists to get exposure for nothing. This is an example of when you want to use the network to distribute, when you want access to your material to be free. That's a choice you can make that has a lot of power."[33] Creativity wants to be paid, true, but it also wants to spread freely, to be known.

FROM THE MUSIC BUSINESS TO THE MUSICIAN'S BUSINESS

A funny thing (humorous, at least, to someone who isn't a major-label exec) is that the music industry itself is responsible for ushering in what it sees as the dark days of downloading. In the 1980s record companies were pushing the digital compact-disc format on the public, but cassette and LP buyers remained unconvinced. CD sales weren't as brisk as they had hoped. Then, in the late 1980s, the major labels instituted an industry-wide no-return policy on vinyl that forced retailers to stop carrying LPs. Because the vast majority of records released fail commercially, a liberal return policy had been an industry norm. Stores could no longer sell LPs without serious financial risk, because they couldn't return them for credit. I was working at a record store during the late '80s, and I remember watching the geographic shift as CDs colonized the majority of the racks over a brief period of time.

Although CDs are in many ways better than cassettes and LPs— in terms of sound quality and portability, respectively—this change was not purely the result of "free market" supply and demand. It was a conscious policy instituted by record companies who wanted to make sure this format took off. The policy generated higher profits and new sales as fans began replacing their vinyl collections with

CDs at inflated prices. And it didn't engender sympathy among consumers when a U.S. court found the nation's largest labels guilty of a conspiracy to drive up CD prices. These companies were ordered to pay back consumers $143 million for a practice called "minimum wage pricing" (which contributed to the steadily increasing retail cost of CDs throughout the 1990s). Also in 2004, New York state attorney general, Eliot Spitzer, revealed that the majors agreed to shell out upward of $50 million in royalties to artists they had neglected to pay.[34] Production expenses fell, consumer prices rose, and artist's royalty rates stayed the same—when artists were paid at all.

Selling CDs meant higher profits, but it eventually allowed fans to easily "rip" songs onto their computers and upload music files to the Internet. Jim Guerinot, manager of the Offspring, a favorite among Napster users in 2000, believes that the industry brought the downloading debacle on itself. He said that when record companies complain about downloading, "I say to them, 'Hey, I'm not the one who went out and had sex without a rubber. This is your problem, not mine.' "[35] The industry opened the door to the digital world, but it was dragged the rest of the way by the consumer-fed file-sharing movement. The rise of digital distribution doesn't mean everyone will suddenly stop purchasing music. It became clear that many consumers were willing to pay for downloads after the debut of Apple's iTunes in 2003 (along with Rhapsody and the too-legit-to-quit Napster 2.0).

Most songs were available for ninety-nine cents a pop, which was considered by most a good bargain, but the low price is deceptive. In the world of digital distribution, there are no costs associated with manufacturing and distributing a physical object, which is built into the retail price of CDs. For a similar price-per-track, record companies can sell their goods with a higher profit margin, but still pay an artist the same per-unit royalty, about ten cents a song. The label takes 65 of the 99 cents, so that Apple—after it pays for advertising, hosting the files, and a workforce that runs the service—makes nothing. But the company can sell iPods, and it has been tremendously successful at doing that, earning millions. Napster 2.0, with no iPods to sell and the same unfavorable business model, immediately began losing millions after its debut.

With the iTunes model, record companies pass along the nonexistent manufacturing and distribution costs to the consumer (who now has less freedom to copy the song because of iTunes' copy-protection technology). However, by finally embracing this new digital-distribution model, major labels are buying into something that may end their market dominance. For a century, the major labels' system dominated the music industry because they owned the means of production *and* distribution. Also by raising overhead costs (publicity, cross-promotion, etc.), the music industry makes it more difficult for indies to enter the market. It just costs too much to get on radio and into stores unless you have big pockets.

Today, the means of producing and distributing music has shifted to individual artists, which means one doesn't need a major-label contract to reach thousands of people. Indie stalwart and Fugazi member Ian MacKaye states, "If there is anything good about the Internet—and there are some things good about it—it kind of cuts out the middleman. It's just a matter of being found."[36] One of the positive things about the iTunes store and similar distribution networks is the fact that they encourage the participation of independent labels, which can more fairly split the revenues with artists. In other words, independent labels can make their music available at little cost, *and* pay artists fairly. Which brings us back to the question: Why do we need the music industry, or at least major labels?

The RIAA is fighting to save a system that rarely treated artists fairly. Following the lead of Ani DiFranco, who began her own independent label in the early 1990s, Michelle Shocked, Aimee Mann, and other artists burned by the major-label system did the same. Similarly, Iowa City's Dave Zollo founded Trailer Records in the 1990s to self-release his solo debut, but it soon turned into something else. It's run much like a collective, with a roster that includes Iowa artists Greg Brown, Bo Ramsey, Brother Trucker, and others. Zollo explains, "It's an organic thing that operates under the philosophy that a family, a community, can go out into the world and support each other, and when something good happens to one member of the family, then everyone benefits."[37]

By sharing knowledge and resources, the Trailer family is able to turn into an advantage what used to be a liability: lack of major-label connections and relative geographic isolation. Trailer obviously isn't the first label of its kind. Other independents such as Touch & Go—home to many classic post-punk records, including dozens that Steve Albini has recorded—operate in much the same way. "Independent labels, generally speaking, operate on a profit-sharing model," says Albini. "That is, as money comes in for a title, a certain amount of the money is used to pay off the expenses associated with that title and then the profits are split halvsies, generally, with the band."

The Def Jux label, home to one of the most talented rosters of today's hip-hop artists, operates under the same principle. "We're a label," says Mr. Lif, "where all the artists are friends and any configuration of us can go out and have a successful tour because we love performing." The recent changes in the industry make it more possible for this model to be one of music's healthy futures. By healthy, I don't just mean economically, but also creatively and culturally. We can hear a greater diversity of expression than what is allowed through the gates of big record companies—with their narrow ideas about what kind of music is profitable.

I don't mean to romanticize indie labels or claim that they *always* behave more ethically than majors, but they do tend to be more closely involved with artists, and are oftentimes run by them. As Berklee College's director of career development Peter Spellman characterizes it, we're seeing a shift from the "music business" to the "musician business." In the early 2000s, major labels had to lay off large chunks of its workforce while—at the same time—many independent labels have seen profits rise (in some cases 50 to 100 percent). This phenomenon materialized because there are huge overhead costs that go into running companies such as Sony Music, with its massive physical infrastructure that employs hundreds of people. At the same time that the major labels' share of the market shrunk, the independent sector enlarged in the United States, the United Kingdom, and elsewhere.

In this shift from the music business to the musician's business, the money generated by music-related sales can be more fairly distributed among those who actually work to make art. There will be less need to deal with and pay for the layers of accountants, lawyers, executives, and others who have populated the music industry for years. Previously, musicians' labor subsidized the salaries of those who made far more annually than the vast majority of the musicians employed by their label. This doesn't mean there will be *no* need for these people, because as long as the products produced by Big Entertainment remain popular for mainstream consumers, they'll have jobs. Britney Spears and other performers like her— those who not only sing, but can appear in films, commercials, televised concerts, *US* magazine, on soda cans, etc.—are the new model for major labels. Only through cross-marketing opportunities, where they can license their properties (both the star and the music), do big record companies believe they can survive.

Today, there is the very real possibility that most musicians can make a living from a small but loyal fan base, and completely by-pass the bloated entertainment industry. "I just think there's sort of a middle ground to it all," says Thom Monahan. "I mean, the Pernice Brothers make all our records in-house and all the money comes directly back to the band, so, you know, we don't really need to sell tons of records in order for it to work." The Pernice Brothers own their own record label, Ashmont, which means they have full control over creative and economic decisions. "If radio wants to play it, good," Thom says. "They can come to us because it's just too much money to mount a radio campaign. It would be pointless. It'd be throwing money out the window to pay people—for what? I mean, where does that money go? It goes into a system that's feeding the rich."

For the first time, new recording and distribution possibilities make it possible for more artist-entrepreneurs to thrive without relying on a self-interested corporation. Also for the first time, the independent sector has a fighting chance to be heard alongside the (admittedly pleasurable, at times) products pumped out by the culture industry. "File-sharing has broadened the audience for all these independent bands," Steve Albini tells me. "All these subcultures and niche types of music—music that's difficult to come by in the conventional record-store environment—it's dead easy to find on the Internet. So, it's exciting people in exactly the same way that the phonograph excited people in the Plains about opera. . . . It's exactly the same way that radio made people sitting at home want to go to the dance hall. The Internet is making people who would never otherwise come across it find music that they like and then buy it."

The music and movie industries were able to survive the home-taping scares of the 1980s and 1990s because a very basic social contract remained intact. You share some things, but you also support others by purchasing their creative work. People will stop supporting musicians and other artists only when the concept of community breaks down, not because of the introduction of a new technology (such as radio one century ago or the Internet). When the owners of VCRs and audiocassette recorders realized they *could* make copies, and never have to pay for content again, it didn't mean the vast majority of people actually did. The same is true of file-sharing networks.

Also, these networks provide an inexpensive way for independent musicians shut out of commercial radio to get their music heard nationally and globally. For instance, Clear Channel Communications owns over thirteen hundred radio stations throughout the United States, which homogenizes music playlists. Clear Channel also excludes musicians who choose not to fully immerse themselves in the corporate music world, which requires them to spend a *lot* of money to ever have a shot at getting airplay. If file-sharing networks were to be shut down, it would have a serious and demonstrably negative impact on many musicians who are increasingly relying on peer-to-peer technologies to get their music heard.

Interestingly, around the same time radio playlists narrowed, there was an increase in the eclectic range of music many young listeners were exploring. Evidence of this can be seen in the wild success of music festivals such as Bonnaroo, which is annually held in Tennessee. The 2004 event drew 100,000 fans and included a dizzyingly diverse array of performers, from jam bands such as Dave Matthews, Gov't Mule, and moe to rock iconoclasts Yo La Tengo, Wilco, and Los Lobos to legends Bob Dylan, Patti Smith, and the Dead. Additionally, there were bluegrass, jazz, blues, African pop, hip-hop, and funk artists—many of whom sell less than one hundred thousand CDs. This, of course, raises the question, how is it that the kids of Clear Channel America can connect these musical dots? The answer I found, after talking to a great number of young music fans, is file-sharing (and other methods of trading music). For instance, most file-sharing programs allow you to look into a peer's music library and download selections. This is a common way fans are exposed to new artists today, and it mimics the informal musical networks of the pre-Internet days—you know, checking out a record collection at a friend's house.

Music is only part of what's distributed on file-sharing networks, which makes possible the spread of information that governments and corporations might wish to suppress. It would have been much more difficult to disseminate the controversial Diebold memos mentioned in the last chapter without the existence of file-sharing. The decentralized nature of these networks made it impossible for the e-voting company to successfully suppress these damning documents, no matter how hard they tried. It's a simple technological and social fact that file-sharing isn't going away; when Napster's head was cut off it sprouted dozens more. Therefore, it's important for us to deal with this reality and to maximize file-sharing's potential to spread creativity while still protecting creators.

First, we need to put the economic impact of file-sharing into perspective. The 2.6 billion downloads per month the RIAA estimates doesn't mean we should adopt an iTunes model that requires consumers to pay out $2.6 billion a month for each download. This far exceeds the music industry's actual revenues, and it would be unworkable. However, just because the recent economic effects of file-sharing seem to be minimal doesn't mean that *no* fees should be paid to copyright owners. On the other hand, these owners shouldn't be allowed to set the terms in an unregulated manner. As we've seen with the history of radio and cable television, there needs to be some third party—governmental or otherwise—that can temper the outrageous prices that businesses inevitably demand when they have the opportunity.

Unchecked monopolies fly in the face of how copyright has been applied by Congress and courts for two centuries. The blanket compulsory-licensing model successfully used to legalize radio and cable television can point us to a future system that would work for file-sharing. This does not mean the new system would be *exactly* the same—for there are qualitative and quantitative differences—but there's also no need to totally reinvent the wheel. In his book *Promises to Keep*, Harvard University professor William W. Fisher has arrived at a workable proposal, similar to a model put forward by the Electronic Frontier Foundation and others. Fisher sees his plan as something that will replace the current intellectual-property system, though I agree with Lawrence Lessig that it would instead complement it.

Boiled down, this proposal goes like this: Given that the movie, gaming, and software industries have grown during a time when their products are freely downloadable—and file-sharing's negative impact on the music industry is highly debatable—additional fees needn't be exorbitant. To generate a dividable annual pot of money in the range of $2 billion, Fisher's plan would require an additional six dollars tacked onto the monthly bill paid by broadband Internet users. The intellectual-property lawyers at the EFF estimate five dollars per month for a file-sharing license. Although the cost of high-speed Internet use would slightly increase, the overall returns would be great. Consumers would have more entertainment options, and artists would be fairly compensated.

"The set of artists who made their creations available to the world at large—and consequently the range of entertainment products available to consumers—would increase," writes Professor Fisher. "Musicians would be less dependent on record companies, and filmmakers would be less dependent on studios, for the distribution of their creations. Both consumers and artists would enjoy greater freedom to modify and redistribute audio and video recordings." He adds, "Finally, society at large would benefit from a sharp reduction in litigation and other transaction costs."[38]

As I said earlier, radio stations don't pay the record companies that own musical recordings, they compensate the publishing companies that own the musical compositions. They pay songwriters, not recording artists. No system is going to be deemed fair by all parties involved; no doubt record companies would love to be paid for the *millions* of individual plays their songs annually receive on radio broadcasts. To do so, however, would put an undue burden on station owners and would stifle the dissemination of culture. When Electronic Frontier Foundation attorney Fred von Lohmann introduced the file-sharing license proposal at a music-law conference in 2004, the RIAA's vice president of government relations David Sutphen condemned the idea. He said the licensing system made no sense because, in part, all music would have the same value; an obscure artist's song would equal "Yesterday," by the Beatles.

Of course, Sutphen's assessment ignores the fact that price controls have been around since the Copyright Act of 1909, but the RIAA has consistently ignored history when it's convenient. What I'm outlining here is just a start; it's by no means perfect, and I'd be lying if I said that hammering out a workable proposal will be easy. It won't. But the alternative option—to do nothing—will continue to criminalize the everyday behavior of millions of Americans and also inhibit the spread of artistic works. Also, if downloading does in fact cause the sales of DVDs, video games, software, and CDs to go into a free fall, which hasn't been the case thus far, there would at least be an adjustable safety net in place to fairly compensate creators. As of now, the extra money will just be icing on the cake for copyright owners.

THE FUTURE WILL BE A LOT LIKE THE PAST

Rick Prelinger believes that the future will be a lot like the past. "You sell some things, but you also give some things away," he says. On the Internet, for instance, you often can download software, then decide whether or not you want to buy it. Software is frequently built on a two-tier system, where the free version allows you to do a limited number of things, but its capabilities expand if you purchase a license. "I think that model is a very old model," Prelinger tells me. "You can read a book in a bookstore, now they've got sofas for you to do it and a café. However, if you want to keep that book, you pay for it, and it works. We still have a book business."

The Internet makes it possible for music, art, video, and other forms of culture to circulate in new ways, but it won't replace the music-industry truism: Start small, and build your fan base. Yes, these changes may be troubling for some artists who crave less ambiguity, but the life of an artist has never been filled with certainty and stability. It goes with the territory. Anyway, the music industry of old didn't exactly provide the most predictable of career paths either, or the most fair and honest ways of being paid. What is clear, though, is that a greater diversity of music is already available today, much more than what previously squeaked through the major-label and broadcasting systems.

Less important than the new medium itself is what is *done* with it, both through public-policy decisions and the moves made by private industry. Communication historians have rightly argued that there is nothing inherent in the way many familiar technologies have wound up being used; in the formative stages of a new medium, much is up for grabs. My esteemed departmental colleague John Peters points out that radio was originally designed to receive *and* send messages, and the phonograph was envisioned as a recording device, not just a machine that could replay sound.[39] The CD, as opposed to the digital audiotape, was enthusiastically embraced by the music industry because it could be used only as a playback format. But to the horror of record companies, it soon turned into a recording medium.

Technologies are designed to encourage certain habits and discourage other activities, argues Jonathan Sterne, another media historian. The habits imprinted onto technologies have much to do with how they are designed and manufactured as consumer hardware. The radio of today can only receive signals because of the way it is put together, but by adding a microphone and rewiring it a little, it's ready to broadcast. But most people don't do that, or don't know how.[40] In the case of radio, only a company's top management and engineers can decide how the hardware will be designed, manufactured, and, therefore, used by consumers. But it's different with the Internet. Yes, you need a piece of hardware, the computer, to process and receive information from the online world, but the Internet's networks of communication are much more malleable. They're soft, as in *soft*ware.

Anyone with basic computer-programming skills and an imagination can potentially alter the habits of millions of Internet users. When the teenage Shawn Fanning patched together his simple Napster program, he pointed to a new way of searching for and retrieving information online. This redesign didn't require an expensive hardware overhaul for every user, only software modifications, which were free. Also, the investment needed to distribute music has gone from *a lot*—which was why a small number of large companies dominated the music industry for a century—to next to nothing. Although there are many elements of the Internet that are quite old, the two things I just mentioned are genuinely new, and much more democratic. Their egalitarian promise is one reason why I can remain relatively upbeat near the end of this book about the dark side of intellectual-property law.

AFTERWORD

freedom of expression®

In the 1984 Betamax decision, the VCR ended up being only *one Supreme Court vote* away from being contraband material, something that would have been a major loss. Imagine for a moment a world without a VCR. Yes, I know, at first it may seem a trivial matter—think of a world without yet another consumer electronics device. But the VCR proved to be extremely important for artists, documentary makers, educators, consumers, and others. The media-literacy movement would have been impossible without the VCR. Educators and students wouldn't have been able to capture, manipulate, and critique the media texts that saturate our popular-culture landscape. Film and television scholars would have been deprived of an important resource. The Media Education Foundation and other similar producers of educational videos would've been without an essential tool. And so on.

The ability to record, comment on, and distribute media content is essential for the survival of a robust democracy and the cultivation of a free culture in the information age. This freedom, granted by the fair-use statute, enables people to build from and transform parts of copyrighted materials without having to ask permission—whether it's open-source or free software, folk parodies, a satirical Web site that targets Dow Chemical, or the documentary *Money for Nothing*. Unfortunately, the promise of fair use often doesn't play out in the real world because wealthy intellectual-property owners think they can spend their way out of ever having to go to court.

"Fair use isn't freedom. It only means you have the right to hire a lawyer to fight for your right to create," said an exasperated Lawrence Lessig during a panel we both sat on for the Illegal Art show. "*Fuck* fair use," the bespectacled, buttoned-down Stanford law professor said. "We want *free* use." It was a variation on his "free culture" argument, also the title of his influential 2004 book. He has a point: Fair use often can come with a hefty price tag. However, it's the fair-use statute that Americans are stuck with, and the only way to make it an effective weapon against overzealous copyright bozos is to use it boldly (though not recklessly). By following the kinds of examples set by intellectual-property activists discussed in this book, we can create safe havens for freedom of expression® in the corporate age. By winning lawsuits—or by not backing down from frivolous legal threats, which is far more common—these people have cleared a space that we should continue to occupy.

After all, freedoms of any kind can easily be lost without exercising them. Some of these copy-fights are costly for those on the front lines, and it's clear why many choose not to resist. To put this into perspective, when organized labor fought to establish a forty-hour workweek and an end to child labor, it came with a price for a number of individuals. Through their sacrifices, these activists made it safer for others to speak up and helped change the internal policies of corporations, public policy, and the law. Tom Forsythe, the artist who won a landmark battle against Mattel in 2004 when it tried to suppress his *Food Chain Barbie* photographic series, believes it was worth the fight. "I always knew I was taking some risk in pursuing the case," Forsythe told me. "At the worst, I would have to declare bankruptcy. Given that other activists lay down their lives for their principles, simple bankruptcy seemed a minor risk."

Courts and Congress have already carved out many safe spaces for freedom of expression® as it relates to intellectual-property law. The problem is that we are often blind to the openings the law provides or we censor ourselves, even when no clear and present danger is imminent. And when an actual cease-and-desist letter or lawsuit lands in our laps, we tend to back down, even when there's a good chance of prevailing. For the most part, this is not the fault of the law itself, but the way it is interpreted by brand bullies and other enemies of creativity. By not defending ourselves, we are complicit in letting our freedom erode when it doesn't have to be so.

However, there are also times when intellectual-property laws very clearly stand in the way of freedom of expression® and creativity. The two worst offenders are the Sonny Bono Copyright Term Extension Act and the Digital Millennium Copyright Act. The Bono Act has helped shrink the public domain, fencing off materials that artists can rework (such as the musical *Les Misérables* or Disney's *Snow White*). And since the DMCA was passed into law, it has consistently created numerous documented barriers to fair use, innovation, and research—for both individuals and big companies.

These are not good laws—if by "good" we mean benefiting society and encouraging creativity. Congressman Rick Boucher's proposed Digital Media Consumers' Rights Act would curtail the most problematic parts of the DMCA. However, it met with such a hostile reaction from the entertainment-industry lobby that it was almost immediately DOA after it was introduced in 2002, though it died a slightly slower death in 2004. "Theft is theft and property is property," said Republican representative Butch Otter of Idaho, taking a dim view of the bill.[1]

The way the U.S. Patent and Trademark Office created new kinds of property—genes and business methods, for instance—can also stifle creativity. In the case of overbroad business patents, the Electronic Frontier Foundation's Patent Busting Project is a good start. The EFF intends to file challenges at the PTO against patents that are used to bully small businesses and nonprofits into purchasing licenses. Near the top of its hit list is Clear Channel's "Instant Live" patent, which gives the music industry giant a monopoly right over producing instant CD recordings of live concerts. "In fighting these patents," says the EFF's Wendy Seltzer, "our first goal is to help clear out specific instances of patents that are clogging the works and then point the way to change the law to prevent future violations."[2]

History has demonstrated that making money and freedom of expression® aren't mutually exclusive. During the second half of the twentieth century, media-entertainment industries exploded at the same time that consumers gained more freedom to play with and reproduce copyrighted material. "Digital" is different and new, yes, but as we saw in the final chapter, a lot hasn't changed. Film, software, and video-game sales only increased at the same time they were heavily traded on file-sharing networks. And when the U.S. economy began recovering in early 2004, there was a rise in CD sales—as well as an increase in file-sharing activity. Even though the potential exists for everyone to get everything for free, this has yet to occur.

That's why the movie industry didn't collapse after the introduction of the VCR, and why the music industry didn't do the same after the introduction of cassette tapes. However, if you believed the rhetoric churned out by these industries twenty years ago, their death was a foregone conclusion. More troubling, if we had followed the entertainment industry's marching orders at the time, creativity would have been far more constrained. As we move from an analog to a digital world, many corporations are using this shift as an excuse to correct what they see as the past wrongs of courts and legislators. As the analog videocassette player becomes obsolescent, they want to prevent its digital equivalent from existing (or at least closely control the way we can use it). Today, these industries have far more power than they did twenty years ago, when they lost almost every important battle in courts and Congress.

These owners want us to view their movies, listen to their music, and read their books, but on their terms. Copy protections make it much more difficult, and sometimes illegal, for people to hijack sounds and images from popular culture for the purpose of criticism and commentary. When so many of our cultural experiences are commercial transactions, and so much of our culture is privately owned, we are in danger of being banished to a world that is not our own. It's a place where culture becomes something that is alien, and a primary cause of that alienation is the way intellectual-property laws are enforced. This leaves us very little breathing room to reshape and react to the popular culture that surrounds us.

Of course, it doesn't have to be this way. The digital future could very well be a lot like the analog past, where people can continue to remix and remake the world in much the same way Woody Guthrie did. Or, for that matter, Marianne Moore, Martin Luther King Jr., Muddy Waters, and others who would be considered plagiarists and copyright criminals today. Echoing numerous court decisions, Supreme Court Justice Sandra Day O'Connor forcefully argued in 1991 for the importance of porous copyright protections—safeguards that aren't so airtight they choke creativity:

> The primary objective of copyright is not to reward the labor of authors, but "[t]o promote the Progress of science and useful Arts." To this end, copyright assures authors the right to their

original expression, but encourages others to build freely upon
the ideas and information conveyed by a work. This result is neither unfair nor unfortunate. It is the means by which copyright
advances the progress of science and art.[3]

The kind of "theft" that intellectual-property owners complain
about today is nothing new. Woody Guthrie's legacy reminds us
that appropriation—whether it's pop art, hip-hip sampling, folk
music, or Situationist *détournement*—makes possible artistic and
political expression that can resonate with many people. For instance, Woody Guthrie wrote a song in 1941 that ridiculed the way
British prime minister Neville Chamberlain appeased Adolf Hitler's
imperial aspirations. Guthrie called it "Adolph & Nevilline," and he
set his parody to the tune of the 1912 song "Frankie and Johnny,"
whose first line goes, "Frankie and Johnny were sweethearts." In his
own version, Guthrie sang mockingly, "Hitler and Chamberlain was
sweethearts / Lordy Lord, how they could love / Swore to be true to
the rich folks / True as the stars above!"

"Frankie and Johnny" still had relevance for those who heard
Woody's version—something that wouldn't be true now if someone referenced a public-domain song like, say, "When Pershing's
Men Go Marching into Picardy." (That 1918 song just barely escaped being "rescued" by the Sonny Bono Act.) Guthrie had the
freedom to sing what he wanted because he lived in a legal culture
that placed fewer restrictions on creativity. It was much more of a
free culture than the one we live in today, something that allowed
him to write "This Land Is Your Land." In a 1941 letter, Woody argued that it was the job of folk singers to make sure that

the seeds are sown which will grow up into free speech, free
singing, and the free pursuit of happiness that is the first and

simplest birthright of a free people. For with their songs choked and their pamphlets condemned, their freedom . . . will just be a rich man's word to print in his big papers and holler over his radio, it won't be real, it will only be a word.[4]

Similarly, I want freedom of expression—minus the ®—to be more than just a comforting, familiar phrase. It needs to be a meaningful concept that guides our political, social, and creative lives, something that enables us to speak back to the world, and make it a better place.

ACKNOWLEDGMENTS

This book would not be what it is without the help and input of many, many people—from those hip-hop artists and scientists and lawyers and everyone else who patiently sat through my research questions to the numerous people who read various versions of this manuscript. I have undoubtedly forgotten some people, so I apologize in advance.

More than anyone else, Doubleday's resident badass, Gerry Howard, played an important role in making this the best book it could be. Even though his reputation as an editor preceded him, I was pleasantly surprised by his attentiveness and enthusiasm; he is a god who walks among us in an industry that has too few deities to worship. Second only to Gerry in the birth of this book is Lynne Nugent, who acted as my de facto editor and continues to be the love of my life. She donated hours that I hope to repay over the years—her command of language and smart questions contributed to a richer manuscript. Also highly deserving of praise is my awesome agent, Sarah Lazin, who saw promise in the project early on, and who captured the interest of top editors in no time flat.

Special thanks to Jay Semel and the Obermann Center for Advanced Studies at the University of Iowa for providing me with course release time and research funds. I was lucky to receive various grants that allowed me to continue my research, including the International Programs Faculty Research Grant, an Obermann Faculty Research Semester Fellowship, and an Old Gold Summer Research Grant. Crucial to this project was an Arts and Humanities Initiative Major Project Grant, which helped fund Ben Franzen's and my documentary *Copyright Criminals,* as well as an Obermann Humanities Symposium Grant that allowed me to mount a conference on collage with Ruedi Kuenzli. Extra special thanks to the four other participants in the Obermann Center's Faculty Research Semester, "Sounding the Voice": Corey Creekmur, Kitty Eberle, Judith Pascoe, and my departmental colleague John Peters, all of whom gave me detailed feedback.

I'd also like to thank the following: Ruedi Kuenzli—Mr. Dada/Surrealism—who has been an invaluable resource; Rick Altman, whose Sound Research Seminar provided me with an early forum to present some ideas contained in the book; my close friend Chris Nelson, with whom I consulted almost every week during the course of writing this book; Louis Schwartz, my intellectual superior and good friend; Sasha Waters, another friend and ally deserving of reverence; Siva Vaidhyanathan, a great tag-team partner; Matt Soar, who influenced my thinking on product placement and other issues; Chuck Eddy at *The Village Voice,* who taught me to be a better writer; Ben Franzen, whose energy and ideas in our documentary collaboration were invaluable; and John Freyer, another source of great ideas and another great friend.

Thanks to all the wonderful faculty and staff in my department, especially Ece Algan, Mark Andrejevic, Barb Biesecker, David Depew, Kristine Fitch, Bruce Gronbeck, Tim Havens, David Hingstman, Randy Hirokawa, and Camille Seaman—all of whom either read parts of the manuscript, involved themselves in discussions about this book, or supported the project in other ways. Mark Andrejevic and John Peters deserve extra-special mentions, for they kick ass and read more. I'm honored that Sam Becker— one of the founders of the field of communication studies—read an entire rough draft; his encouraging feedback meant a lot to me. My research assistants over the years have been great—especially Mike Mario Albrecht, Rachel Avon Whidden, and Nathan Wilson. Also, a shout-out goes to my Ph.D. advisees and departmental grad students who have directly contributed to the ideas in this book, particularly Bekka Farrugia, Hugo Burgos, Judd Case, and, last but not least, Margaret Schwartz.

I should also single out Carrie McLaren, the publisher of the excellent magazine *Stay Free!*, for resparking my interest in art, democracy, and intellectual-property law. She had no reason to mount the Illegal Art show, certainly not fame or money, but Carrie did so because it was an interesting idea and the right thing to do. She is a stand-up person, as is Jason Gross, the publisher of another great 'zine, *Perfect Sound Forever*, who hooked me up with a number of valuable contacts. Thanks also to my winter 2004 class on intellectual-property law and culture—especially Jennifer Zoller, who became my undergrad honors research assistant, and Britanny Shoot, who went beyond the call of duty with her comments.

Sincere thanks also go to—and I realize this reads like an awards show–acceptance speech—Rakesh Satyal, Rosemary Coombe, Lawrence Lessig, Chuck D, Harry Allen, Hank Shocklee, Thurston Moore, Lee Ranaldo, Coldcut, Steve Albini, Wyclef Jean, RZA,

Method Man, Redman, Kool DJ Herc, Grandmaster Flash, DJ Muggs, Bobbito, Mr. Dibbs, DJ Vadim, Eclectic Method, Eyedea & Abilities, Mr. Len, Pete Rock, Prefuse 73, Sage Francis, Treach, Cee-lo, Big Gipp, Killah Priest, Rass Kass, Kool Keith, DJ Premier, Guru, Saul Williams, Paul Miller/DJ Spooky, Vicki Bennett, Miho Hatori, Greg Tate, Qbert, Robin Rimbaud, Dave Marsh, Dave Zollo, Megan Levad, Karla Tonella, Bob Setter, Gary Burns, Jonathan Sterne, Steve Jones, Gil Rodman, Ted Striphas, David Wittenberg, Merrie Snell, David Hamilton, Mark Janis, Laura Rigal, Rob Lathum, Tom Lutz, Thom Swiss, Thom Monahan, Jeremy Smith, Sut Jhally, Nina Nastasia, Kennan Gudjonson, Gordon Mitchell, Nelson Paulosky, Claudia Gonson, Todd Kimm and *Little Village*, Angela Balcita, Chris Doyle, Mark Nugent, David Banash, Tim Eriksen, David Bollier, Helena Chaye, Ann Powers, Joanna Demers, Jessica Clark, Dan Cook, Andrew Herman, Gordon Mitchell, Susan Olive, Courtenay Bouvier, Bruce Busching, David Bromley, Briankle Chang, Justin Lewis, Eric Morgan, Lisa Rudnick, Susan Ericsson, Esteban del Rio, Alicia Kimmitt, Nancy Inouye, Katie Lebesco, Matt Miller, John Sorensen, Brendan Love, Leslie Roberts, Amy Wan, Stuart Downs, Greg Elmer, Matthew Smith, Shirley Halperin, Terry Harrison, Melissa Click, Ken Cmiel, Gigi Durham, Frank Durham, Hanno Hardt, Tim Quirk, Melissa Deem, Gayane Torosyan, Charlie Williams, Philo Farnsworth, Rick Karr, Damon Krukowski, Lorna Olson, Karla Tonella, Dan Maloney, Steev Hise and detritus.net, University of Iowa president David Skorton, Bruce Wheaton, James Twitchell, Ken Wissoker, the kids at KRUI, Electronic Frontier Foundation, Future of Music Coalition, Creative Commons, the Project on the Rhetoric of Inquiry, the Media Education Foundation, and the entire staff of the Prairie Lights bookstore, in whose coffee shop I wrote much of this book—a place where many great books have been written.

Collectively, all of you still turn on my heart light, especially now that I'm caught between the moon and New York City (teaching the children of the corn in the field of dreams). You are the wind beneath my wings; you're the meaning in my life, you're the inspiration, and nothing compares to you. You rock.

NOTES

INTRODUCTION

1.   J. Bercovici, *Media Life Magazine.*
2.   P. Rigden, *Alternatives Journal.*
3.   S. Knopper, *Rolling Stone.*
4.   L. Lessig, *Free culture.*
5.   *Sony Corp. of Am. v. Universal City Studios, Inc.,* 464 U.S. 417, 429, *reh'g denied,* 465 U.S. 1112 (1984).
6.   *NOW with Bill Moyers,* Tollbooths on the digital highway.

CHAPTER ONE

1.   J. Shreeve, *The genome war,* p. 363.
2.   E. Barkley, *Crossroads.*
3.   R. Lissauer, *Lissauer's encyclopedia of popular music in America;* L. Smith, *Los Angeles Times,* 1985; G. Claghorn, *Women composers and songwriters;* J. J. Fuld, *The book of world-famous music;* J. Byron, *Kuro5hin;* V. L. Grattan, *American women songwriters.* Some of this material was presented in my earlier book, *Owning Culture.*
4.   *Chicago Tribune,* Maybe you could get it for a song, 1988, p. C10.

5. I. Ball, *Daily Telegraph* (London), 1988; D. Ewen, *Variety,* 1969; B. L. Hawes, *The birthday,* p. 22.

6. D. Ewen, *Variety,* 1969, p. 4; E. Blau, *New York Times,* 1986; N. Lebrecht, *Daily Telegraph* (London), 1996.

7. J. Zittrain, *Legal Affairs,* pp. 26–35; 27.

8. *Austin American-Statesman,* ASCAP faces the music, 1996, p. J2.

9. L. Bannon, *Minneapolis Star Tribune,* 1996, p. 10E.

10. *Chattanooga Times,* ASCAP chief says scouts controversy part of "shameful agenda," 1996, p. C3; J. Zittrain, *Legal Affairs.*

11. The offenders: Hank Thompson's "Wild Side of Life"; the Carter Family's "I'm Thinking Tonight of My Blue Eyes"; Roy Acuff's "Great Speckled Bird"; Kitty Wells's "It Wasn't God Who Made Honky Tonk Angels"; Reno and Smiley's "I'm Using My Bible as a Roadmap"; and Townes Van Zant's "Heavenly Houseboat Blues." (I've since discovered many more.)

12. J. Klein, *Woody Guthrie,* p. 120.

13. Ibid., p. 82.

14. S. Zeitlin, *New York Times,* 1998, p. A15.

15. S. Fishman, *The public domain.*

16. Ibid.

17. K. D. Miller, *Chronicle of Higher Education,* p. A60.

18. K. D. Miller, *Journal of American History;* B. J. Reagon, *Journal of American History;* R. L. Johannesen, *Southern Communication Journal.*

19. I. Ball, *Daily Telegraph* (London), 1990, p. 11.

20. W. Dixon and D. Snowden, *I am the blues,* p. 222.

21. Ibid., p. 90.

22. S. Vaidhyanathan, *Copyrights and copywrongs,* p. 121.

23. L. Lessig, *The future of ideas.*

24. D. Charles, *Lords of the harvest,* p. 270.

25. G. Zweiger, *Transducing the genome.*

26. *Washington Post,* To own the human genome, 1998; P. Cohen, *New Scientist;* T. Wilkie, *Independent* (London), 1995.

27. J. Gillis, *Washington Post,* 1999.

28. D. Bollier, *Silent Theft.*

29. F. Bowring, *Science, seeds and cyborgs.*

30. D. Charles, *Lords of the harvest,* p. 185.

31. F. Bowring, *Science, seeds and cyborgs.*

32. P. Pringle, *Food, Inc.;* A. Duffy, *Ottawa Citizen,* 1998.

33. *NOW with Bill Moyers,* Seeds of conflict.

34. T. McGirk, *Time* (international edition, Asia); V. Shiva, *Biopiracy;* N. Roht-Arriaza, *Borrowed power,* p. 259.

35. V. Shiva, *Protect or plunder?*

36. Ibid.

37. P. Pringle, *Food, Inc.;* K. Dawkins, *Gene wars.*

38. K. Dawkins, *Gene wars;* P. Pringle, *Food, Inc.;* S. Shulman, *Owning the future,* p. 110; K. E. Maskus, *Intellectual property rights in the global economy.*

39. E. H. Wirtén, *No trespassing.*

40. P. Drahos with J. Braithwaite, *Information feudalism,* p. 10.

41. K. E. Maskus, *Intellectual property rights in the global economy;* V. Shiva, *Protect or plunder?;* P. Drahos with J. Braithwaite, *Information feudalism.*

42. F. Bowring, *Science, seeds and cyborgs.*

43. S. Meyer, *Paradoxes of fame.*

CHAPTER TWO

1.   Many moments in this chapter owe their existence to my *Copyright Criminals* documentary partner, Ben Franzen, who documented dozens of interviews on camera, including a number in Atlanta where I couldn't be present.

2.   D. Hebdidge, *Cut 'n' mix,* p. 14.

3.   R. Barthes, *Roland Barthes by Roland Barthes,* p. 120.

4.   D. Toop, *Rap attack 2,* pp. 63–66.

5.   J. Attali, *Noise,* p. 135.

6. D. F. Wallace, *A supposedly fun thing I'll never do again.*

7. G. Prato, *AllMusicGuide.com*; C. Miller, *Dickie Goodman & friends—greatest fables* (CD booklet).

8. M. MacDonald, *Brahms*, pp. 152–53.

9. E. Cray, *Ramblin' Man*, p. 181.

10. J. Bauldie, *Bob Dylan.*

11. H. Sounes, *Down the highway*; J. Bauldie, *Bob Dylan.*

12. J. Cohen, *Young Bob*, p. 26.

13. S. Hochman, *Los Angeles Times*, 1991, p. F1.

14. S. H. Fernando Jr., *The new beats.*

15. N. Drumming, *Entertainment Weekly*, p. 78.

16. M. Diehl, *Rolling Stone*, p. 138.

17. C. Jones, *New York Times*, 1996, p. B44.

18. S. Morse, *Boston Globe*, 2002.

19. *Mojo*, Rhymin' and stealin', p. 78.

20. P. Bussy, *Kraftwerk*, p. 126.

21. E. Schumacher-Rasmussen, MTV.com.

22. *Rap News Direct*, Ghostface Killah wins copyright infringement case.

23. *Superswell's Sample Law*, Horror stories.

24. J. Cohen, *Billboard.*

25. M. W. Miller, *Wall Street Journal*, 1987, p. 1.

26. J. Derrida, *Limited, Inc*, pp. 31; 34.

27. L. R. Patterson, *Copyright in historical perspective.*

28. J. Litman, *Digital copyright.*

29. J. Jensen, *Entertainment Weekly*, p. 32.

CHAPTER THREE

1. W. Isaacson, *Benjamin Franklin*, p. 95.

2. T. Tucker, *Bolt of fate*, pp. 9–10.

3. W. Isaacson, *Benjamin Franklin*, pp. 96–97; T. Tucker, *Bolt of fate.*

4. H. Richter, *Dada*, p. 114.

5. J. Derrida, *Positions*, p. 42.

6.   T. Tzara, *Seven Dada manifestos,* p. 39.

7.   F. T. Marinetti, *The Futurist cookbook,* p. 13.

8.   H. Wescher, *Collage.*

9.   H. Richter, *Dada,* p. 65.

10. Ibid., p. 66.

11. Ibid., p. 89.

12. Ibid.

13. L. A. Greenberg, *Cardozo Arts & Entertainment Law Journal.*

14. C. White, *The middle mind,* p. 9; L. Bracken, *Guy Debord,* p. 74.

15. S. Plant, *The most radical gesture,* p. 86–87.

16. J. Derrida, *Acts of religion,* p. 236; B. Johnson, Translator's introduction in J. Derrida, *Dissemination,* p. xiv.

17. B. Chang, *Deconstructing Communication,* p. 137.

18. Ibid., p. 139.

19. Negativland, *Fair use,* p. 72.

20. G. Morris, *ARTnews,* p. 105.

21. Ibid.

22. Ibid., p. 104.

23. M. Buskirk, *October;* C. L. Hays, *New York Times,* 1991, p. B2.

24. A. Dannat, *Independent* (London), 1992, p. 20.

25. M. Dickie, *Graffiti Magazine.*

26. Special thanks to NPR correspondent Rick Kerr for tipping me off in an e-mail that this was likely a prank.

27. E. Pouncey, *Undercurrents.*

28. B. Miles, *Paul McCartney,* p. 484.

29. J. Healey and R. Cromelin, *Los Angeles Times,* 2004, p. E1.

30. J. Oswald, *Sounding off !,* p. 88.

31. W. Koestenbaum, *The queen's throat,* p. 66.

32. J. Fricke and C. Ahearn, *Yes yes y'all.*

33. J. D. Peters, *Speaking into the air;* Edison's essay, "The Phonograph and Its Future," *North American Review,* May–June 1878, pp. 527–36, was ghostwritten by Edward Johnson.

34. Plato, *Phaedrus,* p. 81.

35. Ibid.

36. M. Rose, *Authors and owners,* p. 39.

37. M. Woodmansee, *Eighteenth-Century Studies.*

38. M. Rose, *Authors and owners,* p. 115.

CHAPTER FOUR

1. S. Frere-Jones, *New York Times.*

2. D. Smith, *New York Times.*

3. R. Alleyne, *Chicago Sun-Times,* 2003, p. 4.

4. E. W. Joyce, *Cultural critique and abstraction,* p. 75.

5. K. Burke, *Marianne Moore,* p. 127.

6. M. Moore, *Marianne Moore,* p. 30.

7. R. J. Coombe, *The cultural life of intellectual properties,* p. 69.

8. E. Schlosser, *Fast food nation,* p. 50.

9. N. Klein, *No logo,* p. 87.

10. E. Schlosser, *Fast food nation,* p. 56.

11. P. Meredith, Extreme bake sales, *Mother Jones.*

12. A. Quart, *Branded,* p. 43.

13. R. J. Coombe, *Companion guide to law and society.*

14. R. J. Coombe, *The cultural life of intellectual properties.*

15. R. Kelly, *Donnie Darko,* Director R. Kelly's DVD commentary.

16. M. Andrejevic, *Reality TV,* p. 43.

17. *Behind the screens: Hollywood goes hypercommercial,* produced by M. Soar, 2000.

18. M. F. Jacobson and L. A. Mazur, *Marketing madness,* p. 68.

19. F. Rich, *New York Times,* 2003, p. B1.

20. A. Quart, *Branded,* p. 97.

21. L. Skinner, *Billboard,* pp. 1; 100.

22. A. Quart, *Branded,* p. 91.

23. R. Wolmuth, *People Weekly,* p. 38.

24. E. L. Eisenstein, *The printing revolution in early modern Europe;* L. Braudy, *The frenzy of renown;* M. Madow, *California Law Review.*

25. L. Braudy, *The frenzy of renown,* p. 377.
26. S. Soocher, *Entertainment Law & Finance,* p. 5.
27. R. J. Coombe, *The cultural life of intellectual properties,* p. 90.
28. R. A. Stamets, *Federal Communications Law Journal,* pp. 349–50.
29. P. Rojas, *Salon.*
30. G. Meikle, *Future active,* p. 114.
31. Ibid., p. 113.
32. A. Ellin, *New York Times,* 1999, p. C2.
33. G. Meikle, *Future active,* pp. 126–27.
34. M. Richtel, *New York Times,* 1998, p. G6.
35. S. Vaidhyanathan, *The Chronicle of Higher Education.*
36. J. Brown, *Salon.*
37. M. Kotadia, *CNet News.com.*
38. WIPO Arbitration and Mediation Center, 2002, *Vivendi Universal v. Mr. Jay David Sallen and GO247.COM.*
39. G. Fahimian, *Leland Stanford Technology Law Review.*

CHAPTER FIVE

1. J. Bovard, *Sfgate.*
2. J. LiPetri, *Micro Publishing News.*
3. 0100101110101101.ORG, press release.
4. J. Sulston and G. Ferry, *The common thread,* p. 278.
5. J. H. Reichman and P. F. Uhlir, *Law and Contemporary Problems.*
6. D. Bollier, *Silent theft,* p. 30.
7. D. Bollier, *Silent theft;* J. Sulston and G. Ferry, *The common thread,* p. 278.
8. W. Finnegan, *Harper's;* J. E. Stiglitz, *Globalization and its discontents;* S. Jha, *AlterNet.*
9. C. Johnson, *Harper's.*
10. K. Marre, *The Hill.*
11. P. Roberts, *PC World;* A. Orlowski, *The Register.*
12. K. Zetter, *Wired News.*

13. A. Gumbel, *Independent* (London).

14. M. Lewellen-Biddle, *In These Times,* p. 21.

15. A. Gumbel, *Independent* (London).

16. D. Cho, *Washington Post,* 2003, p. B1.

17. I. Hoffman, *Oakland Tribune;* WISH-TV 8, Marion County clerk accuses ES&S of lying, broadcast.

18. R. O'Harrow Jr., *Washington Post,* 2003, p. A1; D. Lindorff, *In These Times,* p. 3.

19. P. Goldstein, *Copyright's highway,* p. 181.

20. D. McCullagh, SunnComm won't sue grad student, *CNet News.com.*

21. R. Lemos, *CNet News.com.*

22. J. Band, *Silicon Valley.*

23. N. Ferguson, macfergus.com

24. D. Bollier, *Silent theft,* p. 35.

25. T. Stephen, *Communication Institute for Online Scholarship,* press release.

26. D. Bok, *Universities in the marketplace,* p. 64.

27. F. Bowring, *Science, seeds and cyborgs.*

28. S. Shulman, *Owning the future,* p. 110.

29. Ibid., p. 111.

30. D. Bok, *Universities in the marketplace,* p. 74.

CHAPTER SIX

1. A. Gilbert, *CNet News.com.*

2. T. Streeter, *Selling the air,* p. 263.

3. L. Lessig, *The future of ideas,* p. 234.

4. D. C. Chmielewski, *Silicon Valley.*

5. D. Gillmor, *Silicon Valley.*

6. S. Jones and A. Lenhart, *Popular Music and Society.*

7. M. Fishbein, S. Middlestadt, and M. Kapp, *A consumer survey: Home taping.*

8. R. D. Gross, *Copy fights.*

9. J. Litman, *Digital copyright.*

10. P. Manuel, *Cassette culture.*

11. J. Fricke and C. Ahearn, *Yes yes y'all;* S. H. Fernando Jr., *The new beats,* p. 12; D. Toop, *Rap attack 2,* p. 78.

12. R. Hall, *Billboard,* p. 68.

13. J. Menn, *All the rave,* p. 144.

14. B. Lew, *Salon.*

15. K. Dean, Schoolgirl settles with RIAA, *Wired News.*

16. T. Shanker, *New York Times.*

17. Selden Patent, *Weird and wonderful patents.*

18. T. C. Greene, *The Register.*

19. D. Wolk, *The Village Voice,* p. 110.

20. J. Howe, *Wired,* p. 138; D. C. Chmielewski, *Mercury News;* A. Veiga, *Yahoo! News.*

21. K. Dean, New spin on the music business, *Wired News.*

22. D. Cave, *Rolling Stone,* p. 17.

23. M. Endelman, *Entertainment Weekly,* pp. 11–12.

24. S. Jones and A. Lenhart, *Popular Music and Society.*

25. L. Lessig, *Free culture.*

26. C. Devenish, *Rolling Stone.*

27. E. Smith, *Wall Street Journal.*

28. J. Pope, *CRN.*

29. J. Van, *Chicago Tribune.*

30. J. Boyle, *Law and Contemporary Problems,* p. 46.

31. E. H. Wirtén, *No trespassing,* p. 144.

32. J. Boyle, *Law and Contemporary Problems,* p. 47.

33. E. Armstrong, *Christian Science Monitor.*

34. D. Marsh, *Rock & Rap Confidential,* p. 6.

35. F. Goodell, *Rolling Stone,* p. 43.

36. J. Guntzel, *Punk Planet,* p. 68.

37. S. Dyas, *Little Village,* p. 10.

38. W. W. Fisher, *Promises to keep.*

39. J. D. Peters, *Speaking into the air.*

40. J. Sterne, *The audible past.*

AFTERWORD

1. D. McCullagh, Congress mulls revisions to DMCA, *CNet News.com.*

2. A. Asaravala, *Wired News.*

3. *Feist Publications, Inc. v. Rural Telephone Service Co.,* 499 US 340, 349 (1991).

4. W. Guthrie, *Pastures of plenty,* pp. 54–55; I changed the incorrectly spelled "wont," as Guthrie originally wrote it, to "won't" in this excerpt.

BIBLIOGRAPHY

0100101110101101.ORG. 2003. Nike scores own goal. Press release, October 28.

Alleyne, R. 2003. Rap's a foreign language, judge rules. *Chicago Sun-Times,* June 6, p. 4.

Andrejevic, M. 2003. *Reality TV: The work of being watched.* New York: Rowman & Littlefield.

Armstrong, E. 2003. File-sharing goes to school. *Christian Science Monitor,* December 16. http://www.csmonitor.com/2003/1216/p11s01-legn .html.

Asaravala, A. 2004. EFF to fight dubious patents. *Wired News,* April 19. http://www.wired.com/news/business/01367,63122,00.html.

Attali, J. 1985. *Noise: The political economy of music.* Trans. B. Massumi. Minneapolis: University of Minnesota Press.

Austin American-Statesman. 1996. ASCAP faces the music. September 1, p. J2.

Ball, I. 1988. Beware if you sing happy birthday. *Daily Telegraph* (London), December 21, p. 6.

———. 1990. Martin Luther King "borrowed ideas." *Daily Telegraph* (London), November 10, p. 11.

Band, J. 2002. Congress unknowingly undermines cyber-security. *Silicon-Valley,* December 16. http://www.siliconvalley.com/mld/siliconvalley/4750224.htm.

Bannon, L. 1996. Birds sing, but campers can't—unless they pay up. *Minneapolis, Star Tribune,* August 24 p. 10E.

Barkley, E. 2003. *Crossroads: Popular music in America.* Upper Saddle River, NJ: Prentice Hall.

Barthes, R. 1977. *Roland Barthes by Roland Barthes.* Berkeley: University of California Press.

Bauldie, J. 1991. *Bob Dylan: The bootleg series, volumes 1–3.* Liner notes. New York: Sony Music Entertainment, Inc.

Behind the screens: Hollywood goes hypercommercial, produced by M. Soar. Northampton, MA: Media Education Foundation, 2000.

Bercovici, J. 2003. In a snit, Fox News drops Franken suit. *Media Life Magazine,* August 26. http://www.medialifemagazine.com/news2003/aug03/aug25/2_tues/news2tuesday.html.

Blau, E. 1986. The antics of Schickele and Borge. *New York Times,* December 26, p. C3.

Bok, D. 2003. *Universities in the marketplace: The commercialization of higher education.* Princeton, NJ: Princeton University Press.

Bollier, D. 2002. *Silent theft: The private plunder of our common wealth.* New York: Routledge.

Bovard, J. 2004. Quarantining dissent: How the Secret Service protects Bush from free speech. *Sfgate.* http://www.sfgate.com/article.cgi?file=/chronicle/archive/2004/01/04/INGPQ40MB81.DTL.

Bowring, F. 2003. *Science, seeds and cyborgs: Biotechnology and the appropriation of life.* New York: Verso.

Boyle, J. 2003. The second enclosure movement and the construction of the public domain. *Law and Contemporary Problems* 66 (1 and 2): 33–74.

Bracken, L. 1997. *Guy Debord: Revolutionary.* Venice, CA: Feral House.

Braudy, L. 1986. *The frenzy of renown: Fame and its history.* New York: Oxford University Press.

Brodeur, S. 1996. Seeing red: The funkadelic Redman continues to bring the outer limits back to the underground. *Source,* December, pp. 85–88.

Brown, J. 1999. Copyright—or wrong? *Salon,* July 22. http://www.archive.salon.com/tech/feature/1999/07/22/scientology/.

Browne, D. 1992. Settling the bill: Digital sampling in the music industry. *Entertainment Weekly,* January 24, p. 54.

Burke, K. 1969. Likings of an observationist. In *Marianne Moore: A collection of critical essays,* ed. C. Tomlinson. Englewood Cliffs, NJ: Prentice-Hall.

Buskirk, M. 1992. Commodification as censor: Copyrights and fair use. *October* 60: 82–109.

Bussy, P. 2001. *Kraftwerk: Man, machine and music.* London: SAF Publishing.

Byron, J. 2003. Exposing the happy birthday story. *Kuro5hin,* June. http://www.kuro5hin.org/story/2003/7/5/112441/6280.

Cave, D. 2004. Don't blame KaZaA. *Rolling Stone,* April 29, p. 17.

Chang, B. 1996. *Deconstructing communication: Representation, subject, and economies of exchange.* Minneapolis: University of Minnesota Press.

Chattanooga Times. 1996. ASCAP chief says scouts controversy part of "shameful agenda." October, p. C3.

Charles, D. 2001. *Lords of the harvest: Biotech, big money and the future of food.* Cambridge, MA: Perseus Publishing Group.

Chicago Tribune. 1988. Maybe you could get it for a song. October 29, p. C10.

Chmielewski, D. C. 2002. Online film piracy cuts into industry profit. *SiliconValley,* May 30. http://www.siliconvalley.com/mld/siliconvalley/3369706.htm.

———. 2004. Music labels use file-sharing data to boost sales. *Mercury News,* March 31. http://www.mercurynews.com/mld/mercurynews/business/8318571.htm.

Cho, D. 2003. Fairfax judge orders logs of voting machines inspected. *Washington Post,* November 6, p. B1.

Claghorn, G. 1996. *Women composers and songwriters: A concise biographical dictionary.* Lanham, MD: Scarecrow Press.

Cohen, J. 2003. Court backs Beasties in copyright suit appeal. *Billboard,* November 11. http://www.billboard.com/bb/daily/article_display.jsp?vnu_content_id =2024875.

———. 2003. *Young Bob: John Cohen's early photographs of Bob Dylan.* New York: powerHouse Books.

Cohen, P. 1999. A liver disorder may have gone unnoticed because of confusion over patents. *New Scientist* 10 (December 25):10.

Coombe, R. J. 1998. *The cultural life of intellectual properties: Authorship, appropriation and the law.* Chapel Hill, NC: Duke University Press.

———. (forthcoming). Commodity culture, private censorship, branded environments, and global trade politics: Intellectual property as a topic of law and society research. In *Companion guide to law and society.* New York: Basil Blackwell.

Cray, E. 2004. *Ramblin' man: The life and times of Woody Guthrie.* New York: Norton.

Dannat, A. 1992. The "mine" field. *Independent* (London), March 23, p. 20.

Dawkins, K. 2003. *Gene wars: The politics of biotechnology.* 2nd ed. New York: Seven Stories Press.

Dean, K. 2003. Schoolgirl settles with RIAA. *Wired News,* Sept. 10. http://www.wired.com/news/print/0,1294,60366,00.html.

———. 2004. New spin on the music business. *Wired News,* May 15. http://www.wired.com/news/0,1294,63474,00.html.

Derrida, J. 1981. *Dissemination.* Trans. B. Johnson. Translator's introduction. Chicago: University of Chicago Press.

———. 1981. *Positions.* Trans. A. Bass. Chicago: University of Chicago Press.

———. 1988. *Limited, Inc.* Evanston, IL: Northwestern University Press.

———. 2002. *Acts of religion.* New York: Routledge.

Devenish, C. 2004. Downloaders pay back Wilco. *Rolling Stone,* April 2. http://www.rollingstone.com/news/newsarticle.asp?nid=19556.

Dickie, M. 1988. Superstar: The Karen Carpenter story. *Graffiti Magazine,* December. http://www.ca.geocities.com/need2bnluv/carpenters/superstar.htm.

Diehl, M. 2003. The making of *Paul's boutique. Rolling Stone,* December 11, p. 138.

Dixon, W., and D. Snowden. 1989. *I am the blues: The Willie Dixon story.* New York: Da Capo.

Drahos, P., with J. Braithwaite. 2002. *Information feudalism: Who owns the knowledge economy?* New York: Free Press.

Drumming, N. 2004. "Kanye, why didn't Lauryn Hill get down?" *Entertainment Weekly,* April 16, p. 78.

Duffy, A. 1998. Biodiversity "crackpot" wins Pearson medal. *Ottawa Citizen,* December 16, p. A10.

Dyas, S. 2003. The Trailer Records saga. *Little Village,* December, pp. 8–14.

Eisenstein, E. L. 1983. *The printing revolution in early modern Europe.* Cambridge: Cambridge University Press.

Ellin, A. 1999. They're king-size issues, whatever you call him. *New York Times,* March 21, p. C2.

Endelman, M. 2004. A little pop! *Entertainment Weekly,* March 5, pp. 11–12.

Ewen, D. 1969. Yanks sing this song most often. *Variety,* January 8, p. 4.

Fahimian, G. 2004. How the IP guerrillas won: (R)TMark, Adbusters, Negativland, and the "bullying back" of creative freedom and social commentary. *Leland Stanford Technology Law Review* 1.

Feist Publications, Inc. v. Rural Telephone Service Co., 499 US 340, 349 (1991).

Ferguson, N. 2001. Censorship in action: Why I don't publish my HDCP results. macfergus.com, August 15. http://www.macfergus.com/niels/dmca/cia.html.

Fernando Jr., S. H. 1994. *The new beats: Exploring the music, culture, and attitudes of hip-hop.* New York: Doubleday.

Finnegan, W. 2003. The economics of empire: Notes on the Washington consensus. *Harper's Magazine,* May, pp. 41–54.

Fishbein, M., S. Middlestadt, and M. Kapp. 1980. *A consumer survey: Home taping*. Warner Communications, Inc.

Fisher, W. W. 2004. *Promises to keep: Technology, law and the future of entertainment*. Palo Alto, CA: Stanford University Press.

Fishman, S. 2000. *The public domain: How to find & use copyright-free writings, music, art & more*. Berkeley, CA: Nolo.

Frere-Jones, S. 2004. The sound. *New York Times*, February 8. http://www.nytimes.com/2004/02/08/magazine/08STYLE.html.

Fricke, J., and C. Ahearn. 2002. *Yes yes y'all: The Experience Music Project oral history of hip-hop's first decade*. New York: Da Capo.

Fuld, J. J. 1985. *The book of world-famous music*. Toronto: General Publishing Company.

Gilbert, A. 2003. iTunes auction treads murky legal ground. *CNet News.com*, September 3. http://www.news.com.com/2100-1025_3-5071108.html.

Gillis, J. 1999. Drug companies, gene labs to join forces: Collaboration aims to probe genetic differences—without proprietary interests. *Washington Post*, April 15, p. E1.

Gillmor, D. 2002. Entertainment industry's copyright fight puts consumers in cross hairs. *Silicon Valley*, February 12. http://www.siliconvalley.com/mld/siliconvalley/2658555.htm.

Goldstein, P. 2003. *Copyright's highway: From Gutenberg to the celestial jukebox*. Stanford, CA: Stanford University Press.

Goodell, F. 1999. World War MP3: It's labels vs. artists in the fight for control of the record business. *Rolling Stone*, July 8–22, p. 43.

Grattan, V. L. 1993. *American women songwriters: A biographical dictionary*. Westport, CT: Greenwood Press.

Greenberg, L. A. 1992. The art of appropriation: Puppies, piracy, and postmodernism. *Cardozo Arts & Entertainment Law Journal* 11.

Greene, T. C. 2003. U.S. senator would destroy MP3 traders' PCs. *The Register*, May 18. http://www.theregister.co.uk/content/6/31287.html.

Gross, R. D. 2002. Copyright zealotry in a digital world: Can freedom of speech survive? In *Copy fights: The future of intellectual property in the information age,* eds. A. Thierer and C. W. Crews Jr., p. 189–95. Washington, D.C.: Cato Institute.

Gumbel, A. 2003. All the president's votes? *The Independent* (London), October 14, pp. 2–4. Consult Lexis-Nexis.

Guntzel, J. 2004. Talkin' 'bout a [platform] revolution. *Punk Planet,* January/February, pp. 64–71.

Guthrie, W. 1990. *Pastures of plenty: A self-portrait.* Eds. D. Marsh and H. Leventhal. New York: HarperPerennial.

Hall, R. 2003. Mix tapes rise from street as hip-hop promo, a&r tool. *Billboard,* April 26, pp. 1, 68.

Hawes, B. L. 1970. *The birthday: An American ritual.* Unpublished master's thesis. University of California, Berkeley.

Hays, C. L. 1991. A picture, a sculpture and a lawsuit. *New York Times,* September 19, p. B2.

Healey, J. and R. Cromelin. 2004. When copyright law meets the "mashup." *Los Angeles Times,* March 21, p. E1.

Hebdidge, D. 1987. *Cut 'n' mix: Culture, identity and Caribbean music.* New York: Routledge.

Hochman, S. 1991. Judge raps practice of "sampling." *Los Angeles Times,* December 18, p. F1.

Hoffman, I. 2004. Diebold knew of legal risks. *Oakland Tribune,* April 20. http://www.oaklandtribune.com/cda/article/0,1674,82%257E1865%257E2095811,00.html.

Howe, J. 2003. BigChampagne is watching you. *Wired,* October, pp. 138–41.

Isaacson, W. 2003. *Benjamin Franklin: An American life.* New York: Simon & Schuster.

Jacobson, M. F., and L. A. Mazur. 1995. *Marketing madness: A survival guide for a consumer society.* Boulder, CO: Westview Press.

Jensen, J. 2004. Comeback? I never went anywhere! *Entertainment Weekly,* April 23, pp. 26–32.

Jha, S. 2002. India's water wars. *AlterNet,* December 5. http://www.alternet.org/story.html?StoryID=14697.

Johannesen, R. L. 1995. The ethics of plagiarism reconsidered: The oratory of Martin Luther King, Jr. *Southern Communication Journal* 60(3): 185–94.

Johnson, C. 2003. The war business: Squeezing a profit from the wreckage in Iraq. *Harper's*, November, pp. 53–58.

Jones, C. 1996. Haven't I heard that "whoop" (or "hoop") somewhere before? *New York Times*, December 22, p. B44.

Jones, S., and A. Lenhart. 2004. Music downloading and listening: Findings from the Pew Internet and American Life Project. *Popular Music and Society* 27(2): 185–200.

Joyce, E. W. 1998. *Cultural critique and abstraction: Marianne Moore and the avant-garde.* London: Associated University Presses.

Kelly, R. 2001. *Donnie Darko.* Director R. Kelly's DVD commentary. Los Angeles: Twentieth Century Fox.

Klein, J. 1980. *Woody Guthrie: A life.* New York: Delta Trade Paperbacks.

Klein, N. 1999. *No logo: Money, marketing and the growing anti-corporate movement.* New York: Picador.

Knopper, S. 2004. Clear Channel limits live CDs. *Rolling Stone*, May 24. http://www.rollingstone.com/news/story?id=6066617.

Koestenbaum, W. 1993. *The queen's throat: Opera, homosexuality and the mystery of desire.* New York: Vintage.

Kotadia, M. 2004. Microsoft: We took MikeRoweSoft too seriously. *CNet News.com*, January 20. http://www.news.com/2102-1014_3 -5143614.html.

Lebrecht, N. 1996. Echoes strike a chord. *Daily Telegraph* (London), May 11, p. 7.

Lemos, R. 2001. Security workers: Copyright law stifles. *CNet News.com*, September 6. http://www.news.com/2100-1001-272716.html.

Lessig, L. 2001. *The future of ideas: The fate of the commons in a connected world.* New York: Random House.

———. 2004. *Free culture: How big media uses technology and the law to lock down culture and control creativity.* New York: Penguin Press.

Lew, B. 2000. Metallica, how could you? *Salon.* http://www.dir.salon.com/ent/log/2000/05/90/metallica_fan/index.html.

Lewellen-Biddle, M. 2004. Voting machines gone wild! *In These Times,* January 5, pp. 20–21.

Lindorff, D. 2003. Still watching: Private industry moves in to compile personal data. *In These Times,* December 8, p. 3.

LiPetri, J. 1999. Owners stretch trademark protection to protect buildings, trees. *Micro Publishing News.* http://www.micropubnews.com/pages/issues/1999/899_trademark_mpn.shtml.

Lissauer, R. 1996. *Lissauer's encyclopedia of popular music in America: 1888 to the present.* New York: Paragon House.

Litman, J. 2001. *Digital copyright.* Amherst, NY: Prometheus Books.

Lockwood, L. 2003. *Beethoven: The music and life.* New York: W. W. Norton & Co.

MacDonald, M. 2001. *Brahms.* New York: Oxford University Press.

Madow, M. 1993. Private ownership of public image: Popular culture and publicity rights. *California Law Review* 81: 125 ff.

Manuel, P. 1993. *Cassette culture: Popular music and technology in north India.* Chicago: University of Chicago Press.

Marinetti, F. T. 1989. *The Futurist cookbook.* Trans. S. Brill. San Francisco: Bedford Arts.

Marre, K. 2003. Rage erupts over profiteering clause. *The Hill,* November 5. http://www.thehill.com/news/110503/profiteering.aspx.

Ma$e. 1999. Stay out of my way. On *Double up* (CD). New York: Bad Boy Productions.

Maskus, K. E. 2000. *Intellectual property rights in the global economy.* Washington, D.C.: Institute for International Economics.

McCullagh, D. 2003. SunnComm won't sue grad student. *CNet News.com,* October 10. http://www.news.com/2102-1027_3-5089448.html.

———. 2004. Congress mulls revisions to DMCA. *CNet News.com,* May 12. http://www.news.com/2102-1025_3-5211674.html.

McGirk, T. 1998. Gene piracy. *Time* (international edition, Asia), November 9, p. 34.

Meikle, G. 2002. *Future active: Media activism and the Internet.* New York: Routledge.

Menn, J. 2003. *All the rave: The rise and fall of Shawn Fanning's Napster.* New York: Crown Business.

Meredith, P. 2004. Extreme bake sales. *Mother Jones,* May/June, p. 46.

Meyer, S. 1995. *Paradoxes of fame: The Francis Scott Key story.* New York: Eastwind Publishing.

Miles, B. 1997. *Paul McCartney: Many years from now.* New York: Owl Books.

Miller, C. 1997. *Dickie Goodman & friends—greatest fables* (CD booklet). Miami: Hot Productions, Inc.

Miller, K. D. 1993. Redefining plagiarism: Martin Luther King's use of an oral tradition. *Chronicle of Higher Education* 39(20), January 20: A60.

———. 1991. Martin Luther King, Jr., and the black folk pulpit. *Journal of American History* 78(1): 120–23.

Miller, M. W. 1987. Creativity furor: High-tech alteration of sights and sounds divides the art world. *Wall Street Journal,* September 1, p. 1.

Mojo. 2003. Rhymin' and stealin'. September, pp. 68–78.

Moore, M. 1969. The art of poetry: Marianne Moore. In *Marianne Moore: A collection of critical essays,* ed. C. Tomlinson. Englewood Cliffs, NJ: Prentice-Hall.

Morris, G. 1981. When artists use photographs. *ARTnews,* 80(1), January: 102–6.

Morse, S. 2002. Setting the new market in sampling. *Boston Globe,* March 3. http://www.boston.com/dailyglobe2/062/living/shtml.

Negativland. 1995. *Fair use: The story of the letter u and the numeral 2.* Concord, CA: Seeland.

NOW with Bill Moyers. 2002. Seeds of conflict. October 4. http://www.pbs .org/now/transcript/transcript_corn.html.

———. 2003. Tollbooths on the digital highway. Produced by Rick Karr. PBS broadcast, January 17.

O'Harrow Jr., R. 2003. U.S. backs Florida's new counterterrorism database. *Washington Post,* August 6, p. A1.

Orlowski, A. 2003. E-voting vendor sued for DMCA takedown. *The Register,* November 11. http://www.theregister.co.uk/content/6/33750.html.

Oswald, J. 1995. Creatigality. In *Sounding off!: Music as subversion/resistance/revolution,* eds. R. Sakolsky and F. Wei-Han Ho, pp. 87–90. Brooklyn: Autonomedia.

Patterson, L. R. 1968. *Copyright in historical perspective.* Nashville, TN: Vanderbilt University Press.

Peters, J. D. 1999. *Speaking into the air: A history of the idea of communication.* Chicago: University of Chicago Press.

Plant, S. 1992. *The most radical gesture: The Situationist international in a postmodern age.* New York: Routledge.

Plato. 1995. *Phaedrus.* Trans. A. Nehamas and P. Woodruff. Indianapolis: Hackett Publishing Company.

Pope, J. 2003. Microsoft holdout Massachusetts opts for open source. *CRN,* September 26. http://www.crn.com/sections/BreakingNews/dailyarchives.asp?ArticleID=44768.

Pouncey, E. 2002. "Rock concrete: Counterculture plugs into the academy." In *Undercurrents: The hidden wiring of modern music,* ed. R. Young, pp. 153–62. London: Continuum.

Prato, G. 2004. Dickie Goodman. *AllMusicGuide.com.* http://www.allmusic.com/cg/amg.dll.

Pringle, P. 2003. *Food, Inc.: Mendel to Monsanto—the promises and perils of the biotech harvest.* New York: Simon & Schuster.

Quart, A. 2003. *Branded: The buying and selling of teenagers.* Cambridge, MA: Perseus Publishing.

Rap News Direct. 2003. Ghostface Killah wins copyright infringement case. http://www.rapnewsdirect.com/Printer/0-205-257646-00.html.

Reagon, B. J. 1991. Nobody knows the trouble I see; or, by and by I'm gonna lay down my heavy load. *Journal of American History* 78(1): 111–19.

Reichman, J. H., and P. F. Uhlir. 2003. A contractually reconstructed research commons for scientific data in a highly protectionist intellectual property environment. *Law and Contemporary Problems* 66 (1 and 2): 315–462.

Rich, F. 2003. There's no exit from *The Matrix*. *New York Times*, May 25, p. B1.

Richtel, M. 1998. You can't always judge a domain by its name. *New York Times*, May 28, p. G6.

Richter, H. 1964. *Dada: Art and anti-art*. Trans. D. Britt. New York: Thames and Hudson, Inc.

Rigden, P. 1997. Companies covet genes: Ethics and profits compete in the patenting of human genetic materials. *Alternatives Journal* 3(23): 8.

Roberts, P. 2003. Diebold voting case tests DMCA. *PC World*, November 4. http://www.pcworld.com/resource/printable/article/0,aid,113273,00 .asp.

Roht-Arriaza, N. 1997. Of seeds and shamans: The appropriation of the scientific and technical knowledge of indigenous and local communities. In *Borrowed power: Essays on cultural appropriation*, eds. B. Ziff and P. V. Rao, pp. 255–87. New Brunswick, NJ: Rutgers University Press.

Rojas, P. 2002. Bootleg culture. *Salon*, August 1. http://www.salon.com/ tech/feature/2002/08/01/bootlegs.html.

Rose, M. 1993. *Authors and owners: The invention of copyright*. Cambridge, MA: Harvard University Press.

Schlosser, E. 2002. *Fast food nation: The dark side of the all-American meal*. New York: Perennial.

Schumacher-Rasmussen, E. 2001. Owners of P-Funk catalog sue over 500 samples. MTV.com. http://www.mtv.com/news/articles/1444406/ 20010611/story.jhtml.

Selden Patent. 2002. *Weird and wonderful patents*. http://www.bpmlegal .com/wselden.html.

Shanker, T. 2004. G.I.'s in Iraq tote their own pop culture. *New York Times*, April 13. http://www.nytimes.com/2004/04/13/arts/music/13TROO .html.

Shiva, V. 1997. *Biopiracy: The plunder of nature and knowledge*. Boston: South End Press.

————. 2001. *Protect or plunder? Understanding intellectual property rights.* London: Zed Books.

Shreeve, J. 2004. *The genome war: How Craig Venter tried to capture the code of life and save the world.* New York: Knopf.

Shulman, S. 1999. *Owning the future.* New York: Houghton Mifflin.

Skinner, L. 2003. Bling! Bling! Ka-ching! Products get play for love and money. *Billboard,* May 31, pp. 1, 100.

Smith, D. 2003. A portrait of the artist's troubled daughter. *New York Times,* November 22. http://www.nytimes.com/2003/11/22/arts/dance/22JOYC.html.

Smith, E. 2003. Can copyright be saved? New ideas to make intellectual property work in the digital age. *Wall Street Journal,* October 20. http://www.online.wjs.com.

Smith, L. 1985. Food servers drafted as birthday warblers. *Los Angeles Times,* April 5, p. E1.

Sony Corp. of Am. v. Universal City Studios, Inc., 464 U.S. 417, 429, *reh'g denied,* 465 U.S. 1112 (1984).

Soocher, S. 1998. Blue velvet. *Entertainment Law & Finance* 14(2): 5.

Sounes, H. 2001. *Down the highway: The life of Bob Dylan.* New York: Grove Press.

Stamets, R. A. 1994. Ain't nothin' like the real thing, baby: The right of publicity and the singing voice. *Federal Communications Law Journal* 14: 347–73; 349–50.

Stephen, T. 2003. CIOS launches free access to communication journals. *Communication Institute for Online Scholarship.* Press release, November 7.

Sterne, J. 2003. *The audible past: Cultural origins of sound reproduction.* Durham, NC: Duke University Press.

Stiglitz, J. E. 2003. *Globalization and its discontents.* New York: W. W. Norton & Company.

Streeter, T. 1996. *Selling the air: A critique of the policy of commercial broadcasting in the United States.* Chicago: University of Chicago Press.

Sulston, J., and G. Ferry. 2002. *The common thread: A story of science, politics, ethics, and the human genome.* Washington, D.C.: Joseph Henry Press.

Superswell's Sample Law. Horror stories. http://www.superswell.com/samplelaw/horror.html.

Toop, D. 1991. *Rap attack 2: African hip-hop to global hip-hop.* London: Serpent's Tail.

Tucker, T. 2003. *Bolt of fate: Benjamin Franklin and his electric kite hoax.* New York: Public Affairs.

Tzara, T. 1977. *Seven Dada manifestos and lampisteries.* Trans. B. Wright. New York: Calder Publications.

Vaidhyanathan, S. 2001. *Copyrights and copywrongs: The rise of intellectual property and how it threatens creativity.* New York: NYU Press.

————. 2002. Copyright as cudgel. *The Chronicle of Higher Education,* August 2. http://www.chronicle.com/free/v48/i47/47b00701.htm.

Van, J. 2003. Motorola to unveil 1st Linux cell phone. *Chicago Tribune,* February 13. http://www.chicagotribune.com/technology/local/profiles/chi0302130228feb13,1,4843889.story.

Veiga, A. 2003. Music labels tap downloading networks. *Yahoo! News,* November 17. http://www.news.yahoo.com.

Wallace, D. F. 1997. *A supposedly fun thing I'll never do again.* New York: Little Brown.

Washington Post. 1998. To own the human genome. May 15, p. A26.

Wescher, H. 1968. *Collage.* Trans. R. E. Wolf. New York: Harry N. Abrams.

White, C. 2003. *The middle mind: Why Americans don't think for themselves.* New York: HarperCollins.

Wilkie, T. 1995. Patent rights "slowing medical progress." *Independent* (London), March 23, p. 4.

WIPO Arbitration and Mediation Center. 2002. *Vivendi Universal v. Mr. Jay David Sallen and GO247.COM, Inc,* Case No. D2001–1121. http://www.arbiter.wipo.int/domains/decisions/html/2001/d2001-1121.html.

Wirtén, E. H. 2004. *No trespassing: Authorship, intellectual property rights, and the boundaries of globalization.* Toronto: University of Toronto Press.

WISH-TV 8. 2004. Marion County clerk accuses ES&S of lying. Broadcast, April 20.

Wolk, D. 2003. Down the hatch. *The Village Voice,* June 25, p. 110.

Wolmuth, R. 1987. Liz Taylor leaps into a vial business with passion. *People Weekly* 28(14): 38.

Woodmansee, M. 1984. The genius and the copyright: Economic and legal conditions of the emergence of the "author." *Eighteenth-Century Studies* 17(4): 425–48.

Zeitlin, S. 1998. Strangling culture with a copyright law. *New York Times,* April 25, p. A15.

Zetter, K. 2003. Students fight e-vote firm. *Wired News,* October 21. http://www.wired.com/news/print/0,1294,60927,00.html.

Zittrain, J. 2003. The copyright cage. *Legal Affairs* (July/August): 26–35; 27.

Zweiger, G. 2001. *Transducing the genome: Information, anarchy, and revolution in biomedical sciences.* New York: McGraw-Hill.

INDEX

ABOUT THE AUTHOR

A journalist, activist, artist, and professor in the Department of Communication Studies at the University of Iowa, Kembrew McLeod is the author of *Owning Culture: Authorship, Ownership, and Intellectual Property Law* and has written music criticism for *Rolling Stone, The Village Voice, Spin, Mojo,* and the 2004 edition of the *New Rolling Stone Album Guide.* He is also the coproducer of a documentary on intellectual-property law, *Copyright Criminals: This Is a Sampling Sport,* which is currently in production, and he worked as a documentary producer at the Media Education Foundation. McLeod was involved in the traveling art show *Illegal Art: Freedom of Expression in the Corporate Age,* which traveled to New York, Chicago, Washington, D.C., and was hosted by the San Francisco Museum of Modern Art's Artist Gallery in 2003. You can download some of his work from his Web site, kembrew.com.